The Art of Being Governed

EVERYDAY POLITICS IN LATE IMPERIAL CHINA

Michael Szonyi

PRINCETON UNIVERSITY PRESS
PRINCETON & OXFORD

Copyright © 2017 by Princeton University Press

Published by Princeton University Press,
41 William Street, Princeton, New Jersey 08540

In the United Kingdom: Princeton University Press,
6 Oxford Street, Woodstock, Oxfordshire OX20 1TR

press.princeton.edu

Jacket art: The images of Ming swordsmen are reproduced from an account of military
training in the seventeenth century *Wubei zhi* [Treatise on Military Preparedness]
by Mao Yuanyi

Library of Congress Cataloging-in-Publication Data

Names: Szonyi, Michael, author.
Title: The art of being governed : everyday politics in late imperial China / Michael Szonyi.
Description: Princeton : Princeton University Press, 2017. | Includes bibliographical
    references and index.
Identifiers: LCCN 2017014806 | ISBN 9780691174518 (hardcover : alk. paper)
Subjects: LCSH: China—Politics and government—1368–1644. | China—History,
    Military—960–1644. | China—History—Ming dynasty, 1368–1644.
Classification: LCC DS753.2 .S96 2017 | DDC 951/.026--dc23
LC record available at https://lccn.loc.gov/2017014806

British Library Cataloging-in-Publication Data is available

Publication of this book was made possible by a grant from the James P. Geiss Foundation,
a private, non-profit operating foundation that sponsors research on China's Ming dynasty
(1368–1644).

This book has been composed in Classic Miller and Adobe Kaiti Std R

Printed on acid-free paper. ∞

Printed in the United States of America

10 9 8 7 6 5 4 3 2 1

For my three teachers:

Tim Brook, David Faure, and Zheng Zhenman

Formal order . . . is always and to some considerable degree parasitic on informal processes, which the formal scheme does not recognize, without which it could not exist, and which it alone cannot create or maintain.

—JAMES SCOTT, *SEEING LIKE A STATE*, 310

Obedézcase, pero no se cumpla (to be obeyed, but not complied with)—Castilian response to a royal command

—RUTH MCKAY, *THE LIMITS OF ROYAL AUTHORITY: RESISTANCE AND OBEDIENCE IN SEVENTEENTH-CENTURY CASTILE*, 2

CONTENTS

ILLUSTRATIONS

Figures

Tables

DRAMATIS FAMILIAE

NUMBERS IN PARENTHESES refer to chapters in which these families appear.

Military Households in the Guards

IN FUQUAN BATTALION

Chen family: originally from Funing in northern Fujian; conscripted in early Ming and assigned to Fuquan; maintained good ties with kinfolk in native place (2)

Jiang family: originally from Anhui; appointed to hereditary commander position for service to first Ming emperor; assigned to Fuquan; ties to smugglers (3)

IN FUZHOU GUARD

Pu family: patriarch Pu Manu; originally from Jinjiang; conscripted in early Ming; accompanied Zheng He voyages; promoted to hereditary officer post (1)

IN GAOPU BATTALION

Huang family: originally from Changle; conscripted in early Ming and assigned to Meihua; later transferred to Gaopu (1)

IN JINMEN BATTALION

Ni Family: patriarch Ni Wulang; originally from Fuzhou; conscripted in early Ming and assigned to Jinmen (1)

IN TONGSHAN BATTALION

Chen family: originally from Putian; conscripted in early Ming and assigned to Puxi, then transferred to Tongshan; members of Guan Yongmao lineage (1, 3, 7)

IN ZHEJIANG GUARDS

He family: hereditary commanders in Puqi Battalion (4)
Pan family: hereditary commanders in Jinxiang Battalion (4)
Wang family: conscripted and assigned to serve in Puqi Battalion;
adopted a monk to serve on their behalf (1)

IN DAPU COLONY

Lin family: originally from Tong'an; conscripted in early Ming and
assigned to Dapu colony; called up to deal with Deng Maoqi
rebellion; claimed connection to Lin Xiyuan; feuded with Ma
family (6)
Ma family: conscripted in early Ming and assigned to Dapu colony;
feuded with Lin family (6)
Tang family: military colonists assigned to Dapu colony (7)

IN HUTOU COLONY

Yangtou Yan family: military colonists assigned to Hutou colony (6)
Hong family: military colonists assigned to Hutou colony (6)
Zheng family: military colonists assigned to Hutou colony (6)
Zhushan Lin family: military colonists assigned to Hutou colony (6)

IN YONGTAI COLONY

Linyang Yan family: patriarch Master Jinhua; originally from
Jiangxi; conscripted and assigned to Yongtai colonies of Yanping
Guard (5)

Military Households in Their Native
Place and Civilian Households

FROM FUQING

Guo family: conscripted in early Ming after being implicated in a
murder; assigned to serve in Shaanxi; fled to Fuzhou after pirate
attacks (1, 2)
Ye family: conscripted in early Ming; assigned to far north; devastated
by pirate attacks (2)

FROM GUTIAN

Su family: civilian household; accused of shirking duties (2)
Yao family: conscripted in early Ming; assigned to Lianzhou in
    Guangdong (2)

FROM HUTOU

Qingxi Li family: powerful family of Ganhua district; one of their
    members conscripted in connection with official misconduct and
    assigned to serve in southwest; family of Li Guangdi (1, 6, 7)
Hu family: conscripted in early Ming; assigned first to Nanjing, then
    to Fuquan, then to Nan'an military colony; family members later
    returned home to Hutou (4, 5, 6, 7)
Lin family: conscripted in early Ming; assigned to Nan'an military col-
    ony; early ancestor Balang brought the Venerated King to Hutou (6)

FROM QUANZHOU

Quanzhou Yan family: patriarch Yan Guantian; conscripted in early
    Ming and assigned to serve in Yunnan (introduction)
Zheng family: fled to Zhangpu in late Yuan; conscripted in early
    Ming (1)
Zhu family: conscripted together with the Yan (introduction)

THE ART OF BEING GOVERNED

A Father Loses Three Sons to the Army

EVERYDAY POLITICS IN MING CHINA

If it is true that the grid of "discipline" is everywhere becoming clearer and more extensive, it is all the more urgent to discover how an entire society resists being reduced to it, what popular procedures (also "miniscule" and quotidian) manipulate the mechanisms of discipline and conform to them only in order to evade them, and finally, what "ways of operating" form the counterpart . . . of the mute processes that organize the establishment of socioeconomic order.

—DE CERTEAU, *THE PRACTICE OF EVERYDAY LIFE*, XIV.

THAT EVERY STATE MUST HAVE AN ARMY—to defend its territory against invaders from without and rebels within—is, sadly, a historical rule with few exceptions.[1] This near universality of the military institution makes it a productive site to study not just how states operate, how they mobilize and deploy resources, but also how states and their subjects interact. For if a state must have an army, then it follows that a state must have soldiers. The need to mobilize manpower for military service is among the most common challenges that a state must address. In almost every state in history there are some people who willingly or not supply labor to the state in the form of military service. *How* a state chooses to meet this fundamental challenge of mobilizing its soldiery has enormous implications for every aspect of its military, from command structure and strategy to financing and logistics.[2] Its choices also have profound consequences for those who serve.

This book is about the consequences of choices about military mobilization in one place and time: China's southeast coast under the Ming dynasty (1368–1644). The focus is not on military or logistical or fiscal consequences but on social consequences, that is, how military institutions shaped the lives of ordinary people. In this book I tell the stories of ordinary Ming families' interaction with state institutions and how this interaction affected other kinds of social relations. At the heart of the book are two simple questions. How did ordinary people in the Ming deal with their obligations to provide manpower to the army? What were the broader consequences of their behavior?

Yan Kuimei, who lived near the city of Quanzhou in the late sixteenth century, has left us a detailed account of how his own family answered these questions. "Alas," he begins,

> the cruelty of conscription is more fierce than a tiger. Our ancestor Guangtian had six sons. Three died [in military service]. Younger brother died; elder brother succeeded him. Elder brother expired; younger brother replaced him.

Kuimei's grievous story stemmed from the status his family held in the Ming system of household registration. The Yan were registered by the Ming state as a military household (*junhu*). For much of the dynasty, this special category of the population provided the core of the Ming army. We will explore this institution in much greater detail below; for the moment it is enough to know that military households had a permanent, hereditary responsibility to supply manpower for military service. This did not mean that everyone in a military household, or even every male, served as a soldier. Rather, being registered as a military household carried an obligation to provide a certain number of men—typically one soldier per household—to the army. The Yan's situation was more complicated. They shared the obligation with another local family, the Zhu. That is, the two families were responsible between them for providing a single soldier, with the Yan family having the primary responsibility. Together they made up what is known as a composite military household.[3] When the two families were first registered as a military household in 1376, the patriarch of the Yan family, Yan Guangtian, took the lead in ensuring that they met their service responsibility. He chose his fourth son, Yingzu, to fulfill the military service obligation. Yingzu was a child of only fourteen *sui*, probably twelve or thirteen years old, when he was sent off to distant Nanjing to serve in the army. He did not serve long; he died soon after he arrived in the dynastic capital. Yan Guangtian then dispatched another young son to replace Yingzu. This boy too served for only a short time; he deserted his post and disappeared. Again Yan Guangtian had no choice but to find a replacement. He now shifted his approach, ordering the eldest of his six sons to become a soldier.

In 1381, Yan's eldest son was transferred to distant Yunnan in southwestern China. He served there for the rest of his life, never once returning home. When he died in 1410, the hereditary obligation kicked in for a fourth time. In his dotage, poor Guangtian had to choose yet another son to serve in the army. This son never even made it to his post. He died somewhere along the long journey across the Ming empire. By the time of Yan Guangtian's own death, four of his six sons had served in the army. Three had died or disappeared soon after being conscripted; the only one of the four to survive had lived out his days in a garrison in the distant jungles of the southwest (figure I.1).

For more than a decade the household's slot in the army remained empty, quite possibly because the clerks in charge of the relevant paperwork had lost track of them. But in 1428, facing a serious shortage of manpower, Ming officials renewed their efforts to make up shortfalls in the ranks. Some officials believed that assigning soldiers to posts that were far from their ancestral homes was partly to blame for the shortfall in soldiers. New soldiers were falling ill or dying while en route to their post, as happened to two of Yan Guangtian's sons; others, like a third son, deserted rather than be separated forever from their families. The army responded with a policy that we might call a voluntary disclosure program. If a man liable for military service came forward willingly, the conscription authorities assured that he would not be sent far away but stationed close to home.[4] One of Yan Guangtian's younger kin took advantage of the policy, presented himself to the authorities, and was duly assigned to duty in nearby Quanzhou. By the time this man died a decade later, the Yan family had been fulfilling their military obligations for more than sixty years.

At the time of his death, there were no Yan sons of an age to serve. So the responsibility now devolved to the other half of the composite military household, the Zhu family. Over the course of the next century, four members of the Zhu family served one after the other.

The need for soldiers on the borders eventually grew too great and the voluntary disclosure policy lapsed. The next soldier conscripted from the Zhu family was sent back to the household's original assignment in the jungles of the southwest. Both the Yan and Zhu families were keen that he stay on the job. Desertion was a serious problem for the Ming army, but it was equally a problem for the military households who would have to

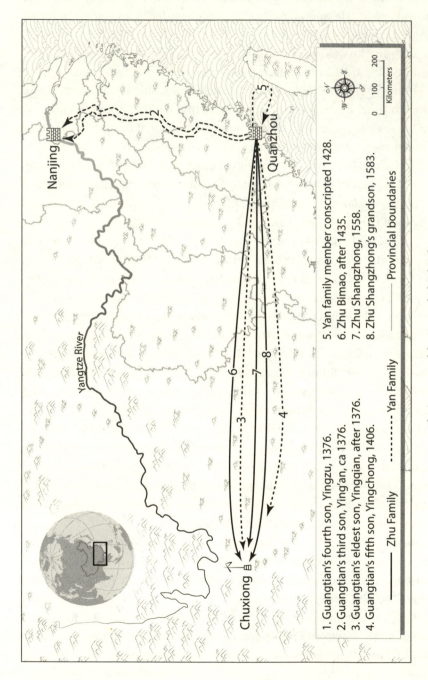

1.1. The journeys of the Yan and Zhu families

1. Guangtian's fourth son, Yingzu, 1376.
2. Guangtian's third son, Ying'an, ca 1376.
3. Guangtian's eldest son, Yingqian, after 1376.
4. Guangtian's fifth son, Yingchong, 1406.
5. Yan family member conscripted 1428.
6. Zhu Bimao, after 1435.
7. Zhu Shangzhong, 1558.
8. Zhu Shangzhong's grandson, 1583.

———— Zhu Family   - - - - - - Yan Family   ———— Provincial boundaries

Yangtze River

Nanjing

Quanzhou

Chuxiong

0   100   200
Kilometers

replace the deserter. To discourage further desertion, the Zhu and the Yan worked out an arrangement to give each new conscript a payment of silver and cloth. Ostensibly this was to cover his expenses; really it was all about persuading him to stay in the army. It did not work. Again and again the man serving in the army deserted. Again and again officials must have descended on the two families to demand a replacement.

By 1527, more than a century and a half after they were initially given the obligation to serve in the military, the two families had grown tired of the uncertainty. They wanted a more long-term solution. Together they drew up a simple contract, the terms of which survive in the Yan's genealogy. The current soldier, a man named Zhu Shangzhong, agreed to remain in the army for the rest of his life (the contract literally reads, "It is his duty to die in the ranks" [*wuyao zaiwu shengu*]). The Yan agreed to pay him for the security of knowing that he was fulfilling their shared obligation.

But this solution was less permanent than they had hoped. In 1558, soldier Zhu Shangzhong came back from Yunnan with a new proposal. He had now been serving in the army for more than sixty years and he wanted out. But he had a deal to offer. He would commit his immediate family and his direct descendants to take on the burden of providing a conscript, in perpetuity, in exchange for regular payments. Shangzhong's eldest son would replace him and then his grandson after him. The effect would be to free the Yan of their hereditary service responsibility, converting a labor obligation into a monetary one. So long as they kept up the payments, the Yan would never again have to fear the arrival of a conscription official seeking to drag one of them off to the wars.

The new contract that the families prepared was more elaborate than the previous version. Its terms—also recorded in the genealogy—covered not only the arrangement between the two families but also the Yan family's internal arrangements for how they would raise the money to pay Zhu Shangzhong and his descendents. Almost two centuries had now passed since Yan Guangtian's family was first registered as a military household. The descendants of the fourteenth-century patriarch probably now numbered in the hundreds. They formed what we would call a lineage. The contract specified that each man in the lineage would make a small annual contribution to a general fund—technically a capitation charge—that would be paid at regular intervals to the soldier off in the far southwest.

The family members must have felt relief at finally resolving this long-standing concern. But the story was still not over. Twenty-five years after the contract was made, Shangzhong's grandson returned to the ancestral home, complaining that the payments were inadequate and demanding the contract be renegotiated. The Yan thought they had no choice but to agree; they raised the capitation charge to cover the new, higher costs.

Yan Kuimei, the author of our account, ends his story in 1593, with an exhortation to his kin to be reasonable and to meet any future demands from the Zhu family. If the serving soldier should ever come back demanding more money, "he must be received with courtesy and treated with generosity, that there be no disaster in the future."[5] His appeal may never have been tested, for half a century later the Ming would fall, replaced by a new ruling house with a very different approach to questions of military mobilization.

Yan Kuimei was an educated man, a successful graduate of the examination system and a state official.[6] But his text was not written from the perspective of a scholar or a bureaucrat; it is neither philosophical rumination nor policy analysis. It is an internal family document, included in the Yan genealogy and intended primarily for internal consumption (although as I will discuss below, Yan was mindful of the prospect that it might one day be read by a judge). It explains and justifies the arrangements that the family developed over the course of more than two centuries, almost as long as the dynasty whose demands they sought to accommodate.

Military Households and Everyday Politics

Documents like Yan Kuimei's account, written by members of families for their own reasons and reproduced in their genealogies, can provide answers to the two core questions of this book. These texts, written by ordinary people to deal with and comment on everyday problems, are perhaps our best source to study the history of the common people in Ming times. They may well be the closest we can get to the voice of the ordinary Ming subject. These texts reveal the mobilization of manpower for the Ming army from the perspective not of the mobilizing state but of the people mobilized. They show how people dealt with the challenges posed and seized the opportunities offered by living with the Ming state. A major inspiration for me in writing this book has been the goal of conveying their ingenuity and creativity. Their strategies, practices, and discourses constitute a pattern of political interaction that I will argue was not unique to soldiers but was distributed more broadly across Ming society, and was not unique to the Ming but can be identified in other times in Chinese history, and perhaps beyond.

To label this type of interaction state-society relations would not be wrong, but it would be simplistic, anachronistic, and anthropomorphic. Society is made up of social actors—individuals and families—but social actors make their own choices. Most of the time they do not act on behalf of or for the sake of society, or even think in such terms, but in the pursuit of their own interests as they understand them. Nor is the state a conscious or even a coherent unified actor. States do not interact with people. Or rather, people rarely experience this interaction as such. They interact with the state's agents—with functionaries and bureaucrats. They follow procedures; they fill out forms and hand over their money. Our own experience tells us that people can behave in different ways in such interactions. I can follow the instructions of state officials to the letter and fill out forms meticulously, precisely, conscientiously, and honestly. Or I can refuse to conform to the process. If pushed, I might even flee the state or take up arms against it. But the vast majority of interactions with the state take place somewhere between these two extremes, and this is as true of people in the past as it is for me in the present.

Moreover, although not all politics involves direct interaction with state institutions or state agents, this does not mean the state is irrelevant to them. The state can matter even when its agents are not even present. Institutional and regulatory structures of the state are part of the context in which people operate. Military officers and conscription officials never once appear in Yan Kuimei's account. But it would be naive to think the state was absent from the negotiations within and between the two families. The conscription system underlay their entire interaction. The state may not have intervened directly in the negotiations between the two families, but it was certainly a stakeholder in them. This sort of negotiation does not fit easily into familiar categories of political behavior, but it would be a mistake not to recognize it as political.

Much political behavior much of the time actually belongs to one sort or the other of this mundane quotidian interaction: it lies somewhere between compliance and active resistance and it does not directly involve the state or its agents. In this middle ground, people interact with state structures and regulatory regimes and their representatives indirectly rather than directly, and by manipulating them, by appropriating them, by turning them to their own purposes. How can we describe the strategies people develop to manage these interactions? We cannot simply follow the official archive and label them as insubordination or misconduct. To move beyond the thin set of choices offered by the binary of compliance versus resistance, I use instead the term "everyday politics."[7] "Everyday politics," writes Ben Kerkvliet, "is people embracing, complying with, adjusting, and contesting norms and rules regarding authority over, production of, or allocation of resources and doing so in quiet, mundane, and subtle expressions and acts."[8]

To speak of everyday political *strategies* is to suggest skills and competencies that can be acquired and transmitted or, in other words, an art of *being governed*. This phrase is obviously inspired both by Foucault's concept of the art of government and Scott's elaboration of the art of *not being governed*. Just as Foucault traces shifts in emphasis in the arts of *governing*, it should be possible to trace histories of the art of *being governed*.[9] I hope that readers will not find my choice for the title of this book, which varies only by one small word from the title of Scott's influential book, to be glib. It is intended to make a serious point. The subjects of the Ming, and of other Chinese states, differed in a fundamental way from the inhabitants of Scott's upland *zomia*. Their art of being governed did *not* consist of a basic choice between being governed or not being governed. Rather, it involved decisions about when to be governed, about how best to be governed, about how to maximize the benefits and minimize the costs of being governed. Everyday politics for Ming subjects meant innumerable calibrations, calculating the consequences of conformity or non-conformity and evaluating those costs in relation to the possible benefits.[10] Taking these calibrations seriously does not mean reducing people in Ming times to automatons driven by rational choice but rather treating them as purposive, thoughtful agents who made self-conscious efforts to pursue what they saw as their best interests. Nor does it mean dismissing their efforts as simply instances of "working the system . . . to their minimum disadvantage."[11] Working the system is probably universal in human societies—but how and why people work the system, the resources they bring to bear to do so, and the way that working the system reshapes their social relations, are meaningful, even pressing, subjects for historical enquiry. To study these questions is to credit ordinary people with the capacity to perceive their relationship with the state and to respond to it, in other words to make their own history.

This book explores everyday politics in Ming through the stories of several military households. We will meet the Zheng family, who solved the problem of choosing which member of the family to serve in the army by revising their patriarch's will; the Ye family, who fended off pressure from local bullies by maintaining ties to kinsmen serving on a distant frontier; the Jiang family, who took advantage of their military rank to engage in smuggling and piracy, and many others.

Table I.1. The art of being governed: a typology of strategies for interaction with the state

Degree of formalization	Degree of perceived compliance/resistance	
	Not perceived as resistance	Perceived as resistance
Formalized	*Everyday politics*	*Rebellion/coup*
Ad hoc	*Everyday resistance*	*Mutiny/desertion*

The set of strategies that these families had for dealing with the state can be classified along several axes, as shown in table I.1. I have already mentioned the continuum from compliance to resistance. (These are relative terms; what they really mean is compliant or resistant from the perspective of the state.) A second continuum relates to the degree of deliberation in the strategy, from ad hoc expediency on one side to deliberate, formal strategizing in advance on the other.

The ultimate expressions of resistance in the military are desertion and mutiny. I do not discuss strategies like these in any detail here, not because they were not part of Ming everyday politics, not because Ming soldiers never mutinied or deserted, but because for obvious reasons Ming soldiers rarely wrote down such strategies. Desertion was hugely consequential for the Ming dynasty. In order to deal with high levels of desertion, the dynasty gradually shifted to reliance on hired mercenaries, and the resulting fiscal burden has often been blamed for the eventual fall of the Ming.[12] But there are almost no sources that convey desertion from the perspective of the soldiers themselves.

Military households must also have had many other strategies that involved responding flexibly and expediently to challenges as they arose. Pilfering, foot-dragging, desertion, and mockery are among the "everyday forms of resistance" through which people everywhere defend their interests as best they can against claims by superordinate groups and states.[13] Practitioners tend not to record these sorts of ad hoc strategies either; to understand them from the perspective of their practitioners is easier for ethnographers and anthropologists than it is for historians. So I will not consider such strategies in detail here either.

The tools of history lend themselves best to the study of the everyday political strategies in the upper left quadrant: strategies that are both formal and perceived as being compliant or at least not opposed to the state. They are strategies that tend to be recorded in writing by the people who used them, and indeed, the fact of their being recorded is often part of what makes them work. This is the subset of strategies I focus on here.

Institutions, Deterritorialization, and Social Legacies

Military institutions move people around. The army transfers soldiers from one place to another—to attack, to defend, to communicate a signal, or for a host of other reasons. When it moves soldiers, the army dislocates them from the social settings they know and from their existing social relations. It decontextualizes them or, to use language popularized by Deleuze and Guattari, it deterritorializes them (Deleuze and Guattari might say that the army is a deterritorializing machine).[14] But transfers of troops simultaneously generate counterforces for their reterritorialization. Even as commanders seek to facilitate one type of mobility, deployment, they impose mechanisms to limit another type, desertion. Soldiers themselves produce other counterforces for reterritorialization. When soldiers and their families are sent to a garrison far from home, their existing social networks are weakened. But they soon begin to form new social ties with the people around them, both their fellow soldiers and others living around them in their new assignment.[15] So the military is actually also an institution that creates new social relations. These new social relations—unintended consequences of state mobilization policies and popular responses—are the second main theme of this book. They constitute a second kind of everyday politics, less obviously strategic but potentially equally important.

The institution I am concerned with here, the Ming system of military households, came to an end with the fall of the dynasty that established it. But we will see that many of the social relations that arose as unintended consequences of Ming military policies endured even after the fall of the institution that produced them. They survived the fall of the dynasty that created the institution (in 1644), the fall of the entire dynastic system (in 1911), and even the fall of the succeeding republic (in 1949). So while the institution itself died multiple deaths, the social relations that it spawned remained, and remain, alive. The history of the institution can thus illuminate historical processes behind social networks that are still active today. A brief visit to the town of Pinghai will show what I mean.

Every year the townspeople of Pinghai, a former garrison just north of Quanzhou, perform a grand ritual to commemorate the Lunar New

1.2. Temple of the God of the Wall, Pinghai

Year. They carry their God of the Wall in a procession around the town on the ninth day of the new year. (The Chinese term *Chenghuang* is usually rendered in English as the City God; but Pinghai is not a city, so in this case the more faithful translation is also the more accurate.) The festival is a riot of sensation—firecrackers and handheld cannons fill the air with flame and smoke; the colorful costumes of the god's bearers and hundreds of accompanying horsemen come in and out of view through the thick incense smoke; the women of the village chant prayers as they sweep the road in front of the procession and take lit sticks from the god's heavy incense burner (figures I.2–I.4). The walls of Pinghai have long been destroyed, but the procession stays within the area that used to be demarcated by those walls and does not enter the surrounding villages. Every year as he tours the precincts of the town to receive offerings from his devotees and to expel evil influences and ensure good fortune in the coming year, the God of the Wall thus also marks Pinghai residents off from the villages of the surrounding area, even centuries after the military base at Pinghai itself was disbanded.

In many places in China, the God of the Wall is anonymous. No one knows his name or how he came to hold his position as tutelary deity. But in Pinghai, the god is a familiar if forbidding figure. He is the apotheosis of a real historical person named Zhou Dexing. Zhou Dexing,

1.3. The God of the Wall, Pinghai

the Marquis of Jiangxia, was one of the oldest and closest supporters of the founding emperor of the Ming. When the emperor needed a reliable lieutenant to set up defenses on the southeast coast of his empire, it was Zhou to whom he turned. In the 1370s, Zhou Dexing marched his forces to Fujian. They uprooted tens of thousands of men from their home villages, conscripted them, registered their families as military households, and forced them to labor building the walled forts where they would ultimately serve. Pinghai was one such fort, built by the ancestors of the very people who live there today. When the fort was first established, a temple to the God of the Wall was built and an image of the god installed in it. At some point in the succeeding centuries, the people of Pinghai came to the realization that the God of the Wall of their own town was none other than the spirit of Zhou Dexing. So when the people of Pinghai today parade their god in the hopes of ensuring good fortune in the year to come, they are not simply repeating a timeless expression of Chinese culture. They are also commemorating a historical moment, the foundation of their community centuries ago. Their commemoration in the twenty-first century speaks both to the formation of local identity and to remarkable historical continuity. History has produced this ritual. The procession is—among other things—a story of the ancestors' interaction with the Ming state.

1.4. Pinghai procession festival

On Ming History

The Ming was founded by a strongman who arose in the chaotic waning years of the Mongol Yuan dynasty. After eliminating his rivals and establishing the new dynasty, Zhu Yuanzhang (r. 1368–98) set about implementing an ambitious agenda to rebuild Chinese society after decades of foreign domination and internal turmoil. Zhu and his advisers invoked ancient Chinese models in order to draw a clear line between the Ming and its Mongol predecessor. But in reality they also relied extensively on Yuan precedents, including some parts of the system of hereditary military household registration.[16]

A second major distinctive feature of the Ming was Zhu's personal imprint. Zhu Yuanzhang, unusual among dynastic founders in Chinese history, came to power with a social policy, "a grand design for the establishment and maintenance of the social order."[17] Zhu's vision involved more than just creating or reviving the right government institutions. He also wanted to create (or recreate) a utopian rural order in which most of his subjects would live contented lives in self-sufficient villages, supervised not by state officials but by their own kin and neighbors.

Like all leaders, Zhu worried about his legacy, and he ordered that the rules and principles of government that he and his ministers had devised—what we might call the Ming constitution—were to remain in force, inviolate, for all eternity. Historians have often described this commitment as a third distinctive feature of the Ming and invoked it to explain the Ming's supposed inability to respond to changing circumstances. But the principle of the inviolability of the constitution was not unique to the Ming.[18] The principle may have been especially strong in the Ming, but the system still had various ways of adapting to changing times. How else could the dynasty have endured for almost three centuries? In its actual operation, the inertia or path dependency of the Ming state may not have been fundamentally different from other polities or even modern states— though of course the rationale and institutional structure that created the inertia was very different. Zhu Yuanzhang's constitution matters to the history of the Ming, to be sure, but we cannot simply take it at face value.

Though in Zhu's bucolic ideal of society the rural communities would mostly govern themselves, realizing his vision actually required a program that was highly interventionist. In its ambition, if not in the technological capacities available to realize that ambition, his regime has often been compared to that of Mao Zedong many hundreds of years later. For much of the twentieth century the Ming was seen as the height of Chinese autocracy, and this view still persists among some scholars.[19] But the prevailing view has changed as we have learned more about the burgeoning economy and vibrant society of the mid-Ming. The commercialization of the economy, spurred by highly productive agriculture and a massive influx of silver caused by global demand for Chinese products, had a transformative effect on social, cultural, and political life. Today many scholars see late Ming society, especially in wealthy urban areas, as having been basically unconstrained by the state. Some even describe it as liberal.[20] The dominant narrative arc of the Ming has thus become one of a shift from the state at the center to the market at the center.[21]

Here I want to suggest a history of the Ming in which neither the state nor the market, neither emperor nor silver, is the principal agent. This book argues that both the earlier autocracy thesis and its liberal society antithesis are overstated. The history of state-society relations in the Ming is better told as a story of changing roles for the state and changing consequences of state presence, not the disappearance of the state.

About This Book

Librarians will probably shelve this book under the classification of Ming dynasty military history, but this is not quite what it is about. Though this book is about the Ming army, it describes no battles and has little to say about the classic themes of military history such as strategy, logistics, or weapons. Much of the huge literature on these topics concentrates either on the rise of the dynasty or its fall. That is, military historians are primarily interested in how the first Ming emperor won the empire or in how his descendants lost it.[22] Military weakness is central to many narratives of Ming decline—as an emblem of decadence, misplaced priorities, political factionalism, or crushing fiscal burden.[23] But like other scholars of the Ming military who have gone beyond narrowly military concerns to examine foreign policy, strategic culture, ethnicity, or violence, I study the military institution not for its own sake, but in order to shed light on something else, the everyday politics of ordinary Ming subjects.[24]

This book is about a particular institution, the Ming military, but my goal is not to elucidate the formal rules of the institution and their operation over time. It builds on and differs from a substantial literature on the military household system by scholars such as Zhang Jinkui, the leading expert on the field in the People's Republic of China (PRC), because I treat the military institution primarily as a topic of social history. It builds on and differs from the work of Yu Zhijia, Zhang's counterpart in Taiwan, because I attempt to situate the topic within a specific local ecology (though to be fair, it is often only with the help of her more general work that I was able to make sense of the local case, and some of her more recent work is set in a specific locality).[25] I explore the system not as it was devised by the central state—though this is necessary background—but rather as it shaped and was reshaped by the people who interacted with it, how they inhabited, appropriated, manipulated, and deformed it. In other words, this book traces both the everyday politics of the institution and the role of the institution in everyday politics more broadly. It considers some of the ways in which the institution as it was experienced changed over time, the degree to which it was and was not self-reinforcing, and the factors endogenous and exogenous that affected the degree to which it was self-reinforcing.

This book is a work of local history, but it is not the history of a locality. Rather, it explores historical phenomena in relation to a specific local microecology. Clifford Geertz famously wrote that anthropologists do not study villages, they study in villages.[26] This work likewise is not the history of a place in China; it is a history of everyday politics in China using evidence drawn from one place. My "village" lies far from the northern and western frontiers, the focus of Ming military priorities and most previous scholarship. Strategic importance does not necessarily signify for social history. My "village" is also rather larger than what Geertz had in mind: the geographic scope of the book, encompassing coastal Fujian but also extending north to southern Zhejiang and south to northeastern Guangdong, follows from my goal of considering institutions in the political, social, and ecological context within which they are experienced.[27]

The key distinguishing feature of the southeast coast's ecology is the presence of the sea. The sea was the source of livelihood for many of the region's residents, who fished on it, cultivated shellfish in its shallows, and traded and smuggled across it. They crossed it to reach Taiwan, Okinawa, Japan, and Southeast Asia. Like other frontiers, the sea offered possibilities for flight when circumstances grew too dire. Residents of the coast, soldier and civilian alike, could and sometimes did flee to Taiwan or simply to one of the many offshore islands.

The sea was a source of danger as well as opportunity; the region was ravaged many times by attacks from the sea, and the main military function of the families discussed in this book was to defend against such attacks and keep peace on the seas. But the coast was a relatively peaceable frontier. Unlike in the north and northwest of the empire, army units along the coast did not face constant, immediate, and pressing military threats over the entire course of the Ming. Being less central to the chief military priorities of the empire, they were also not a constant focus of attention by the court.

A second distinguishing element of the region is the relationship between the coast and the inland periphery. Linked by navigable rivers to the coastal plains, upland regions were the main breadbasket for the military bases by the sea. Commercialization driven by maritime trade penetrated these areas, and they were more prosperous and more commercially oriented than the far more isolated counties further in the interior.

The local history of this region has been told by other scholars; just as the major influence for the institutional part of my story is the work of institutional historians of the Ming military, the major influence for the regional part of the story is the recent flowering of local history. I integrate these two bodies of literature, institutional history and local history, to yield a local institutional history, one that reveals how everyday politics in the military institution was conditioned by and in turn conditioned the local physical and social microecology and its legacies.[28]

Most of the research for this book is drawn from about twenty Ming garrisons, or guards, along the Fujian coast, though at times I venture further up or down the coast (figure I.5). One can still see many physical legacies

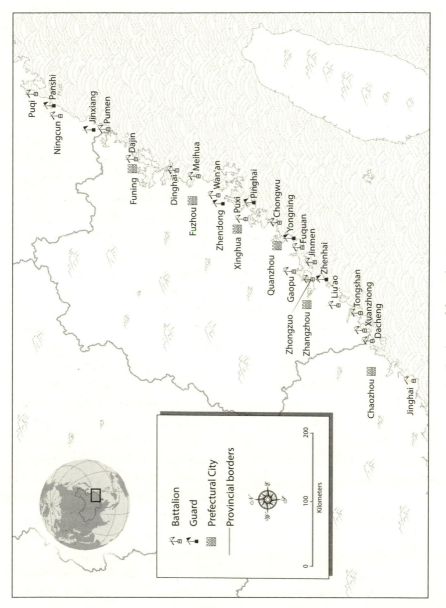

I.5. Garrisons of the southeast coast

of the Ming period on the sites of some of these garrisons, even those that have subsequently been completely surrounded by larger settlements. The Ming layout of Yongning Guard, for example, with its long narrow lane of old paving stones extending almost a mile from one former gate to another, still survives though today the guard is just a small corner of the vibrant city of Shishi. Other former bases, such as Zhenhai, situated on a remote peninsula and atop steep cliffs, have largely been bypassed by recent prosperity. Zhenhai's temples were most recently rebuilt in the eighteenth and nineteenth centuries, and these reconstructions are still intact.

For practical and intellectual reasons, most of the guards discussed here are rural. There were also guards in major cities such as the provincial capital of Fuzhou. The reason that these guards don't appear much in this book has to do with my sources. As I discuss in further detail below, the genealogies of former military households like the Yan family are one of the main sources for this book. The best way to gather such genealogies is simply to go to the former garrisons and look for the descendants of these households. In many rural guards, much of the population still consists of the descendants of Ming soldiers. Such an approach could never work in Fujian's major cities, whose population now numbers in the millions. Moreover, guards located in urban centers never dominated local social, economic, and political life in the way they did in rural areas— though this of course is not to say that the guards did not have an impact on urban society.[29] So for the purposes of isolating the consequences of the institution, the rural guards are a better choice. If we think of the military households as a kind of natural experiment in how people interact with state institutions, the experimental conditions are better where the guards were relatively isolated from the noise of urban life.

This book is also a work of local history because it relies heavily on fieldwork—not the ethnographic fieldwork of an anthropologist who spends a long period of time living in a single community, but fieldwork in the sense that it uses sources collected in the field and interpreted in the local context. In spite of the considerable efforts by more than one state, the historical archive in China has never been fully nationalized. Vast quantities of historical texts are only accessible to the researcher who takes the time to visit the places where these texts were created and used, and where they survive today.[30] Most of the sources used here were not found in libraries or government archives, but in private hands or otherwise in situ. Collecting such sources is one of the great pleasures of this method; it means finding people, often elderly, who are interested in talking about and sharing their history; typically the only cost to the researcher is to be the guest of honor at a meal. Fieldwork literally created the historical archive that I use in this book.

Second, fieldwork means reading the newly created archive in its local context, with particular attention to the local conditions that produced it, and taking advantage of local knowledge that people today, often the descendants of the authors of the text, can bring to bear on it. This can be as simple as locating the plots of land listed on a land deed so as to learn about the work of the farmers who bought and sold them, or clarifying the local terms used in a tax register so as to better understand the actual burden of the tax. Or it can mean cross-referencing a stone inscription at a village temple against local genealogies to understand the kinship connections between the temple's patrons. Or, as we shall see in chapters 6 and 7, it can mean following the procession festival of a local deity as a means of tracing out the boundaries of a community.

With its small scale and focus on local experience, the methodology of this book in some ways resembles the microhistory practiced by scholars such as Robert Darnton and Carlo Ginzburg. Microhistory was intended as a challenge to social-science approaches to history that seemed to efface human agency and human experience. Like microhistorians, my goal here is to trace human agency "beyond, but not outside" the constraints of larger structures, to ask "large questions in small places."[31] While the scale of the stories here is certainly "micro," unlike microhistories of the West few of the sources I use are the product of people's unwilling encounters with agents of the state or other institutional powers. There are few depositions, arrest records, or inquisition reports here. The local documents here were produced for the most part willingly and with more obvious strategic intent. This means they can be more easily used for social than cultural history. The stories here tend to be revealing of behavior rather than *mentalité*, of action more than interpretive framework. They favor narrative over structure. They help us understand political strategies more than political culture.

This book, to summarize, is a social history of a Ming military institution in a local context, based on sources gathered and explored through fieldwork. It proposes a typology of everyday political strategies within a particular microecology, on the basis of which it builds a more general argument about everyday politics in Ming and in Chinese history.

The body of the book consists of four parts, each set in a different place and time. Part 1 is set in the late fourteenth century, when the Ming system of military households was first established, and in the native villages of the soldiers who served in the Ming army. The second and third parts deal with the operation of Ming military institutions in their maturity, mainly in the fifteenth and sixteenth centuries. Part 2 is set in the military bases to which the soldiers in part 1 had been assigned, part 3 in the agricultural colonies where others of them were stationed. Part 4 returns to the garrisons after the fall of the Ming.

Part 1 explores the recruitment and conscription system itself. Chapter 1 opens with the story of the Zheng family, whose creative solutions to the challenge of choosing a family member to serve in the army introduce us to the sophisticated strategies through which families in the military system addressed their obligations to provide labor to the army. Their regulatory position was straightforward—they had to provide one soldier for military duties—but their actual situation could be complex. They developed elaborate strategies to manage the difference between the two, to make their obligations more predictable, to reduce their risks, and to distribute the benefits of their registration as widely as possible while minimizing the costs.

Registration as a military household entailed more than simply providing soldiers to serve in the army. It carried valuable tax exemptions. It exposed the household to potential threats and blackmail from their neighbors. So households had strong incentives to maintain ties to their relatives serving in the army, who could confirm that they were in compliance with the rules of the system. One such family is the Ye of Fuqing, whose most famous member, Grand Secretary Ye Xianggao, has left us an account of how his family tried to restore contact with their soldier-kin on the northern frontier.

Parts 2 and 3 shift the focus from the native villages of the military households to the garrisons in which they were stationed, and from the early years of the dynasty to the middle and later periods. In chapter 3 we meet the Jiang family, hereditary commanders of the garrison at Fuquan. At least one of their members was both an officer and also a smuggler and pirate. His story shows how families took advantage of their special position in the military system to gain advantage in illicit commerce. Their proximity to the state and their ability to negotiate the differences between the military and commercial realms using their special position gave them a competitive advantage in overseas trade. Soldiers stationed in the garrison had to adapt to the new contexts in which they found themselves and build new communities. Chapter 4 explores soldiers' marriage practices, the temples at which they worshipped, and the Confucian schools at which some of them studied to show how soldiers and their families became integrated into the societies where they were garrisoned.

Part 3 moves from the military garrisons to the military colonies that supported them. In these colonies, groups of military households worked the land to feed their colleagues in the garrisons. The tragic story of the Yan family of Linyang illustrates how soldiers of the colony became highly adept at turning the differences between their land and ordinary land to their own benefit. Commercialization of the economy generated complex patterns of landownership and usage, and households in the colonies tried to draw on these patterns for their own purposes. But everyday politics in the colonies involved more than manipulating the land regime. Just like their counterparts in the guard, households stationed there also had to integrate with the communities around them. Chapter 6 explores this process. Some tried to move between different regulatory systems. Others tried to enter into and even take over existing social organizations. A small temple in the village of Hutou provides an illustration of how these new social relations could endure.

In chapter 7, I return to the garrisons after the fall of the Ming. Even after the Ming military institution no longer existed, it continued to matter to the people who had lived in it. Some refused to let the institution die, seeking to maintain the prerogatives they had enjoyed under it. Others found they had inherited obligations that survived the change in dynasty and had to find ways to manage those obligations. Still others tried to adapt elements of the Ming institution to suit the new context. They found ways to make themselves legible to the Qing state, and they did so using language that Qing officials could accept, even though the language described social institutions that were actually very different from what they seemed.

Together the episodes in the four parts suggest some of the ways Ming families dealt with their obligations to provide labor service to the state. On the basis of the discussion, I propose in the conclusion some broader ways of thinking about the art of being governed in late imperial China and beyond.

PART I

In the Village

CHAPTER ONE

A Younger Brother Inherits a Windfall

CONSCRIPTION, MILITARY SERVICE, AND FAMILY STRATEGIES

THE ZHENG FAMILY lived not far from Yan Kuimei's family, in the city of Quanzhou itself. The mid-fourteenth century was a chaotic time for them. As the ruling Yuan dynasty tottered, local soldiers took up arms against their Mongol rulers. The rebels were crushed after much violence by a loyal Yuan general; his army would soon fall in turn to the rising power of Zhu Yuanzhang. The patriarch of the Zheng family was among the countless victims of the turmoil. His widow fled the city with her four sons, hoping to find safety in more isolated Zhangpu county to the south. In the 1370s when a measure of stability had returned, she sent two of her sons back to Quanzhou, ostensibly to tend to their father's grave. The other two sons stayed by her side in their new home in Zhangpu.

In 1374, two years before the Yan family, the widow and her two remaining sons came to be registered as a military household—probably as part of a general draft, but we do not know for sure the precise circumstances. The family was required to provide one soldier to serve in the army in a far-off garrison. They had to decide which of the two brothers would serve. The decision might seem straightforward, but it generated some complex negotiations. These involved not only the issue of military service itself but also questions of inheritance or, to use the Chinese term, "household division" (*fenjia*).

Inheritance in premodern China was patrilineal and partible. When members of a family decided they no longer wanted to live in a common household, pooling their property and income together—a decision taken most often on the death of the parents—the household estate was divided up evenly among the sons. Families might make provisions for specific circumstances, but they generally adhered to this basic principle, and indeed it was required by law.[1] According to an account in their genealogy, the Zheng family did things very differently. The two brothers in Zhangpu divided the whole estate between themselves; the two brothers sent back to Quanzhou got nothing. Nor did the two sons in Zhangpu divide the property evenly, as partible inheritance would require. The elder brother received only one-quarter of the value of the estate. The bulk of the estate, three-quarters of the total value, went to the younger brother. The genealogy explains why. The younger brother received the lion's share because he took responsibility for the family's military service obligation. He was the one who went off to join the army. In effect, the elder brother used half of his inheritance to buy himself an exemption from military service.

This decision would have consequences not just for the two brothers themselves but also for their descendants in the generations to come. For the agreement, like the military service obligation itself, was hereditary. Only the younger brother's sons and grandsons would be liable to serve in the army; the elder brother's would be exempt.

Many years later when the younger brother had grown old, the question arose of who would replace him in the ranks. Both brothers had three sons; there were six males in the third generation. The initial, unequal division of the original household estate meant that the three sons of the elder brother were free of any obligation to serve. So the crucial question was which of the younger brother's three sons would go to the army. A second round of negotiations ensued. The family might have simply repeated the solution of the previous generation and given a larger share of inheritance to the son who agreed to serve. They did not, perhaps because the estate was no longer big enough to persuade anyone to become a soldier. Instead, this round of negotiations was all about prestige and ritual.

The result of the negotiations was that the second eldest son of the second brother was appointed the "descent-line heir" (*zongzi*). This was already an archaic term in Ming times. It gestured back to classical antiquity, when noble families practiced a form of primogeniture called the descent-line system (*zongfa*), whereby in every generation the eldest son inherited the political and ritual privileges of his father. From the Song

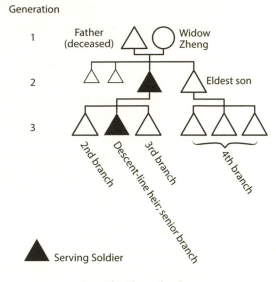

1.1.The Zheng family

onwards, some neo-Confucian thinkers had been calling for this system to be revived and extended to the common people. They recognized that the world of the ancients was gone forever, that primogeniture would never again replace partible inheritance. But they hoped that giving the eldest son in each generation a special ritual role could provide a much-needed sense of order and hierarchy in their own troubled times.[2] The Zheng were one of many families in Ming Fujian who adopted the practice of appointing a descent-line heir. But they did not give the title to the eldest son of the eldest son. They gave the title to the second son of the second son. Why? Because he was the one who replaced his father in the army. His descendants became the "senior" branch; his sons and their sons would forever take precedence in sacrificial ritual. Whereas the first generation had traded inheritance rights for service obligations, the second generation traded ritual precedence for service obligations (see figure 1.1).[3]

On Genealogy

Like the story of Yan Guangtian in the introduction, this story of the Zheng family is drawn from their own internal account of how family members dealt with the challenge of fulfilling military service obligations over the course of generations. They were not alone in facing this challenge. One widely cited though probably exaggerated early Ming source puts the proportion of military households at 20% of all households. By the late Ming, there were four million registered soldiers, which meant four million registered households.[4] The rules that governed this immense system are recorded in the Ming dynasty's statutes. But how did these rules actually matter to these people's lives? We can answer this question only by turning to the documents produced by ordinary people and in many cases still in the hands of their descendants. The Zheng genealogy shows that for this family the consequences of military registration went well beyond military service itself, shaping inheritance practices and property relations, internal family structure, and even ritual behavior.

In sheer volume, the number of (written) characters they contain and the number of (human) characters they describe, genealogies are the greatest surviving source for Chinese history in Ming and Qing times. The term *genealogy* encompasses everything from a handsomely printed and bound multivolume work to a handwritten scrap of paper on which successive generations of barely literate family members have written names of ancestors. Today, it can also mean a reprint of an older genealogy that a lineage member has found in a research library, a photocopied version used to replace a personal copy lost in the Cultural Revolution, or even a virtual genealogy that exists only online. A typical Chinese genealogy consists mostly of family-tree charts and biographies of the male descendants of the founding ancestor, and sometimes their wives and daughters. For most descendants, this is the kind of information that is most useful if one needs to perform sacrifices to one's ancestors—a typical entry consists only of dates of birth and death and the location of their tomb. But many genealogies contain much more information—property deeds and contracts that shed light on the material conditions of the lineage members; prefaces commissioned from prominent men, illustrating the lineage members' social networks, and essays on such diverse topics as family origins, construction of ancestral halls, and even taxation matters. The story of Yan Kuimei's family is taken from one such text, as is the tale of the Zheng of Zhangpu.[5]

Not every family in Ming had a genealogy, and no genealogy is the product of the collective efforts of every family member. Rather, genealogies were compiled by certain members of certain families, with their interests in mind. But all this means is that genealogies, like any other historical source, need to be read carefully and critically. As Maurice Freedman wrote, the genealogy is "a set of claims to origins and relationships, a charter, a map of dispersion, a framework for wide-ranging social organization, a blueprint for action. It is a political statement."[6] Every genealogy is produced by a concrete group of people in a concrete historical setting, driven by concrete historical concerns. Genealogies are texts in which power relations, real and potential, have been inscribed. The genealogy is not solely or even primarily a vehicle for making political claims, but it often does serve this purpose. Since genealogies are records maintained by the members of military households themselves, their political claims illustrate the family's interaction with the state from their perspective, showing what it meant to them.[7]

We need not take these texts at face value as true accounts. Better to think of them as what Zemon Davis called "fictions"—meaning not texts that are false but texts that have been deliberately formed into narratives.[8] An account of how a family dealt with its obligations may not be simple description but rather retrospective construction or argument. The sources shed light on the organizational resources and approaches that people used to deal with their problems. That these strategies appear in the genealogies suggests, at a minimum, that people found the logic of these strategies valid. They show us solutions that were culturally and politically acceptable. We also know from the appearance of these same strategies in legal documents that certain people did indeed make use of such strategies and found their logic valid and persuasive. Ming judges adjudicated cases about precisely the same practices as are described in the genealogies. Whether a given family actually used a given strategy is for our purposes largely irrelevant. Families made use of certain narratives to explain a situation; at the core of this analysis is the question of why they chose these narratives rather than others.

Military Households of the Ming

The families discussed in this book shared one thing in common: they were registered by the Ming state as military households. They probably had other things in common with one another (and for that matter with our families today). They must have worried about the harvest, worried about money, worried about their children's future. They squabbled and they celebrated. Not every aspect of their lives is accessible to the historian. But from their genealogies we can learn quite a lot about one particular element of their common experience, the way they were registered with the Ming state.

"Registration" here means several things.[9] First, it has a concrete sense. The name of the family's ancestor (usually a late fourteenth-century ancestor) was recorded in a particular type of state file, known as a Yellow Register (*huangce*). One copy of the file was housed together with other state documents in a vast archive located, to protect against fire, on a small island in a lake near the modern city of Nanjing, the site of the capital in early Ming. All military households in principle had an entry in a Yellow Register. An additional set of records, known as a Military Register (*weixuanbu*), was maintained for households that held hereditary officer rank.[10] Figure 1.2 is a reproduction of one such Military Register for a household headed by a man named Pu Manu. Copies of these files were housed in different archives, in the Board of Military Affairs and the Palace Treasury.

From 1381 to the fall of the dynasty in 1644, thousands of officials and clerks maintained the vast state archive of such documents, receiving, copying, updating, filing, and transmitting its records. The Ming used various technologies to ensure the security and integrity of its data. The registration archive was protected not only by location but also by redundancy. Household registration data was kept in different forms in multiple locations—in the county offices, or *yamen*, in the place where the household had originally been registered and in the military base where members of the household were garrisoned—and periodically updated so that mistakes in any one version could be corrected.[11] Like any historical document, a personnel file has a material existence, and the story of how the file came to be—of its circulation, collation, and copying, of its storage and transmission—could be the source for a different kind of history. And it has a strategic existence. The story of how a file was deployed, manipulated, faked, or even deliberately lost, tells yet another history. An alternative version of this book could be written as a history of these files, of their creation, retention, and disposal and their movements across the land.

Registration in the state archive had practical political consequences; it implied certain obligations to the state. Military household registration specified a permanent, hereditary obligation to provide labor for the Ming military at a location of its choosing. Pu Manu, a native of Jinjiang county, was conscripted in 1383 and assigned to nearby Quanzhou, the original home of the Zheng family, and the same guard where a member of the Yan family was briefly stationed during the period of the voluntary disclosure policy.[12] In 1388 Pu Manu was transferred up the coast to Fuzhou. Later, in the early fifteenth century, he served on a naval expedition to Southeast Asia (on this expedition see chapter 3). His meritorious performance earned him a promotion to the rank of company commander (*baihu*). The promotion was hereditary; with some conditions every subsequent member of the household who served in the military also held the rank of commander.

Pu Manu retired from active duty in 1425. By that time his eldest son had already died. So he was replaced by his grandson. The personnel file continues for five more generations, through another of Manu's grandsons, who replaced his deceased brother and served for almost fifty years, through that man's own sons and grandsons, to the seventh-generation member of the lineage, Pu Guozhu, who took up his position in 1605. With each transition, authorities in Fuzhou sent word to the central board, where the archive clerks updated the file. The updating of the records only lapsed after Pu Guozhu's time, in the waning decades of the Ming, probably because by then the whole Ming institutional system was collapsing.[13] In the way it traces lines of descent back to a distant ancestor, specifying the relationship between the members of each generation, the personnel file resembles a genealogy. But it is a genealogy of a special sort. It is a genealogy of service to the Ming state.

These two senses of registration, the concrete sense that one's name or the name of an ancestor was recorded in a particular type of file in a particular archive and the service obligation that this implied, had social consequences. People at the time recognized that families who were registered as military households shared these rights and obligations. So a third meaning of registration is to describe a class or category of persons and families. This was an indigenous category, not one invented by historians after the fact. Military household (*junhu*) and military-registered (*junji*) are the terms most often used to describe this category, and people in Ming times knew what these terms meant. This third sense of the term was not only social—because it affected social relations within military households and between military households and other people—but also cultural—because people shared ideas about the category of people who had the status.

In this chapter and the next, I explore how families responded to these various implications of registration, and how the social implications of the various meanings of registration changed over time. Registered households strategized about how to interact with the military registration system; this chapter is about the strategies they came up with using the organizational and cultural resources they had at their disposal, and how their actions in turn affected that repertoire of resources.

蒲氏選譜武

一外黄查有

衛所百户

一草蒲媽奴　已載前黄

二草蒲榮　舊選簿查有

三草蒲壽奇　舊選簿查有

四草蒲英　舊選簿查有

五草蒲威　舊選簿查有

六草蒲茂　舊選簿查有

七草蒲國柱　年九歲係福州右衛後所故世試百户

1.2. Pu Manu's archival record

PU MAO: PROBATIONARY COMPANY COMMANDER

The external Yellow [Register] contains the record:

Pu Ying, of Jinjiang.

Great-great grandfather Pu Manu. 1383: conscripted to serve as soldier in Quanzhou Guard. 1388: transferred to Fuzhou Right Guard Rear Battalion. 1406: promoted for merit to Squad Commander. 1414: promoted for merit to Probationary Company Commander. 1425: [retired due to] age. [Ying's] Great-grandfather Qing died without succeeding to the position.

Grandfather Rong, descendant in the main line of descent. 1435: [Rong] died.

[Ying's] uncle Fu, descendant in the main line of descent. He was a minor and [therefore] received a stipend, superior grade. 1455: died without issue.

[Ying's] father Shou was Fu's younger brother... 1459: came of age and succeeded to the position. 1507: [retired due to] age.

Ying, eldest son in the main line of descent, succeeded to the Commander position.

FIRST GENERATION: PU MANU

Recorded in previous Yellow [Register] [i.e. above]

SECOND GENERATION: PU RONG

Previous Register of Appointments records:

1434, tenth month: Rong, age 17 *sui*, senior grandson of Fuzhou Right Guard Rear Battalion Probationary Company Commander Manu, who was originally Platoon Commander, and who went to the Western Oceans on state business and was promoted from his original position on his return, [is now] specially appointed by imperial favor as Probationary Company Commander.

THIRD GENERATION: PU SHOU [TRANSLATION OMITTED]

FOURTH GENERATION: PU YING

Previous Register of Appointments records:

1507, twelfth month: Ying, of Jinjiang, eldest son of Company Commander of Fuzhou Right Guard Rear Battalion Shou, [retired due to] age, is appointed by imperial favor to the hereditary position

FIFTH GENERATION: PU MINCHENG [TRANSLATION OMITTED]

SIXTH GENERATION: PU MAO

Previous Register of Appointments records:

1548, tenth month: Mao, age 8, of Jinjiang, second son of deceased hereditary Company Commander of Fuzhou Right Guard Rear Battalion Mincheng.

Father Mincheng: originally Probationary Company Commander. 1545: promoted to Company Commander in accordance with regulations... 1552: died; stipend suspended.

1555, twelfth month: Mao, age 15, second son in main line of descent... came of age and succeeded to the position of Probationary Company Commander

SEVENTH GENERATION: PU GUOZHU

Age 9, eldest son of deceased hereditary Probationary Company Commander of Fuzhou Right Guard Rear Battalion Mao. 1597, second month: selected to receive full stipend, superior grade . . . 1605, eighth month: Guozhu, age 17, eldest son of Mao, deceased, appointed [Probationary Company Commander], second rank . . .

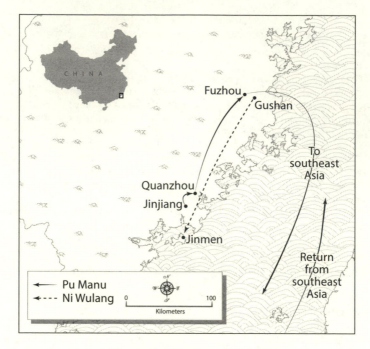

1.3. The stories of the Pu and Ni families

How the Ni Family Came to Jinmen: An Introduction to the Institution

To begin our discussion we need a more thorough understanding of the military institution itself. Rather than convey its mechanics through a dry institutional summary, let us instead look at the story of a single soldier, an ordinary man named Ni Wulang. He is not an invented or composite figure but a real person, though not a person about whom we know very much. In the next few paragraphs, I will fill in some of the blanks around his life as a way to show the basic operations of the military household system. I use Ni's life history to shed light on four elements of the institution: the systems of recruitment and household registration, of assignment and transfer, of succession, and of permanent settlement. Along the way, I will also use his story to explain some of the specialized vocabulary that I use in the rest of the book.

Recruitment and Household Registration

Ni Wulang almost certainly had an entry in the Ming archive, but only a tiny fragment of that archive survives, and unfortunately his name is not in it. The only historical source we have about the man himself is a brief biographical notice in a genealogy compiled by his descendants. The most recent edition of that genealogy, probably written about a century ago, tells us that Ni was born east of the city of Fuzhou, at a place called Gushan Mountain. "In the twenty-fourth year of the Hongwu reign (1391), in order to defend against pirates, he was stationed at Jinmen Battalion. Thus he laid the foundation [of the family] on Jinmen. He married a woman née Ruan. The anniversary of his death is the third day of the twelfth month. He is buried outside the south gate of the battalion wall, at the place called Kengdilun."[14]

These few sentences are the whole of Ni Wulang's presence in the written historical record. But even this very short record is enough to situate Ni Wulang in relation to the institutions of the Ming state. Though the genealogy never says so explicitly, the fact of his assignment to Jinmen Battalion makes it all but certain that his family was registered as a military household.[15] We can think of the process by which a family became registered as a hereditary military household as a channel for *recruitment* into the Ming army.

There were four main channels of recruitment into the Ming army, or ways one could be registered as a military household. Two were specific to the founding of the dynasty. Like most dynastic founders in Chinese history, the Ming founder came to power through military triumph. Once he declared himself emperor and established the Ming dynasty in 1368, many of the men who had joined his army over the years were registered as military households. They were known as "fellow campaigners" (*congzheng*). Some became hereditary officers, and if they survived the purges of Zhu's later reign, they became commanders of garrisons in places like Pinghai or Jinmen. The second channel recruited the armies of Zhu's defeated foes, including both Mongols and other rival claimants to replace the Mongols. Their soldiers too were registered as military households and incorporated into the Ming system as "submitters" (*guifu*). The numbers of "fellow campaigners" and "submitters" were essentially fixed after 1368; no new households were recruited to the military through these channels after the dynasty was founded.

A household could also be recruited into the military as a consequence of conviction for a crime. Recruitment into the military registration was on the books as a punishment throughout the Ming, but it was only in the early part of the dynasty that large numbers of convicted criminals and their families were registered as hereditary military households. By the fifteenth century, recruitment by criminal conviction was no longer typically hereditary. It applied only to the convict himself, and the obligation to serve in the military died with him. Conviction for a crime could be and increasingly was redeemable by a payment of a fine or provision of labor service for a specified period.[16]

The fourth main recruitment path was through a draft (the reason I use this term rather than conscription will become apparent in a moment). As Zhu Yuanzhang's forces swept across the land in the mid-1360s, "fellow campaigners" and "submitters" were left behind to garrison newly pacified areas as they came under Zhu's control. After the conquest, troops could still be moved around to meet operational needs but there was no longer a pool of forces that could be permanently transferred to one location without creating a shortfall in another. Nor was there a large number of convicted criminals waiting to be assigned to new units, even if anyone had thought that a good policy—which no one did. So to provide military manpower for newly pacified areas like the southeast coast, Zhu's lieutenants implemented drafts. In these drafts able-bodied men were impressed from the general population and they and their families registered as hereditary military households.[17] The genealogy does not tell us explicitly how Ni Yulang was recruited. But the circumstances and timing make it all but certain that he was recruited through the draft.

The *Veritable Records of the Ming*, the imperial annals compiled for each emperor's reign by a staff of historians under the subsequent emperor, provide the story of the drafts on the southeast coast from the court's perspective. An entry from early spring 1387 reports that Zhou Dexing, who we met in the introduction as the God of the Wall of Pinghai, drafted more than fifteen thousand soldiers in Fujian and built sixteen garrisons to which they were assigned. Several months later Zhou's counterpart up the coast in Zhejiang reported similar results. "From each household with more than four registered males one person was recruited to serve as a soldier. In total more than 58,750 men were obtained." Most of the people we will meet in this book were descendants either of the men conscripted at this time, of members of the military households that were registered when their ancestors were drafted back in the 1380s, or of their officers.[18] Ni Wulang was one of them.

Assignment and Transfer

When Ni Wulang was drafted, he would have been assigned to a unit known as a guard (*wei*), under the command of a guard commander (*zhihui shi*). Guards, with a nominal size of 5,600 men, were subdivided into five battalions (*suo*), each with 1,120 men. There were also independent battalions (*shouyu qianhu suo*), units administered by a guard but physically separate from it. Battalions were further subdivided into companies of one hundred men. Lower officers' ranks were named for the number of men under the officer's command. Battalions were led by "thousand [household] commanders" (*qianhu*); Companies by "hundred commanders" (*baihu*), the rank held by Pu Manu.[19] Because guards and battalions were the main peacetime operational unit, Chinese scholars often use the term "guards and battalions" (*weisuo*) as a shorthand term for the Ming army; I will further abbreviate the term to just "Guards."

The Ni genealogy tells us that Wulang was assigned to serve in Jinmen, a small island located about three hundred kilometers to the south of his native place near Fuzhou (figure 1.3). Jinmen, also sometimes known as Quemoy, was an independent battalion under Yongning Guard. Some of Ni Wulang's descendants still live there today. I have talked to them, and they tell me that Ni Wulang came to Jinmen because he was "transferred" (*diao*) there. Historians are trained to be skeptical of the stories people tell about even their own experiences, let alone those of their parents or recent ancestors. It would be reasonable to dismiss out of hand an oral tradition about the military career of an ancestor who lived more than six hundred years ago. But it turns out that the story these descendants tell is almost certainly true. We know this because it is also recorded in the *Veritable Records*.

According to the *Veritable Records*, only a few years after the massive drafts of the 1380s, the emperor began to receive troubling reports. Because they were stationed near to their homes, the newly drafted troops were well connected to local society and found it easy to evade duty or even desert, slipping back to their villages and disappearing. Or they took advantage of their position to make trouble in their home communities. The emperor took decisive action. Applying a kind of military version of the rule of avoidance that forbade officials from serving in their native place, he ordered that all soldiers be transferred to bases far from their homes. He saw that the solution to the problem lay in deterritorializing the new soldiers, removing them from their existing social networks. But it soon became apparent that the cost of implementing the policy would be prohibitive. So the policy was modified. Troops were rotated within a single region, sent far enough away to resolve the problem of tension with local communities but near enough to limit the material and personal costs.[20] This is how Ni Yulang ended up in Jinmen (the genealogy is off by a couple of years on the date).

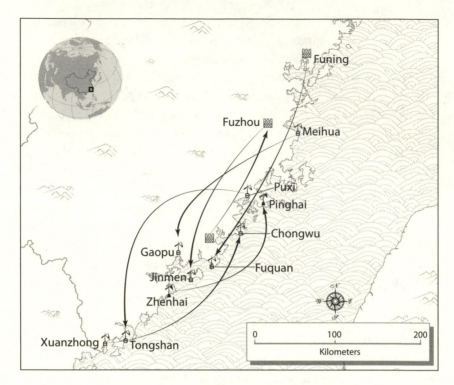

1.4. Troop transfers in fourteenth-century Fujian,
according to genealogies and oral history

The Ni family's legend of their ancestor's transfer from Fuzhou to Jinmen is common among former military households in the region. Many
people living in former garrisons today tell a similar story of ancestors
being transferred from elsewhere in Fujian in the late fourteenth century. Their genealogies confirm the story; so do the gazetteers. This evidence lets us trace several other circuits of movement from this period,
filling in the details of the spare entries in the *Veritable Records* (see
figure 1.4). Besides the transfer of troops including Ni Wulang from the
Fuzhou area to Jinmen, troops from Puxi were sent south to Tongshan
and troops from Xuanzhong north to Chongwu. The troops of Zhenhai
were transferred to Pinghai and troops from the Quanzhou area to the
north of the province, including to Fuzhou where they replaced soldiers
like Ni Wulang who had been transferred to Quanzhou (figure 1.4).[21] The
consistency between the oral tradition, the genealogical record, and the
official documents about this historical episode is powerful confirmation that oral history, at least on certain issues, should not be summarily
dismissed as fanciful.

Succession and Conscription of Replacement Soldiers

Ni Wulang's registration as a military household would have triggered the creation of a new entry in the local population registers, which would then have made its way upwards to the archive in Nanjing. In some records the name at the top of the entry was actually the name of a real person who served in the army; in others it was a pseudonym or an invented name. Ni's entry does not survive so we don't know which it was in his case. As we have already seen, a registration entry did not mean that all members of the household were soldiers or liable for military service. Rather, it signified that the family had an obligation to provide one adult male for military service. This man was known as the *serving soldier* (*zhengjun*). Each military household was responsible for ensuring that there was one serving soldier associated with their registration on duty at all times.

The obligation to provide a serving soldier had no fixed term; it was permanent and continuous. When the incumbent died or became incapacitated due to illness, injury, or old age, or if he deserted, he had to be replaced. In a sense, the registration entry created a slot or position and specified the pool of people who were responsible for filling the slot when it became empty. I use the term *conscription* to describe the process whereby an empty slot was filled by a replacement soldier, or in other words what happened when one serving soldier was replaced by another. Thus a family was recruited into the military institution when it was registered as a military household; individual members of the family were conscripted when they actually served as soldiers. I use the term *regulars* to describe actual serving soldiers in guards and battalions so as to distinguish them from soldiers recruited through other channels, such as mercenaries and local militias.

What about members of military households who were not themselves serving as soldiers? The Ming state used different terms to describe these family members depending on the type of household in which they were registered. Family members in hereditary officer households were known as housemen (*sheren*) and in ordinary soldier households as supernumeraries (*junyu*). These terms originated in the early Ming system, when they referred to an individual family member who would accompany the serving officer or soldier to the guard to provide assistance. (The term *houseman* actually goes back to antiquity, but meant something very different then.) I use the term *military kin* to describe both groups.

When a slot became empty, the registered household had to find someone to fill it. Registration thus entailed rights and obligations that extended beyond the soldier himself to his household, to his kin, and in theory to all of the people descended from the ancestor in the archive. The registered household in this sense survived beyond the lives of its individual members; the obligation was inherited by the descendants of the original soldier and by their descendants in turn.

Ni Wulang was buried outside the walls of Jinmen Battalion. His biography tells us the day on which he died, because it was important for the family to know when to offer sacrifice to his spirit, but not the year. He was survived by two sons. The younger left Jinmen and moved to the mainland, settling outside the county seat of nearby Tong'an. The family lost touch and the genealogy does not tell us what became of him. But we can make an educated guess about the elder son. He is known to posterity by the sobriquet or courtesy name "Gentleman of the South Battalion." He followed his father into the army.

Household registration was required of every imperial subject. As the author of a seventeenth-century gazetteer of Fujian put it, "In the early years of the dynasty, when Fujian was pacified, the people were ordered to make a truthful report of their household . . . The people were ordered to take on the registration that corresponded to their occupation." The occupational categories—the most important of which were civilian, military, craftsman, and saltern (responsible for producing salt)—were fixed and hereditary. Households in most categories were supposed to report any changes to their situation when the population records were recompiled every ten years. But the rules for military households were slightly different. They were forbidden from dividing their household.[22] This did not mean that all of Ni Wulang's descendants—who already by the time of his great-grandson's generation numbered more than twenty males—were forever expected to live together with their wives and children and hold their property in common. Rather, it meant that all the descendants of the original household had to remain under their original shared registration. The entry in the Nanjing archives with Ni Wulang at the head specified an obligation that fell on everyone who was descended from him, forever.

This poses a terminological challenge because Ming sources use the same term household (*hu*) to refer both to the registration status implying a fiscal or labor obligation and the social group responsible for that obligation. This is not such a problem when we are talking about the early years of the dynasty when the two were basically coterminous. But it becomes a problem for later periods when the two phenomena had diverged. The household in the sense of a domestic unit was the main organization responsible for production, consumption, and property ownership. But responsibility for labor service inhered in the patriline, consisting of all the descendants of the first ancestor to be registered, down through the generations. A single household (*hu*) in the latter sense might be comprised of many households (*hu*) in the former sense. To deal with this problem I use the term *household* to describe the unit of tax obligation and *family* for the social group. Later, the kinship group descended from the original family might grow very large and consist of multiple, even many, families living separate lives. I use the term *lineage* for such groups.[23] The law forbidding military households from dividing really meant that everyone descended from an early Ming soldier was required to remain registered under a single household registration. Thus the Zheng family, with whom the chapter opened, was not technically in violation of the rule. They divided the household only in the social sense, while remaining part of a single household in terms of their registration.

The purpose of the rule on household division was to maintain the strength of the armed forces at early Ming levels. If the several sons of a military household divided their household and registered separately, the archivists could have created a new entry for each new household and issued multiple conscription orders. The size of the armed forces would then grow needlessly due to natural population increase. We might think that maintaining an accurate record of the number of members of military households should have been a state goal in itself. Zhu Yuanzhang in his wisdom saw no need for this. From the perspective of the center, it was easier just to forbid the original household to divide and leave the problem of finding a replacement to the descendants of the original household collectively. In effect, the policy delegated the administrative challenges of finding replacement soldiers to the registered households in the hope of reducing overhead costs. This policy decision is precisely what created the possibility for families to strategize about how best to meet their obligation.

When Ni Wulang died, just as when any slot became empty through death, injury, or desertion, a bureaucratic procedure would have been initiated. Clerks would consult their copy of the personnel file associated with that slot. Underneath the name at the head of the file was a description of how that person came to serve, his place of registration, the garrison to which he was assigned, and the person's current situation. By analogy with surviving archival registrations for officers—such as the one we just saw for Pu Manu—we can reconstruct Ni Wulang's entry. It must have read something like "Ni Wulang, recruited by draft, native of Gushan in Fuzhou, assigned to . . . . , later transferred to Jinmen Battalion." In the early fifteenth century, the clerk would have added the notation "deceased" to his file and then initiated the procedure to conscript his replacement. In early Ming, the first step in the procedure was ordinarily to notify the authorities in the original native place that there was a vacancy that needed filling. Local clerks would identify the household with the obligation to provide the replacement and make arrangements for the replacement to be conscripted and sent to his assignment. The name of Ni's eldest son in the genealogy, "Gentleman of the South Battalion," suggests that the replacement process in this case was straightforward. The son's name was added to the entry in the government archive, underneath that of his father, and he reported for duty. One of the reasons that the replacement was so straightforward in this case was that there was no need to go back to the original native place to conscript a replacement. Ni's son was already with him in the battalion. This was the result of an early fifteenth century innovation to the system, one with enormous consequences for our story.

Permanent Settlement and Localization

Fuzhou, where Ni Wulang was born, is only about three hundred kilometers from Jinmen, the post to which he was assigned. But in much of China, newly conscripted serving soldiers were assigned to garrisons far, sometimes very far, from their native place. Moreover not all of the military households registered in one place were assigned to the same garrison. This may have been a deliberate effort to keep soldiers from one locality from serving together, or it may simply have been the result of operational transfers that moved some soldiers to new garrisons to meet immediate military needs.[24] One single county in central China, Gushi in Henan province, had 1,730 registered military households. They were assigned to 358 different guards, which as shown in figure 1.5 were distributed all over the empire. So at least in the early Ming, when the system was functioning as planned, a death in Yunnan triggered a bureaucratic process that led to the eventual conscription of a man more than two thousand kilometers away, in Henan. The great historian of the Ming Ray Huang likens the overall system by which the Ming requisitioned labor to "drawing water from a deep well, not merely bucket by bucket but also drop by drop." The analogy applies well to the specific system of conscription.[25]

A memorial by the military reformer Yang Shiqi (1365–1444) describes systemic problems that would have been all too familiar to Yan Guangtian:

Men from [provinces of north and northwest China] are transferred to the furthest borders of the south to fill the ranks. Men from [provinces

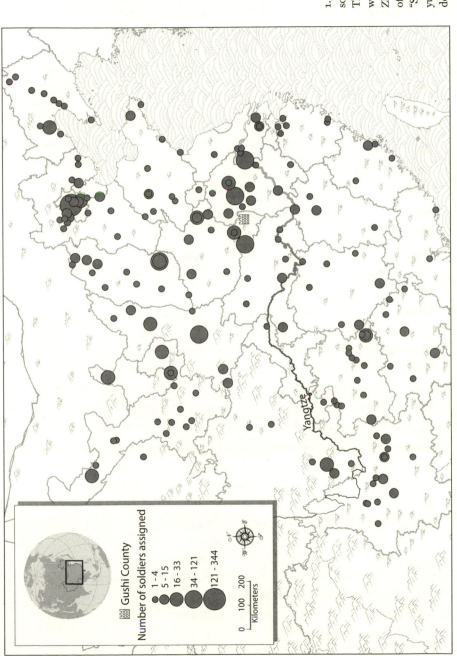

1.5. Assignments of soldiers from Gushi. The data for this map was compiled by Yu Zhijia on the basis of Gushi gazetteers. "Shilun Mingdai weijun yuanji yu weisuo fenpei de guanxi," 409 *ff.*

Yangtze

Gushi County

Number of soldiers assigned

1 - 4
5 - 15
16 - 33
34 - 121
121 - 344

0   100   200
Kilometers

of south and southwest China] are transferred to the distant borders of the north to fill the ranks. In both cases they are unaccustomed to the local conditions. The men of the south perish from cold; the men of the north die of malarial diseases. The garrison may be ten thousand *li* [about six thousand kilometers] or seven to eight thousand *li* [four to five thousand kilometers] from their native place. The travel is extremely difficult, and they cannot get supplies. Most desert or die en route, and so only a few reach the garrison.[26]

This assignment policy first began to change in the early fifteenth century when the Yongle emperor transferred the capital to Beijing. With an eye to developing the new capital region and ensuring his own security, he ordered that new serving soldiers conscripted in the Beijing vicinity should not be sent to the far-off post to which their family was originally assigned but simply stationed in one of the many guards being established near his new capital. His successors generalized the rule, ordering that while replacements for deserters must still be sent to the original post, newly registered military households could be given assignments near to their native place. Yang Shiqi wanted this to become a general rule. His proposal was accepted, and the principle that newly conscripted troops should be assigned to duties close to home became law.[27] This was the beginning of the voluntary disclosure policy that allowed Yan Kuimei's ancestor to serve in Quanzhou, close to his home, and avoid the southwestern jungle.

Officials also worried about what to do with the wives and dependents of conscripted soldiers. They wrote memorials about it and debated the best policy. This was the Ming version of the problem of "camp followers," a perennial issue for armies in world history. Put simply, the issue involves the costs and benefits of having family members and other civilians in close proximity to soldiers. On the one hand, civilians can reduce costs by providing services that the military might otherwise need to provide. On the other, the presence of civilians expands the size of the camp community, creating new logistical burdens and new possibilities for illegality.[28] Zhu Yuanzhang made clear his own policy preferences back in 1374, when he ordered "in all cases where the soldier husband is dead and the widow has no one to support her, let her be sent back to her native place. Let those who wish to remarry or rely on their kin do as they please." A decade later, the emperor noticed an influx of officers' family members, neighbors, and followers to the capital. "Send them back to their villages!" he told the Chief Military Commission. "Let only their parents, their wives and their children" remain with them.[29]

But by the early fifteenth century, military officials were noticing that the benefits to having family members with the serving soldier in the garrison outweighed the costs. Whenever men were transferred to a new garrison the desertion rate went up. "Because they have no dependents they repeatedly desert."[30] Encouraging the soldier to put down roots might help. Having family members in the garrison would also make things easier when the time came to find a replacement for the regular (that is, the serving soldier). If a son or younger brother could be found in the garrison, then much cumbersome bureaucratic procedure could be avoided. The conscripting officer would only have to send a note to the central archive and to the county magistrate in the household's ancestral home, advising them to update their records. The whole complex process of issuing a conscription order to the ancestral home, finding a replacement there, and transferring the replacement to the guard to begin service as a regular could be avoided.

By the 1430s, local officials were encouraging newly assigned soldiers to marry and take their wives with them to the garrison. In 1436 this became general policy. The practice of looking for replacements for serving soldiers in the garrison first before going back to the native place gradually became well established. In 1531, a new rule required that if it was necessary to go back to the native place to find a replacement, and if the replacement who was found was unmarried, his relatives should pay the costs for him to take a wife and for her to accompany him to the garrison. This would remain the general rule for the remainder of the dynasty.[31]

These reforms help us understand why Ni Wulang's wife was by his side in Jinmen. But the genealogy does not give us any information about her background. Was she originally from the Fuzhou area and came with her husband to Jinmen or was she from Jinmen herself and married a new arrival? The Ni genealogy tells us only that she was surnamed Ruan. There are only a few people with that surname in Jinmen today, and they are all recent immigrants (one is a Vietnamese mail-order bride). None of them has a genealogy. So we cannot use genealogical sources to determine where Ni's wife came from. The one thing that is sure is that Ni and his wife and their family had settled more or less permanently in Jinmen. They began to build social relationships with the people around them; they became reterritorialized. Their descendants would eventually begin to intermarry with local women from civilian households; the genealogy records that his seventh-generation descendant married a woman from the Zeng household of Anqian.

An Operatic Interlude

The late Ming play *Record of the Double Pearl* conveys a sense of how people towards the end of the dynasty viewed this system. Shen Jing (1553–1610), an influential though not terribly successful dramatist, set his play in the Tang dynasty, but it is clearly anachronistic. Shen and his audience knew that the world of the play was their own. Scenes 4 and 5 are a dramatic rendition of the very processes described above. The characters even read aloud from personnel files—quoting the text of government documents was apparently not fatal for dramatic tension in Ming opera. As the scene opens, a clerk rushes onstage to see the prefect. He reads from the document he is carrying:

From: The Office of the Military Commissioner of Jinghu Circuit

Re: Inspection and resolution of conscription issues

In compliance with an order from the Ministry of War to investigate the troop situation, the validity of said order having been duly confirmed . . .

Yunyang Guard has issued a report that soldier Wang Yi has died. This has created a shortfall in the ranks

Investigation shows that this soldier's registered native place is Zhuozhou. Let conscription be carried out.

The village elders are summoned and told to produce their own copy of the archive, the local version of the documents in Nanjing. They consult the register and learn that Wang Yi's household includes two other adult males, his brother Wang Jin and his nephew Wang Ji. Wang Jin has already died. "Wang Ji must be conscripted. Seize him and his wife and send them off!"

The action now shifts to the home of Wang Ji, where the handsome young scholar is preparing to take the civil service examinations. Such a man, the audience knows, will be sure to impress the examiners and receive an official post. But the audience also knows that disaster looms. The soldiers burst in and grab Wang and his wife and son. Before they know it, they have been sent to the distant frontier. In the way of Chinese drama, this sets off a chain of lugubrious and improbable events: Wang is framed for murder; his wife seduced by a general; a deity intervenes to prevent her suicide; their fortune turns; Wang saves the empire, and their son places first in the imperial examination.[32]

Happy endings happen only in operas, and not even always there. People in Ming China were familiar with the conscription system and knew that no good generally came of it. Registered families knew that they had to deal with the practical consequences of officials and clerks bursting in on their domestic life and seizing a member of the household. They developed strategies to minimize the disruption to their lives. Official sources typically describe their responses in negative terms—as efforts to evade or shirk their legal obligations. These sources have been used to good effect in traditional institutional histories that explain the problems of the system and the weakness of the Ming army. But such sources are all but useless in shedding light on the motivations of the people involved. Luckily private records in genealogies describe interaction with state institutions from their perspective, showing what the system meant to them and how they strategized within it.

Family Strategies

In many genealogies the descriptions of recruitment and conscription are tantalizingly brief. We read that this family member "was recruited to be a soldier and therefore became registered as a military household," or that "this son was sent on campaign and did not return." Sometimes the reference is even more oblique: "he moved away to Yunnan" in the very year when the official sources tell us that soldiers from Fujian were transferred there to deal with some local uprising. Each such summary must represent an individual or family trauma or tragedy.

Some genealogies give more detail. In one family, the eldest of two sons might choose to serve because his parents "could not bear to be separated from their younger son"; in another a younger son barely into his teens might be chosen to serve. But even these longer accounts tell us almost nothing about how registration affected people's inner lives. There is little on how military registration interacted with notions of loyalty. Such evidence typically emerges only in traces—the anguish of the *paterfamilias* whose son is lost to the army, the righteous indignation of an elderly woman demanding that familiar rites not be tampered with. What the genealogies do tell us is something about people's practical solutions to the problems they faced, about their capacity to identify and seize on opportunities. Of course, the sources do not describe their strategies as such. They tell in a matter-of-fact way what people did. Or they reproduce a formal agreement or contract. So we need to intuit why they did what they did and to what end.

The simplest strategy for dealing with conscription was desertion, but as I explained in the introduction I will not cover that subject here. There are many official accounts of the problem, speculating on the causes and proposing solutions. Sources from the Ming describe root-less men who seem to come from nowhere, hiding out in the wilds and emerging to rob and plunder, or gathering in the *demi-monde* of the growing cities.[33] No doubt many of these people were deserters. But for obvious reasons we have no records from deserters in their own voice, telling us why they made the choices they did and what the consequences were. On the other hand, tens of millions of people in Ming did not desert. Their genealogies tell us about how they strategized about their military obligations, about how they tried to minimize their costs of not deserting, about what they hoped to gain from not deserting, and therefore about the broader consequences of military registration over the course of the Ming and beyond.

Members of military households in early Ming Fujian had three basic strategies for dealing with conscription. We can label these strategies of concentration, rotation, and compensation. They were not mutually exclusive but overlapping; many lineages used two or even three strategies simultaneously. In a concentration strategy, the shared obligation was concentrated on a single individual. One member of the family took full responsibility, sometimes on his own behalf and sometimes on behalf of his descendants, for the service obligation of the entire household. We've seen two examples of concentration already: the brave second son of the Zheng family and the more venal Zhu Shangzhong (of course, the reason for the different treatment is that we know of the former from a source internal to the family and the latter from a source external).

The logical extension of concentration was substitution. Families soon realized that the person on whom the obligation was concentrated did not need to be a family member. An outsider could be persuaded, usually by payment of a consideration, to serve in the army on the family's behalf.

The second basic approach was rotation. Different groups within the family, and later the lineage descended from the original family, took it in turns to provide service. Substitution strategies almost invariably involved some kind of payment or compensation; rotation strategies might but need not involve payment of a consideration. To review, the Zheng of Zhangpu used a combination of concentration and compensation strategies, while the Yan used a combination of rotation, concentration, and compensation. Whether it was to support a concentration strategy or a rotation strategy, there were two basic ways in which families financed compensation. They either levied a capitation charge on all members of the lineage or they established a permanent estate and used the income from the estate to pay the compensation.

The Guo of Zelang was registered as a military household due to criminal conviction. In 1395, the local magistrate was murdered. Guo Yuanxian's son Jianlang was implicated, convicted, and sentenced to conscription (the genealogy assures readers that it was all a frame-up and their kinsman was not really guilty). The name at the top of the family's entry in the national registration archive was Guo Jian, presumably an abbreviation for Guo Jianlang, but subsequent events make clear that all the descendants of his father were registered in a single household. Guo Jianlang was sent to far-off Shaanxi in the northwest (figure 1.5). He traveled alone, leaving behind his son and grandson. In 1405, he died there, alone. The same interest in bureaucratic detail that we saw in the *Double Pearl* is found in the Guo genealogy. "Because there was no adult male to replace him, a document was issued to conscript [a replacement]." The document worked its way back to Zelang.

The basic principle of the conscription system was that father would be replaced by son. In this case this was impossible. Guo Jianlang's son had already died, and his only surviving grandson was still a child. But the obligation on the household remained. Their slot was empty; it had to be filled. To solve the problem, the surviving brothers and nephews decided to hold a lottery. Guo Jianlang's adult male nephews drew lots. Cousin Guo Wei drew the short straw. His name was reported to the authorities. They duly recorded it in their own registers and sent word to Nanjing to have it added to the entry under Guo Jian. But it was not the spirit of fairness alone that made Wei accept his fate. "The whole lineage appreciated his righteous actions, so they gave him a reward to encourage him."

After he was conscripted and set off for the northwest, Wei took a curious step. "After he entered the army, on his own authority Wei altered the name on the registration from Guo Jian to Guiqing." It is not entirely clear what he was up to. The likely explanation is that this was another case of a family combining concentration and compensation strategies. The "reward" he received functioned something like the Zheng family's uneven distribution of the household estate. It was understood by all parties to be a hereditary consideration, compensation not just for Wei's own service but for his assumption of the military obligation of the household in perpetuity. Wei's descendants would serve, freeing his brothers' and cousins' families from the duty. The change of name on the registry was intended to insulate the other descendants of Yuanxian from the risk that they would be called upon to serve.

This interpretation gains some force by events that took place a decade later. In 1416, Wei returned home. "It was decided to collect fifty *taels* to

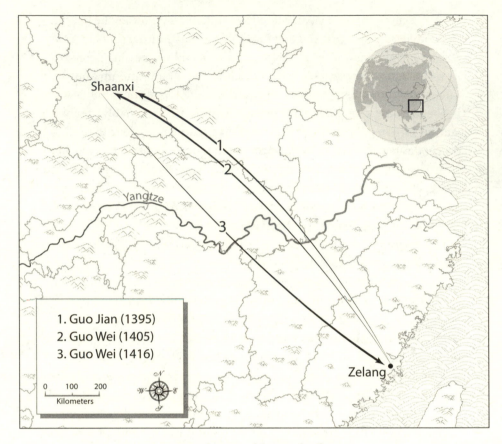

1.6. The story of the Guo family

give him. He was required to personally write a receipt, guaranteeing that he would not return to the ancestral home to try to obtain more money ever again." When Wei returned to his duties in Shaanxi, he took his own younger brother with him, so that he could replace Wei in the ranks when the time came. The essay that narrates this story, "How Gentleman Zhike Came to Be Registered in the Military" is not simply a "just-so story" that explains how things came to be the way they are. It is a contractual agreement.[34] As we will see below, this is precisely how it was used in the centuries to come.

Like the Zheng family with which this chapter opened, the Guo effectively sought to calculate the monetary value of an indefinite and potentially infinite term of military service. The obligation to serve was assigned to a single member of the family in exchange for payment of that amount. This relieved all the other descendants of the registered ancestor of the service obligation. The obligation to serve had been concentrated on a single family member and his descendants, who received compensation for their efforts.

The Guo family's strategy is simply the military household equivalent of more common patterns of household diversification. In elite families in Ming, one son might study for the examinations, another manage the family property, and a third engage in trade. In poor families, one brother might rent land as a tenant and another hire himself out as day labor. Among military households, one son shouldered the army service obligations so that the others could devote themselves to other aspects of maintaining the family. The main difference is that the diversification was formalized by an internal family contract and involved payment of a consideration.

The obligation for military service did not need to be concentrated on the family of the regular (that is, the family member who served as a soldier). Families could also look beyond biological kin to implement this strategy, in effect finding a substitute descendant. This is what the Wang of Yingqiao in Wenzhou chose to do. According to their genealogy, after the family was recruited in the great drafts of the late fourteenth century:

> Gentleman Qiaoyun lacked brothers, so he had his adopted son (*yi'nan*) Hu Qianyi and servant Wu alter their [original] registration from that of monks. They served in the army in Ningcun Battalion. Later they were transferred to Puqi Battalion and later to Longshan Battalion of Ningbo. Qianyi's descendants took on the Wang surname and continued to fulfill the military obligation in perpetuity.[35]

This text raises interesting but unanswerable questions. How did adopted son Hu and servant Wu come to be registered as monks? Was this prior registration itself a strategic move? The text mentions Hu (later Wang) Qianyi's descendants. Did he renounce his vows and marry, had he never actually taken Buddhist vows, or did he perhaps continue the pattern of recruiting a replacement from outside his own biological kin? Whatever the answers to these questions, the use of a substitution strategy freed the rest of the Wang family from the obligation of hereditary military registration. They were no longer personally liable to fill the slot that was created through the draft in 1388. Though they remained registered under the name at the head of the personnel file, the duties arising from the registration had been transferred to other people through substitution.[36]

Substitution strategies were sufficiently common that families found ways to abuse them, and officials developed responses to address the abuses. In 1429, a memorial was submitted to the emperor concerning conscription of "adopted sons and sons-in-laws." If someone was willing to serve in the army to fulfill his adoptive father or father-in-law's hereditary obligation, "it is up to them." But when that person died, the replacement must be sought within the original registration.[37] With the emperor's approval, the memorial then became a *tiaoli*, a codified precedent or substatute with the force of law, which is why it was included in legal compendia and transmitted to us today.[38] Such substatutes were created when administrators responding to particular local conditions raised issues that eventually received imperial approval. At least two editions of collected substatutes on military matters were published, one in 1552 and the other in 1574. Together these collections tell us the response of Ming law to the strategies deployed by ordinary households; they are the counterstrategies to household strategies. While my focus here is on family rather than state strategies, the reality was that families and bureaucrats interacted in ways that meant the institution was always in flux. Clearly what gave rise to this particular issue was that people were trying to evade military service on the argument that an ancestor of theirs had been replaced by a surrogate, an adopted son or a son-in-law, and that the hereditary obligation had therefore been transferred to the descendants of that surrogate.

Wang Qianyi's decision to accept the charge of serving in the army relieved the family of their most pressing obligation. But they had to ensure that Qianyi's descendants continued to fulfill the responsibility that he had taken on. If they did not, then the obligation for military service would revolve back to the original family. To address these concerns, Qiaoyun set aside some of his property as a permanent estate, committing the rental income from it to go in perpetuity to support Qianyi and his descendants.[39] In other words, rather than a one-time payment as in the case of the Zheng or the Guo, Wang Qiaoyun created an estate with a continuous revenue stream to compensate the serving regular. The Wang family thus combined concentration and compensation strategies.

So did the Qingxi Li of Hutou in Anxi county. They were a family of some wealth and influence in the early Ming. Zecheng, a member of the fourth generation, was an examination graduate who held a minor official post. To Zecheng's lifelong misfortune, his superior was convicted of some malfeasance. Zecheng was found guilty by association and sentenced to conscription and registration as a military household. "At that time, the dynasty was newly established and so the rules were applied strictly." (This is probably less a bottom-up perspective on institutional decline than a post-facto explanation of why Zecheng did not commute his sentence by paying a fine.) Zecheng was sent off to a garrison far away in the south-west, in the remote highlands where the provinces of Guangxi, Guizhou, and Hunan meet. There he died. The fate of his replacements was no happier. "For successive generations if the descendant [serving as a soldier] did not die in the ranks then he was buried in the bowels of fishes [i.e., died en route]." Eventually one descendant appointed to the slot appealed for mercy from his kin. "To travel great distances to fulfill corvée is truly onerous . . . Is there no one who can take my place?" Two of his cousins were men of means, and they came up with a solution. In 1455 they endowed an estate to provide for the needs of the serving soldier in the future.[40]

Genealogies of many military households in Ming Fujian refer to estates to pay the costs of compensating the soldier who served on their behalf. There are several possible institutional antecedents for such estates. Their founders may have been inspired by the corporate lineage estates that neo-Confucian scholars promoted to encourage cohesion among agnates or by "charitable service estates" that some people had established in the Song to pay for village tax obligations or perhaps by the tradition of endowing estates to support Buddhist monasteries, academies, and village schools.[41] They were part of the organizational repertoire that Ming military households could bring to the challenges of being governed by the Ming state.

In the preceding examples, the descendants registered in a military household sought to specify more clearly who should serve in the army and provide adequate compensation. Their strategies took advantage of the discrepancies between the simple logic of the system and the reality of complex families. They also made use of the discrepancies between a recruitment regime based purely on kinship and the reality of a market for labor.

The other basic method that households used to deal with their obligation was rotation. This strategy was possible because the recruitment regime expected son to succeed father but the reality was that, in at least some families, with each passing generation there were more and more descendants capable of serving. The concentration strategy recognized the principles of the market—the idea that labor can be recruited by adequate compensation. The rotation system rested on the principle that all the descendants should share the obligations inherited from the ancestors. Like the endowment of estates, the rotation strategy has multiple possible institutional antecedents. It may have been adapted from earlier practices for the management of corporate estates, or perhaps from the Ming system of assigning corvée responsibilities to civilians, a topic discussed in chapter 6.

The Cai of Dalun, near Quanzhou, implemented a rotation strategy to deal with their military obligation. The family was registered as a military household in 1377, having been caught up in Zhou Dexing's general draft. The initial conscript was assigned to the capital in Nanjing. In 1428, the serving soldier had to be replaced. The living members of the lineage agreed that the "rules decided by the ancestors" should determine who was liable for service. These rules—a strategy made explicit—provided for various exemptions, people who should under no circumstances be compelled to serve: the descent-line heir, households with few male members, examination licentiates and their fathers. The actual assignment of responsibility was handled through rotation. By this time the lineage was divided into six branches. Each branch of the lineage was responsible for providing a soldier for a fixed term. When one branch's term began, its eligible adult members would draw lots to decide who would serve. If the serving soldier became incapacitated before the branch's term was finished, the branch would again draw lots to find a replacement to serve out the term. The senior branch took the first term, then the responsibility rotated through the remaining branches by order of seniority. When every branch had served one term, the rotation cycle began anew. This was thus an arrangement combining rotation of responsibility through the subdivisions of the lineage descended from the ancestor who was first registered and the drawing of lots as practiced by the Guo. In order to keep the serving soldier content, it was agreed to pay him a sum of money each year. "Each year [the descendants] come to a collective agreement on the amount to be paid." This amount was then raised by allocating a levy on all of the adults of the branch (or perhaps the lineage as a whole; the text is not clear).

The Cai family's system worked smoothly for several decades. In 1484, it was again the turn of the senior branch to provide a soldier. The lineage members gathered to discuss an adjustment to the rules. They agreed to change the period of the rotation to thirty years. This obviously had implications for the man chosen by lot to be the serving regular. Drawing the short straw now meant soldiering for one's entire adult life. Cai Yujie, the man appointed to serve, actually ended up in the army for almost fifty years. By the time he withdrew from service (or died), the system had changed again, and he was replaced not by a distant cousin from another branch, but by his own descendant. The localization policy that encouraged serving soldiers to relocate to the garrison with their families had taken effect; Yujie obviously had married and had at least one son with him in the guard.[42]

We can sometimes deduce a rotation strategy even if a genealogy does not explicitly mention one, by mapping the pattern of service onto the structure of the genealogy. The Huang family of Jinmen, for example, were first registered as a military household in 1426. A preface to the genealogy identifies their channel of recruitment—"because of the matter of the draft"—but this seems unlikely. If the date is correct then it is more likely that they were recruited through criminal conviction (and explains why they mentioned the circumstances at all—to obscure the real reasons). Eventually they were assigned to Jinmen, where they would have served together with Ni Wulang's family. When the family was initially registered as a military household and required to produce a soldier, they "drew lots." Yu, the first serving soldier, was assigned to Nanjing. Sometime later, he was found to have been lax in guarding prisoners and was transferred to the northwest.[43] There he died. An uncle replaced him; he too died. A second uncle replaced him and died without issue. An order to conscript a replacement was issued. This time it was Yu's cousin who served. The genealogy does not explain how the family chose each of these men, but it is clear from their position in the genealogical tables that there was a rotation system in which the three branches of descendants each served a term. This explains why Yu was replaced not by his brother or son but by his two uncles in succession. On the death of the second uncle, the rotation returned to Yu's branch, who determined, presumably again by drawing lots, who should serve next.[44]

The Rong of Jinghai must also have used a rotation strategy. A summary of the service records of individual serving soldiers shows that soldiers retired from service and were replaced by relatives in 1579, 1589, 1599, 1609, 1619, 1629, 1632, and 1639. This can only mean that a rotation system was in operation and continued to operate until the very last years of the dynasty (the anomaly in 1632 is most likely due to the death of a serving soldier).[45]

While military officials must have been happy to see slots filled by serving soldiers, the rotational approach was open to abuse. Like many other aspects of the conscription, problems appeared in the early decades of the fifteenth century, as the long-term implications of the everyday politics of the system started to become apparent. In 1436, an official in north China noticed that military households had set up rotation systems as a way to get out of their obligations. "Fathers, sons, and brothers are illegally arranging their own transfers. [The officers] in the guards to which they are assigned accept bribes and allow them to replace one another. Each person serves for a year, and rotates one after the other. The one actually serving whiles away his time and before his term is over he deserts. Every year conscription must be implemented, but the ranks stay empty for a long time."[46]

Arrangements like those of the Dalun Cai or the Jinghai Rong were not attempts to beat the system so much as attempts to comply with it in ways that the family members could more easily accept. Their strategies reduced uncertainty and enhanced predictability. When this type of strategy worked as planned, it increased the likelihood that slots would remain filled, that serving soldiers would always be on station. It relieved state agents of the burden and costs of monitoring and ensuring compliance. Perhaps some officials felt that the strategy had a certain appeal because it was consistent with fundamental orientations of the Ming constitution. It assigned the costs of keeping the state running to the lowest possible level of society, relying on local initiative to get the job done. But abuses multiplied, and eventually in 1553, a substatute titled "Soldiers may not surreptitiously replace one another" came into force. It declared, "only when a soldier is old or weak can he request to be replaced. It is not permitted to present a private document agreeing to a ten year or five year rotation through branches."[47]

Neither rotation nor concentration could reduce uncertainty entirely. For it was always possible that the man whose turn it was in the rotation to serve would refuse to go or desert. This is why rotation systems were also often backed up by payments. In practice military households chose from a repertoire or tool-kit of methods to address the issue of payments to the serving soldier. (To us these various strategies seem like multiple solutions to deal with a single problem; this does not mean that they conceived of the problem or its solutions in the same way). Some households, like the Zheng family of Zhangpu, made a lump-sum payment, to compensate for military service either for the lifetime of the soldier or in perpetuity. Others, like Yan Kuimei's family, promised a permanent income stream funded by levies on living relatives. Still others established permanent estates. This last solution was the functional equivalent of an annuity. Without a permanent estate families like the Zheng and Wang had to estimate the value of service each year. To use a modern analogy, they chose a variable rate on their mortgage. Families like the Cai who established an estate avoided one of the challenges faced by the Zheng and the Wang, of estimating the actual present value of service in perpetuity.

The size of the compensation in such strategies could vary considerably. There is no evidence of consistency or standard amounts.[48] How did the huge income generated by the Li estate compare to the size of the younger Zheng son's inheritance? Was the fifty tael payment to Guo Wei comparable in value to the income of the estate whose income served former-monk Hu Qianyi? Agricultural yield and productivity in late imperial China is a highly contentious subfield of Chinese economic history, but a few very rough estimates can help give us some sense of the examples discussed above. Let us estimate average yield in Fujian at two bushels (*shi*) per mu, about in the middle of the range of estimates for the Ming (though these estimates are usually made on the basis of nearby Jiangnan) and average farm size as twenty mu.[49] The harvest would be forty bushels. Three bushels of rice is about what the average adult consumed in a year in Ming (the Ming state assumed that one bushel was adequate for one person's consumption for one hundred days). The estate established for Hu Qianyi, recall, was thirty mu in size, slightly larger than the average farm, and would have produced a yield of around sixty bushels. If we estimate rent at 40%, then this estate would produce rental income on the order of twenty-four bushels, enough to support a family of eight at bare subsistence level. The estate of the Li of Hutou yielded an income of either six hundred or eight hundred baskets (*lao*)—both figures appear in the genealogy. The *lao* was a local measure equivalent to about half a bushel. So this was a considerable property, enough to support dozens of people. Wealthy members of military households were obviously willing to forgo property of substantial value in order to free their descendants from the burden of military service, just as poorer members of the lineage were willing to take on the task of serving as the soldier in exchange for this income.

Though they would not have used this language, military households in early Ming seem to have had an understanding of what perpetual military service was worth in real terms and been able to calculate the net present value of an income stream. In fact their calculations were even more complex because of two additional sources of risk. The first was the risk of default. The rest of the family could never guarantee that they would never be called upon to fulfill the military service that they had paid someone else to fulfill. If the soldier deserted and disappeared, and the authorities arrived to conscript a replacement, then the payment would be for naught. Moreover, there was always the possibility that the army would conscript a *second* member of the household due to some urgent military need. We shall see below that this did indeed happen occasionally. So what families actually calculated was the value of concentrating their military obligation on a single member of the family, discounted by some risk factor.

The responsibility for service and the responsibility for payment did not need to be part of a single strategy but could be unbundled. This is what the Huang of Changle chose to do. Huang Zhulang was conscripted in 1392. He was initially stationed at nearby Meihua and later transferred to Gaopu Battalion, an independent battalion under Yongning Guard. Members of the family continued to serve until at least 1516. The genealogy explains that the eight branches of the lineage together set up a system whereby each branch was responsible in rotation for an annual payment of 2.4 taels. The downside of unbundling was that it introduced new uncertainties. Not only was there a possibility that the serving soldier would fail to fulfill his part of the bargain, but so too whoever was responsible for payment might not fulfill his side of the deal. The solution was to endow a permanent estate. By 1506, one family within the larger registration had become quite successful and produced a scholar. He "reflected that [some of] the descendants of the original registration were impoverished and in difficult straits." So he purchased an estate of fourteen mu. It earned a net income after taxes of 4.1 taels, considerably more than the traditional subsidy. In this family, the estate was managed directly by the serving soldier himself, perhaps to reduce the risk of default, perhaps to insulate the rest of the family from the obligations of the registration. In 1516, when the serving soldier died, his replacement took over management of the estate and its tax obligations.[50]

Local contingencies introduced further variation into an already complex system. In some places, soldiers went to the garrison with a second family member, known as a supernumerary (*junyu*), who could replace him if necessary. Elsewhere, two or sometimes more than two households shared the responsibility to provide a soldier, forming a composite household. We have already encountered this system in the story of Yan Kuimei. The composite household was another inheritance from the Yuan dynasty. Under the Mongols, many military households were actually composite households, made up of two or more families, one regular (*zheng*) and the other auxiliary (*tie*). The regular household had the primary responsibility to supply a soldier, but if the regular household ever lacked an adult male, the auxiliary household had to provide one temporarily. Another regional variation is families who were registered simultaneously as military households and saltern households, responsible for providing salt to the state. The Wang family of Wenzhou is actually an example of this sort of registration, which may have been a deliberate strategy to optimize tax obligations. Other families deliberately took on multiple registrations in the hopes of taking advantage of the system.[51]

Conclusions

Countless states in human history have required some of their subjects to serve as soldiers. Soldiers and their families everywhere have sought to minimize the costs and uncertainties of their military service while maximizing the prerogatives they enjoyed. This chapter is a specific illustration of this general theme.

Whether a family held its own registration, shared a single registration with another family, or held multiple registrations, there was a common goal to its strategies—to minimize the possibility that a position that became vacant due to death, injury, old age, or desertion could not be promptly and mechanically filled at minimal cost. Families took advantage of the discrepancy between the rules of the system and the reality of their situation, and between the rules of one system and the logic of other systems, to optimize their fulfillment of the military service obligation in relation to their own interests.

As it happens, there is a term in economics that corresponds closely to these behaviors: regulatory arbitrage. The term has come into more frequent use since the 2008 financial crisis; some scholars have argued that regulatory arbitrage in the financial sector lay behind the collapse of the mortgage market.[52] But it is an old idea, and a simple one to grasp. To engage in arbitrage is to take advantage of differences between two markets. The same asset—the same thing—may be valued differently in different markets. Buying an asset in one market where it is cheap and selling it in another market where it is dear is the simplest form of arbitrage. "Regulatory arbitrage" refers to efforts to take advantage of differences in regulatory regimes or of differences between one's real situation and one's regulatory position, that is, how one is perceived by a regulatory regime. For a very simple example of modern regulatory arbitrage, consider the inventor of a new herbal remedy. If she chooses to label and market the product as a drug, then it is subject to a restrictive regulatory system. If instead she chooses to market the product as a food, a category with a lower regulatory threshold even though she knows that people are buying it for its purported medicinal purposes, then she is using regulatory arbitrage (of course, the practices that led to the mortgage crisis were much more complicated than this simple example). Again and again in this chapter, we have seen military households trying to take advantage of the differences between the institutional regulations and their own reality in service of their interests. These strategies are the expression of Ming regulatory arbitrage.

The Ming state never decisively resolved the problem of desertion. Huge numbers of soldiers deserted and were not replaced. By the latter part of the dynasty, especially on the strategically crucial northern frontiers, garrisons were chronically understaffed, and paid recruits—mercenaries—eventually became the core of the standing army. For this reason, the Ming conscription system is often treated by scholars as a failure. But here we are not interested in explaining the system's problems. Rather, the focus is on those people who remained within the system, how they worked in and around the institution as it evolved over time, and how they turned its features to their best advantage.

The Ming conscription system, initially devised on earlier models to meet the immediate concerns of the dynastic founding and later reformed to accord with changing realities, operated according to its own logics. The system was genealogical and algorithmic with respect to law. The law stated that the obligation to serve was hereditary and outlined how hereditary was to be interpreted. In theory, each time a serving soldier retired or died, his replacement was to be determined through the application of an algorithm. In its simplest form, the algorithm stated that a serving soldier was replaced by his son. If every serving soldier at the time of the founding emperor had had one and only one son, the algorithm would have remained in this extremely simple form. But society is more complicated than an algorithm.

The households registered in the system operated according to different logics that the algorithm could not comprehend. The countless internal family debates over who should go to the army next were each of them articulations of these different logics. From the perspective of the household, the selection system was an object of decision-making and strategy. The question of who from a larger group of eligible kin should fulfill the military service obligation was recognized as an internal matter for the kin to decide. It is also clear that once such a decision was taken, state agents were expected to accept it, and even, as the various disputes show, to enforce it. The various statutes, substatutes, and precedents relating to conscription in Ming legal texts were basically efforts to revise the algorithm to deal with greater social complexity.

Households enacted their own strategies for managing their relationship with the agents of the state, keeping them at bay wherever possible; finding ways to comply with them at minimal cost and, as we shall see in subsequent chapters, manipulating the resources created by compliance to gain advantage in other spheres. What generalizations are possible about these strategies? The first core principle of their strategizing was to insulate family members from state impositions by specifying or concentrating them as narrowly as possible. (As we will see below in chapter 2, this was coupled with efforts to secure and distribute the benefits of compliance as widely as possible.) A multilevel calibration and negotiation of interests lies behind each of the accounts we have looked at. The individual who ultimately became the serving soldier calibrated the costs and benefits of his service and his own interests against those of the family. The rest of the family calibrated the costs and benefits of the various possible modes of engagement with the military institution.

A second core principle of this strategizing was to increase predictability, to avoid the nightmare that faced the hero of *The Double Pearl*. Whether it was by hiring a surrogate from outside the kin group or securing the agreement of one kin member to serve, or by arranging a fixed-term rotation through a specified group, all of these strategies made it easier to know in advance whether one was likely to have to serve, and if so when.

The third core principle was that all descendants of the patriarch should share in the inherited obligations. This might be called an ethic of fairness in military service, though that is not how the sources present it. The ethic of fairness is implicit in rotation strategies. When a family member took on the responsibility of military service that the rest of the family need not, he should be compensated, whether in property, rights to income, ritual precedence, or in some other form. Having been compensated, he and his descendants should continue to fulfill that responsibility. This fairness ethic was not absolute but was shaped by culture, for example when lineages spelled out exemptions for certain types of people. It also seems to have varied from family to family. Absent entirely from the documents is mention of any ethic of service or loyalty to the state. This was simply not part of the internal considerations of the family.

These strategies were not perfect, of course, for the person who was supposed to serve might desert or become incapacitated, and it sometimes happened that additional family members were conscripted even when the household's slot was already filled. But they aimed at and on the whole must have succeeded at reducing uncertainty. It is hardly surprising therefore that they resemble strategies used in the marketplace to mitigate risk or uncertainty. Selecting and compensating a single lineage member, or an outsider, concentrated all of the risk of being a soldier on him, freeing the rest of the kin group from risk. Rotation systems reduced uncertainties of timing; they allowed people to predict when they or the lineage subdivision to which they belonged would become responsible for military service. Establishing dedicated estates created reliable streams of income; they allowed people to predict in advance their ability to meet the expenses associated with military registration, including both compensation for the soldier's service and payments of subsidies.

Contracts were central to this risk mitigation. Much family strategizing was accomplished through the use of instruments that are recognizably contracts in the sense of agreements intended to be binding in which one party agrees to do something in exchange for a consideration. In the examples I have cited here, the consideration is spelled out explicitly, but in many of the more spare accounts in the genealogies we are told only that "so-and-so went to serve." It is impossible to say how often such a consideration was paid. The sources often explain that all the relatives appreciated the contribution of the serving soldier. In other words, there was a moral value to taking on the family's burden. But for many families there was also a recognition that service had a monetary value for which the soldier should be compensated. Together the two approaches index the relationship between the moral and market economies of Ming China.

In the standard narrative of Ming history today the market is a central player. According to this narrative, widespread commercialization in the fifteenth century led to a habituation to the market and this in turn had manifold effects, including changes to popular culture and the distribution of new skills that served further economic development. But a cultural pattern of seeing the world in terms of things that could be bought and sold already long had been part of everyday life in Fujian. Did the people of the region develop their strategies and contractual solutions by applying their previous experience with commerce to political relationships? Or did they devise through practical and discursive work innovative solutions in response to the challenges of their political relationships, and then apply these same solutions to commercial challenges? In other words, did the economy of state obligations precondition families to find solutions that turned out to work well in the market economy? This is of course a chicken-and-egg argument whose implications are no less profound for the argument's being unsolvable. It complicates the notion of a natural moral economy that precedes and is undermined by market penetration. It suggests that long before the systematic efforts of modern state regimes penetrated Chinese society, ordinary Chinese people had developed a sophisticated economy of state interaction, a system of managing state exactions and expectations. In the genealogies we can see them trying to figure out the best way to inhabit the institution, to live up to its letter while maximizing their own interests, and using the appearance of compliance to their advantage in other negotiations.

Once soldiers were encouraged to settle permanently in their assigned guard, the overall calculus changed. The goal of the settlement policy reforms was to incorporate guard soldiers more completely into the state structure, deterritorializing them from their native village and making it easier to deploy them to meet immediate military needs. But these policies in turn set up new cycles of reterritorialization as soldiers put down roots in their assigned guards and began to construct new communities. For the families in the original native place (*yuanji junhu*), the focus of concern shifted from providing manpower to securing evidence that their slot was filled. This evidence could then be useful in local political disputes, as we shall see in chapter 2. The first era of strategizing was ended. The focus of strategizing now became the family in the guard, and we shall see the patterns of this era of strategizing in chapters 3 and 4.

CHAPTER TWO

A Family Reunion Silences a Bully

NEW SOCIAL RELATIONS BETWEEN
SOLDIERS AND THEIR KIN

YE XIANGGAO (1559–1627) grew up in a military household in Fuqing, midway between Quanzhou and the provincial capital of Fuzhou. Ye's ancestor had been conscripted in early Ming and assigned to a guard in Jiangsu. Later he was transferred to a distant garrison in the far north. In all likelihood, the reassignment was either a routine transfer for operational needs or possibly a form of discipline for some malfeasance. That is not how the family remembered it. A family legend explains that the serving soldier had taken a principled stand against the Yongle emperor's usurpation in the early fifteenth century. The new emperor was furious and inclined to have him executed. But since he could ill afford to lose the services of such a righteous man, he had him assigned instead to the harsh northern frontier, a punishment close enough to a death sentence.

"Because of the great distance," the genealogy continues, the kin back in Fuqing lost contact with the soldier in the north. We know from chapter 1 that the real reason for the breakdown in communication, though it goes unmentioned in the genealogy, was probably that the principled soldier had settled down with his wife on the frontier. When it came time to replace him, conscription officers looked to one of his sons in the garrison to fill the empty slot rather than send back to Fuqing to find a replacement. The consequence of the localization reform was that the two sides fell out of contact.

Meanwhile some of the relatives back in the ancestral home in Fuqing had become rich, possibly from the surreptitious maritime trade that was the source of much local prosperity (and is the main focus of chapter 3).

In the mid-Ming, some scoundrels came up with a scheme to blackmail a particularly successful member of the family. They threatened to go to the magistrate and "denounce him as belonging to a military household." The idea, obviously, was to claim either that he was an actual deserter or that the family's slot in the guard was empty and he was shirking his responsibilities. These plotters were local men who had been deputized to collect taxes and corvée labor from the rest of the populace, which is why their schemes were so alarming. The registration documents that might have saved the day were out of date. The only solution was to somehow show that the claims were false.

Luckily a plucky member of the family was willing to take action. He traveled to the northern frontier in search of the current serving soldier. Unfortunately the genealogy provides no information about the journey; we know from other sources that it must have been an odyssey lasting months, perhaps years.[1] He found his long-lost relative, received a warm welcome, and gave him a gift of money. When he returned to Fuqing, he brought with him a document, probably a copy of the household's military register, that proved that the household slot was filled, and therefore there was no wrongdoing on the part of the Fuqing side of the family. Once the document was made public, "the bullies gave up and did not dare say a word."

With contact restored, the family of the soldier in the north began to pay return visits to the ancestral home (figure 2.1). The children of the lineage called the visitors "soldier-uncles" (junshu). The kinfolk in Fuqing gave them gifts of silver. Since they had been serving for generations without a subsidy, the gifts must have been consideration not for their military service but for their willingness to attest that the relatives in Fuqing were not shirking their duty, or perhaps both.

Then in the mid-sixteenth century, the whole southeast coast was ravaged by piracy and banditry, a topic discussed in more detail in chapter 3. Fuqing was hard hit. The next time the visitors from the north came for a visit, they found lineage members impoverished and desperate. Uncomfortable with accepting gifts and adding to the burden on their kin, they decided to stop visiting the ancestral home. This was the last the Ye of Fuqing would hear of their cousins on the northern frontier.[2]

In the previous chapter, we saw how beginning in the early fifteenth century newly conscripted soldiers were encouraged and eventually required to bring their wives with them to their assignment. The officials who implemented this change had martial not marital considerations in mind. They sought not to maximize soldiers' conjugal bliss but to

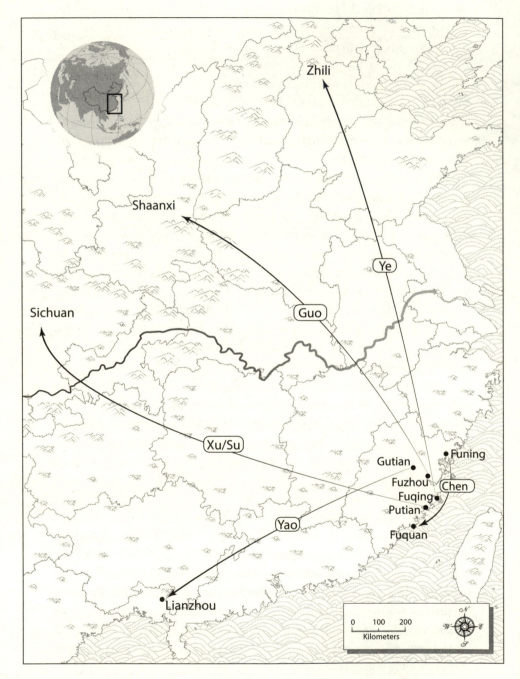

2.1. Long-distance family ties

maintain troop strength and reduce overhead. The effect of the reform was to tie serving soldiers more closely to the guard in which they served, further deterritorializing them from their native place. This would have consequences not only for serving soldiers and their immediate families in the garrison but also for their kin still living in the place from which the family had originally been recruited. The fates of military households now diverged; those who remained "home" in the original place of registration followed one path and the descendants of the serving regular another. But their relationship was not completely severed. Despite the distances that separated them, new relationships developed between the two groups. Military households used such ties for a variety of purposes, to protect themselves, to challenge their rivals, and to claim tax exemptions. This chapter tells the stories of how several military households in Fujian used long-distance ties to family members serving in the military in other places to their advantage.

Ties between serving soldiers and family members in the place of formal registration could be maintained for purely practical considerations (emotional ones, too, perhaps, but these do not appear much in our sources). When soldiers were rotated, reassigned far from home and made to settle with their family in the guard, they must have had no idea how long the new policy would be maintained. Might it one day be reversed? Might they eventually be able to return to their home village? If they owned property they had to decide what to do with it. Should they hold on to it in the hope of an eventual return? Or should they liquidate so that they would have cash in hand when they arrived in the new assignment? Where soldiers were assigned thousands of miles from their native place, on the northern frontier or in the jungles of the southwest, it probably made sense to sell. But the pattern of recruitment in Fujian, with the initial draft of the 1380s followed by the rotation of assignments a decade later, coupled with the voluntary disclosure system, meant that most soldiers were assigned at some distance, but not impossibly far, from their place of registration. Many newly transferred soldiers must have decided that it was best to hold on to their property. (It may not have been possible to find a buyer immediately, and the sudden transfer of so many soldiers would have depressed the local market). When a member of the Chen family from Funing, in the north of the province, was conscripted and sent south to Fuquan in 1394, he carried with him "contracts and wills recording the mines, houses, mountain lands and fields located in Funing." Over the years, family members of the serving soldier returned periodically to Funing—a distance of about four hundred kilometers, which in the

Ming probably meant a travel time of a few weeks—to collect the rental income from these properties.[3]

As we saw in the previous chapter, military households often tried to reduce the risk of desertion by paying a subsidy or establishing an estate to incentivize the serving soldier to stay in service. Such a financial arrangement typically did not end just because the serving soldier came to be more permanently settled in his guard. This same Chen family of Funing had an ongoing arrangement to provide a subsidy to the serving soldier in Fuquan. Along with the deeds to his own property, the first serving soldier sent to Fuquan took with him a copy of the subsidy agreement. The genealogy frames this as a deliberate effort to maintain unity among the kin, a plan "which the ancestors established in order that the descendants of later generations should forever keep in contact, know that they are links on a single chain, and treat kin as kin ought to be treated." For eight generations, the family of the serving soldier in Fuquan regularly sent members back to the ancestral home, to collect the rents and the subsidy. But after the original contracts and deeds were destroyed in a fire, the visits ceased. Then, "since there was nothing to rely on for proof, [we] did not dare return to the ancestral village to visit the relatives or the ancestral tombs."[4] The noble sentiment of uniting the kin obviously needed to be leavened with the incentive of material benefit.

Such financial arrangements, whereby family members in the original native place sent funds to their kin, as one genealogy put it, "in compensation for [their] arduous labor and incalculable hardships" could last indefinitely.[5] A late Ming story tells of an old soldier accompanied by his son traveling from his garrison in Beijing to his hometown in Shandong to collect his subsidy, with which he intends to pay the costs of his wife's funeral. Early in the story the old soldier dies on the road, which must have raised questions in readers' minds about why the son is not worried about being conscripted to replace him. The mystery is solved in the climax of the story, when the son is revealed to be a daughter in disguise.[6]

State officials may have encouraged soldiers to put down roots in their garrison, but they were still happy to rely on family members back in the village to cover some of the soldiers' costs. In the closing years of the Ming, a judge in Fujian adjudicated a case involving a financial arrangement that had endured for at least several decades and possibly much longer. Ever since the ancestor of Xu Tingchun had been conscripted and sent to Sichuan, the serving soldier had returned regularly to the ancestral home in Putian to collect a subsidy. In 1615, this arrangement was confirmed in a written contract. Recently, a certain Su had shown up and demanded payment. (The case record does not explain why a man named Su was try-ing to collect on money owed to a soldier named Xu. Perhaps the soldier had hired Su to go back to Putian on his behalf. A more intriguing possi-bility is that Xu had sold his rights to the subsidy to Su, which would mean that the subsidy contract had become a kind of financial instrument). Su explained that the 1615 contract had been lost, but he had in his posses-sion an earlier version dated 1585. Xu Tingchun refused to pay. The judge found in Su's favor. He questioned why Su would have come all the way to Fujian unless there was some basis for his claim. He also found it very convincing that Su could accurately recite the Xu genealogy, without any discrepancy from the version held by the Putian kin. Su must have had access to their military registration documents. Xu was ordered to pay the subsidy. To allow otherwise would be to "let the sons and their wives become rootless."[7] Here as in so many of the legal cases involving military households, the judge based his decision in part on the existence of a writ-ten contract between the different parts of the family.

The Xu story illustrates why soldiers in the guard might maintain ties with family members in order to secure compensation payments. If this were the only reason to maintain such ties, we could imagine that family members back home would be less keen to keep the connection. But fam-ily members back home had their own reasons to maintain ties with their distant kin in the guard. There were at least two such reasons: to protect themselves from further conscription and to assert tax privileges.

The most common reason that the two sides of a single household would maintain relations despite the separation of time and distance was to manage the risk of further conscription. Under normal circumstances the members of a military household who lived in their old place of reg-istration should have been largely free from this uncertainty. In the early Ming, if a family had strategized effectively using the methods discussed in the last chapter, they would be able to predict when conscription was coming and make advance preparations. Later, after the policy of settling soldiers permanently in the guard was in place, they could expect that under normal circumstances the serving soldier's descendants would be conscripted to replace him, freeing them of the risk. But as we have seen from the story of the Ye of Fuqing, they were never completely safe. Con-scription officials always found it more convenient and cost-effective to replace an aged serving soldier with his immediate descendants in the guard. But these sons and nephews were still only the more easily acces-sible representatives of a military household that was still registered back in the original native place. This is why the guard registers continue to describe serving soldiers as "Native of place X, serving in guard Y" even ten generations after a serving soldier had settled in the guard and himself become the patriarch of a large lineage with many descendants. This is why the personnel files in Nanjing still had to be updated. Ultimate responsibility to fill the soldier's slot remained with the original household in the original place of registration. So no matter how well a family had planned things, there was always the possibility that their strategies would come to naught. The serving soldier in the garrison might have no descendants. Pressing military needs, an overzealous conscription official, or even a simple bureaucratic mistake might lead conscription officials to conscript a second member of the family. When this happened, anyone with even a remote connection to the registered household could fall into the snare. The conscription process was notoriously corrupt, as sources from above as well as below, from both within and without the system, attest. Zheng Ji, a prominent member of the Putian gentry in the fifteenth century, wrote in a pained letter of the disastrous consequences for local society of the appointment of an ambitious new official:

> Last year the Board of Military Affairs issued a duly-verified order requiring that three of every ten deserters be replaced. Censor Guo pressed down on Fujian, hoping to earn special merit and raise his reputation . . . In some cases [the records indicated] that certain people were descended from previously registered soldiers. Their genealogical charts were checked [and they were conscripted]. These were called "soldiers by virtue of having the same surname" (*tongxing jun*). There were cases of people who had purchased the land of soldiers with no posterity. Other people who wanted to acquire this land reported them [and they were conscripted]. These were called "soldiers by virtue of having acquired property" (*deye jun*).[8]

These claims of abuse might seem exaggerated, but the identical problems are also discussed in official documents. Almost a century after this letter was written, in 1572, the emperor received a memorial calling for prohibitions against "reckless conscription and reckless dispatching [of conscripts to their assignment] in violation of the statutes." The memorial mentions some of the very same problems as Zheng Ji: "people of the same surname" but who have no kinship connection being conscripted and "tenants conscripted to replace a soldier [identified as the owner of the land they worked]."

Even if a serving soldier was on station fulfilling his duty, the memorial continued, the conscription officials might still come calling on his distant relatives. "It even happens that supernumeraries are conscripted even though there is no shortfall in the ranks." It might be that a serving soldier was transferred permanently to another guard but the original assignment or slot had never been eliminated and the files never updated. This could be the result of an honest mistake or official corruption. It was very much in the interest of the officers in the original guard to leave the registration untouched. If the transfer went unrecorded, they could collect and embezzle the absent soldier's pay. So double or even triple conscription on the basis of a single slot was a perennial problem. It appears in the *Veritable Records* as early as 1426, with a report that two or three soldiers were being conscripted from a single household, and an imperial order to show mercy in such cases.[9]

Maintaining ties with serving kin could be useful as a way to demonstrate and document that one's slot was filled and thereby stave off additional conscription demands. A petition submitted to the magistrate of Gutian in 1462 shows that the consequences when a military household was accused of failing to provide a soldier could be grave. Li Ren-yuan found this document copied into petitioner Su Duo's genealogy and has analyzed it in terms of the various genres of written texts that people of Gutian used in the Ming. Here I use it to a different end—to consider the social relations between serving soldiers and those in the original native place. Su Duo claimed that his great-great-grandfather had registered as a commoner household in the early years of the dynasty. At roughly the same time, a nearby family with the same surname was also registered as a military household. The serving soldier from that household had recently returned home to collect a subsidy payment. His own relatives were obviously poor—they had been selling off portions of the property that was supposed to fund the subsidy—while Su Duo's family was rich. So, according to Su Duo, the soldier came up with a plan to swindle them. He reported to the authorities that it was actually Su Duo's family that was registered as military household, and they had been shirking. Su's father and his neighbors were taken into custody for questioning. The elder Su protested that the two households were completely separate. But no one believed him. The family decided that their only hope was to try to bribe the official in charge. Su Duo was sent home to sell off their land and house. But he could not immediately find a buyer. The official grew impatient and ordered the prisoners be tortured. After several days of having his limbs pressed with a heavy stick, Su's father sickened and died. The death of the leading witness made resolution of the case quite straightforward. Su Duo and his close relatives were attached to the military registration of the serving soldier's family, thereby making them liable for military service. Su Duo then appealed to higher authorities, begging them to reflect that "if ordinary people are falsely combined into a military registration, the burden falls on the descendants for generations," and entreating them to check the archives, correct the registration records, and overturn "a true injustice."[10]

The surviving document is Su's petition. It is written from his perspective, and so we should be cautious of our natural inclination to sympathize. Certainly the sorts of abuses Su Duo writes about did happen. Some thirty years earlier, an official had complained to the emperor about "military households who consort with local bullies holding office as tax captains or village elders. When conscription takes place they bribe the officials, the clerks and those who do the conscripting in order to harm weak commoners and muddle the registration. There are also village elders who themselves have military registration. Year after year they engage in trickery, making false reports."[11]

Regardless of the facts of this case, the poorer of the two Su families was certainly using its ties to the visiting soldier from Nanjing to benefit its interests. If Su Duo was telling the truth, then it was these ties that made it possible for his enemies to pursue their nefarious schemes. If Su Duo was lying, then these ties helped them to reduce their own share of the overall responsibility by distributing it more broadly and fairly.

The accusation that a slot was unfulfilled due to desertion was a common and apparently often effective tool for embezzlement in mid- and late Ming. As we saw in the previous chapter, since the early fifteenth century the service obligation of the Guo of Fuzhou was being filled by their kinsman in the northwest. More than a century later, the village headman came up with a scheme to extort money from the Guo by threatening to report them as deserters. As it happened, the great-grandson of the original soldier who was transferred to the northwest was visiting (the story of Ye Xianggao's family at the start of this chapter suggests one possible explanation for this extraordinary coincidence—perhaps Guo family members had gone looking for him). The visitor "reported [to the magistrate] that our family had members in Shaanxi who fulfilled the responsibility, so it was unnecessary to conscript someone in the place of original registration." The visiting soldier was able to secure a certificate from the magistrate, probably in the form of a copy of the magistrate's judgment of the case, that the family could use if troubles ever arose in the future.[12]

The kinfolk in the garrison provided an invaluable service by guaranteeing that the family in the ancestral home was not in violation of their obligations. Such a boon deserved to be compensated. When the original visitor's own great-grandson returned to the ancestral home in 1575, he received an additional payment, supplementing the funds given to his ancestor Wei back in 1416. This was not simply a military subsidy paid to the serving soldier, for this visitor was not even a soldier. He was a merchant who had business in the Fujian interior and had simply seized the chance of being nearby to pay a visit to his kin (or was he perhaps seizing an opportunity to extort them?)

The story did not end there. Like so many of the families in this book, the Guo were devastated by the piracy of the late sixteenth century. Most of them abandoned their ancestral home and fled to the comparative safety of Fuzhou city. Unlike the more charitable relatives of Ye Xianggao, the descendants of the Guo family members who had gone off to the north so many years before showed no pity for those who remained in the south. In 1602, soldiers from the north tracked them down in Fuzhou and demanded money. Guo Zhike used the documents that had accumulated over the ensuing centuries to resist their claims. "I showed them the family contract, so that they would understand that their liability for military service is due to obligations they have inherited. It is not a matter of [our] being unfair. They should not come and demand money from us."[13] Here a contract was being used not to fend off demands from outsiders, but to fend off demands from within the family. Guo Zhike was telling his distant relatives that their ancestor had agreed to take on the military service responsibility on behalf of the family and had been duly compensated. The relatives in Shaanxi had inherited this responsibility; it was no concern of his.

Li Ren-yuan has found a second case from Gutian of social ties being maintained or recovered between the original native place and the garrison. According to the genealogy of the Yao of Ruiyun, in 1376 a member of the family was conscripted and assigned to Lianzhou in western Guangdong. It was the younger brother who should have gone, but the family could not bear to be separated from him. So heeding his father's instructions elder brother Zirun and his wife set off for the garrison. Some parts of the story don't quite add up. Soldiers recruited from Fujian through the draft in the first decade of the Ming were typically assigned either close to home or to the capital, not to Guangdong. Since elder brother Zirun went off to serve, it seems unnecessary to even mention the more beloved younger brother. Perhaps the family was registered in the military through criminal conviction of the younger brother, and Zirun served in his stead.[14]

Because of the distance between Gutian and Lianzhou, the two branches of the family had lost contact. The group that remained in Gutian prospered in the early Ming and attracted the jealous attention of their neighbors. A village headman hoped to use the threat of exposing them as a military household as a vehicle for extortion. The threat was more immediate than it had been for the Ye or the Guo. There was no time to search for kin in Guangdong and return with proof. Instead the Yao found a relative who was willing to go to Lianzhou and fill the "empty" slot and raised funds to compensate him.

But when this man arrived in Lianzhou, he found that the slot was not empty after all. Zirun had flourished there. He had even been promoted. "His descendants were numerous and prosperous; they had become a prominent family." (This may be a slight exaggeration; there is no trace of Zirun in official sources from the Ming.) The visitor remained in Lianzhou for over a year before returning home to Gutian with the funds intact and, most importantly, with a document that confirmed the situation. This must have been a copy of the family's military registration. The extortion scheme immediately collapsed. "The village bully did not dare say another word."

The compiler of the Yao genealogy, a non-lineage member who was hired to do the job, weighs in occasionally with his own perspective. (He was, incidentally, a native of Fuqing and knew Ye Xianggao, with whom this chapter opened, well enough to request a preface to the genealogy from him.) One of his two comments on this part of the story is obviously sardonic. Noting that the Yao in Guangdong have become famous, he finds it regrettable that the man sent to Guangdong worried so much about bringing back the money back while neglecting to bring back a copy of the family tree. This could have added luster to the Gutian Yao's own genealogy. His other comment is an insightful one. Most people consider military service to be the worst kind of obligation. "One must serve generation after generation without ceasing." But in this case, the Yao relatives in Guangdong fulfilled the military obligation. So "the rest of the lineage relies on them to gain peace. This is a case of the outer being sufficient so the inner gains relief."[15]

Being able to confirm that the household's slot was filled, whether to avert conscription or to defend oneself against local rivals, was not the only potential benefit from maintaining ties with one's kin in the guard. Being able to confirm that one belonged to a military household in good standing could bring positive benefits. The conventional wisdom in Ming studies is that military registration was seen in very negative terms and

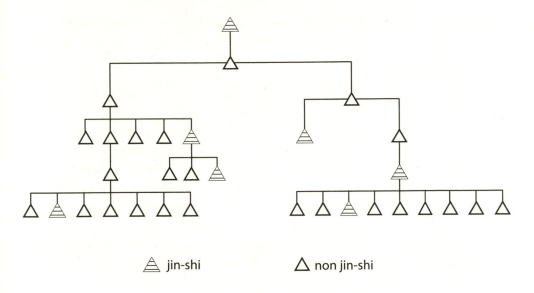

△ jin-shi   △ non jin-shi

2.2. The Lin family of Putian
Adapted from Wang Weichu, "Families and Regions of Ming *jin-shi* Degree Holders," 13.

that military households therefore had low status. But Yu Zhijia and Zhang Jinkui have debunked this conventional wisdom by showing that members of military households frequently, perhaps even disproportionately, rose to the very heights of the social and political order.[16] In later life, Ye Xianggao of Fuqing became grand secretary to the emperor (and incidentally patron to the Jesuit mission in China), proof positive that military registration was not an insurmountable obstacle to social success.

By analyzing Ming lists of degree holders, Wang Weichu has been able to identify the family connections of more than ten thousand members of the Ming elite. Only fifteen families of the thousands of families she identifies produced seven or more *jinshi* degree holders. One of these was a military household from Putian, surnamed Lin. In six generations, seven family members attained the highest examination degree, sure evidence that their military status was not fatal to their prospects (figure 2.2). Clearly this family was not handicapped by its registration status.

It stands to reason that as the size of the household grew while the obligation remained fixed, the likelihood of being conscripted and therefore the negative consequences of having a military registration for any given family member declined. But even soldiers themselves did not always find their status unacceptable. While millions upon millions of soldiers deserted their posts in the Ming, many more millions remained. If military registration meant low status, surely people would have avoided it as much as possible. That they did not must mean that there were advantages to the status, or at the very least that the disadvantages were not insurmountable.

To understand why this mattered to their kinfolk, we need to expand on our earlier discussion of the Ming tax system. Military households were not unique in having hereditary service obligations. In fact, all of the registration categories of the Ming were in principle hereditary: members of saltern households had a hereditary obligation to supply salt; members of artisan households had a hereditary obligation to supply labor in imperial workshops. Civilian or commoner households had a hereditary obligation to supply corvée labor as well as taxes in kind or in cash. Corvée labor was coordinated through the *lijia* system. Based on the results of the first Ming census, the population had been divided into units of 110 households called *li*, then further subdivided into ten units of ten households each, or *jia*. Parallels with medieval England suggest the terms "hundreds" and "tithings" as translations for *li* and *jia*.[17] The ten largest and wealthiest households (in fact, the ten households with the highest tax obligation) in the *li* were named headmen (*lizhang*), and given responsibility for coordinating corvée labor assignments from the tithing households in a decenial rotation. The "village bullies" who made trouble for the Ye, the Guo, and the Yao were actually *lizhang* headmen—informal agents of the Ming state who sought to use their power to their advantage, and who inspired counterresponses from the people whose relationship with the state they were supposed to mediate. In principle, the assignment of households to *li* and to *jia* was to be revised every ten years when a census and land registration was conducted. In practice, households assigned to a status in the beginning of the Ming retained that status for the whole dynasty, even as the group of people covered by the registration grew through population increase or shrank due to poverty.

Military households paid tax on their landholdings just like ordinary civilian registered households. But they enjoyed an exemption from corvée labor service. Like much of the Ming system, the corvée labor system was designed to keep the government running at the lowest possible overhead cost. Ordinary peasants provided labor in rotation to staff the magistrate's yamen, to collect and transport grain tax, to man local police stations, and so on. When the system was initially set up, households in the *lijia* system were assessed corvée labor obligations based on the number of adult males (*ding*) in their household. Military households received a corvée exemption for one adult male, on the principle that the serving soldier provided labor service in the garrison. Families with corvée exemptions jealously guarded and even tried to expand their prerogatives. Examination graduates enjoyed a corvée exemption on the principle that the state could hardly ask a scholar to serve as a policeman or a yamen courier. Their families often manipulated this privilege, claiming an exemption for the whole household and not simply the scholar. Military households did the same. They asserted complete exemption from corvée obligations not just the single exemption to which they were entitled.

Over the course of the Ming, both labor service and ultimately the land tax were gradually converted into cash payments. Labor service obligations were converted twice—first from labor to cash, and later from a separate levy to a surcharge on the land tax. So eventually the special privilege that a military household enjoyed was exemption from a surcharge. Miscellaneous corvée duties, whether levied in labor or commuted to cash, grew and grew over the course of the dynasty. Eventually, the land tax might become only a minor part of a family's overall tax obligation relative to the corvée surcharge. So the relative advantages of corvée exemption grew with the passage of time. This meant that military registration, and the ability to document fulfillment of the responsibilities associated with it, was potentially grounds for significant tax relief. This was one of the advantages that kept people in the system when they might have sought to avoid it entirely.

So the document that the Yao family member brought back from his kin in Lianzhou had other benefits besides eliminating the threat of extortion. It provided the basis for a claim to an exemption from corvée labor obligations. It also provided another unexpected benefit some time later. In 1603, the county magistrate ordered a reassessment of the county's registration data and tax rolls. By that time, some of the Yao had moved to the county town. Others remained back in their native village of Ruiyun. Still others had settled in a neighboring county. These various groups now decided to take advantage of the reassessment to register separately as independent households, probably because to them it made no sense to remain under a single fiscal registration. Why would the magistrate allow this? Wasn't this a violation of one of the basic rules about household division? The answer to these questions is that the document brought back from Guangdong enabled the Yao to demonstrate that for them to divide their registration would not violate the spirit of Ming law. The law was intended to prevent household division from leading to empty slots and shortfalls in the number of troops. The Yao were able to demonstrate that their slot was being filled without issue. Since their military obligations were already being fulfilled in Lianzhou, allowing them to register separately would have no impact on it. Their efforts took advantage of the difference between the relatively simple rules of the system and the more complex social reality in which they lived.

Conclusions

It was obviously in the Ming state's interest to monitor military households both in the place of registration and the place of service. Keeping track of both groups increased the likelihood that when a slot became empty a replacement could be conscripted successfully. Serving soldiers had their own reasons to want to maintain ties with their kinfolk in their original native place. Serving soldiers wished to continue to receive subsidies from their kin back in the village from whence their ancestor had first moved to the guard. The kin back in the ancestral village also had good reasons for maintaining relations with their relatives who had settled in a distant military base, though the financial incentives worked the other way. Being able to demonstrate that one branch of the household was fulfilling the obligations of military registration was a useful political resource for the other branches in their own everyday politics. When this demonstration was used to fend off blackmail, or even worse, the attentions of conscription officials, the resource could be vital protection. When it was used to negotiate for a more beneficial arrangement for the payment of taxes and corvée, the resource became a way to take advantage of the complexity of the Ming state system for personal gain. On the other hand, maintaining ties carried risks too. Soldiers in the guard could also exploit the vulnerability of their relatives in the village, extracting payments in return for providing confirmation that these relatives were not liable for military service.

State agents relied on bureaucratic procedures to monitor military households. But the archival records produced by these procedures were useful for the people who were documented as well as for the state that sought to monitor them. Some of the exploitation schemes that created so much trouble for the families discussed in this chapter hinged, in turn, on the expectation that the families could not produce the documentary evidence that would disprove the rumors being spread about them. Being able to demonstrate that one was in compliance with the statutes on military households was a valuable resource in a system in which access to state documents was costly and uncertain. At the same time, the case of the Xu family and the visitor from Sichuan shows that documents such as contracts that were produced internally by the family had a legal standing.

Magistrates adjudicated disputes on the basis of these contractual records of the informal arrangements that these families made.

Thus one unintended consequence of the hereditary conscription system and the troop settlement policy was to incentivize widely separated kin to maintain relations with one another over time. There is nothing "natural" about maintaining such ties. Centuries later, scholars would notice that Chinese emigrant families also managed to maintain unity even when they were dispersed around the world. Philip Kuhn and others have argued that this capacity must have been honed by the long experience of sojourning scholars, merchants, and laborers migrating within China.[18] The policies of the Ming military may also have provided another precedent for the patterns of family behavior that would later shape Overseas Chinese society. State institutions lay behind this type of historical experience of deterritorialization and family dispersion, and state institutions also shed light on the incentives and strategic opportunities that encouraged dispersed families to create and maintain long-distance social relations. The people involved in these relations invoked the rhetoric of family, to be sure, but their choices were motivated by strategic considerations and not simply cultural predispositions.

Three distinct regulatory regimes affected everyday life for military households. There was the civilian household registration regime, access to which insulated a family from conscription at the cost of higher corvée exactions. There was the original conscription system, whereby family members in the home village were vulnerable to conscription. And there was the reformed conscription system after the localization policy was put in place, which effectively insulated the family from conscription and enabled them to reduce their corvée obligations. Members of military households through means fair and foul circulated amongst these regulatory systems, trying to ensure that they were treated under the regime most favorable to their interests at particular times. The tales in this chapter, of men traveling across the empire carrying contracts, genealogies, and other documents attesting to their family's status, bolstering claims that they belonged under one regulatory regime and not another, challenging similar claims made by other families, are an expression of the everyday political strategies of people in Ming times.

PART II

In the Guard

CHAPTER THREE

An Officer in Cahoots with Pirates

COASTAL GARRISONS AND MARITIME SMUGGLING

IN THE SUMMER OF 1529, hungry soldiers from Panshi Guard in south-ern Zhejiang abandoned their posts. Enraged by months of unpaid rations, several hundred of them seized a local official and demanded to be paid. The kidnapped official's superior could only persuade the mob to release him and disperse by promising to make good the arrears out of public funds. The uprising naturally prompted an investigation, the results of which reached the Jiajing emperor that winter. The news was probably dispiriting even to an emperor with a reputation for taking little interest in affairs of state. For the dereliction of duty in Panshi went far beyond unpaid wages and rioting troops. It turned out that the commander of the guard and two of his officers had been in league with smugglers and pirates, permitting them to trade illegally in foreign goods and even to pillage coastal villages. The officers might even have been directly involved in smuggling themselves.[1] It was their bad luck to be exposed by an incident unrelated to their crimes (or perhaps it was not completely unrelated. Perhaps the rioters wanted their share of the profits of the illegal trade).

A similar report reached the Jiajing emperor about twenty years later, in 1547. Once again it was investigation of a seemingly unrelated matter that led to the discovery of official malfeasance. Portuguese vessels, *Folangji* (Franks) as the Chinese called them, had been raiding the coast near Zhangzhou. Coastal security forces successfully drove them off. But follow-up reporting revealed that local officers, including the commander of Wuyu Fort, a forward post under Jinmen Battalion, had taken cash and foreign goods from the Portuguese. These officers were guilty, in the evocative language of the report, of "selling the harbors" (*maigang*).[2]

This juxtaposition of soldiers and smuggling—troubling as it must have been to senior officials in the capital—was in fact a regular feature of the Ming. It was a logical, even a predictable, result of the long-term evolution of the institutions set up at the start of the dynasty. This chapter explains why. In chapters 1 and 2, I showed how members of military households in their place of registration used complex and sophisticated strategies to manage their military service obligations in ways favorable to their interests, to optimize their relations with the state. In this chapter, I show how some of their descendants in the garrisons used their proximity to state institutions to serve their interests, even though these strategies could undermine the very institutions in which they served.

Life in the Coastal Guards

A more traditional military history of the guards might recount the battles in which their soldiers fought, a more traditional institutional history their organizational structure and their position in the hierarchy of Ming government.[3] Neither of these is our primary focus here. Rather, our interest is the everyday politics the military institution generated for the people who served under and lived in it.

Just as the tale of the Ni family of Jinmen can shed light on the history of military households in the early Ming, the story of another family can help us understand how families developed after they were settled permanently in the guard. As in chapter 1, I have deliberately chosen a case of an ordinary soldier rather than a hereditary officer. Genealogies of officer households tend to provide more detail about the family's military service, for two reasons. First, military service is typically more important to the reputation of an officer household, though for this same reason the information in the genealogy is often hagiographical. Second, for an officer household military service was a privilege rather than a burden, so the genealogy is often a mechanism to show that the privilege has been transmitted fairly or according to lineage rules. For both these reasons, genealogies of hereditary officer households survive in disproportionate numbers.

The genealogy of the Nanyu Chen family of Tongshan is quite unusual because it provides details about the military service of an ordinary soldier household for almost the whole of the dynasty. Between 1387, when the patriarch of the Chen family was conscripted by Zhou Dexing, and 1625, when his descendant passed the highest level of the civil service examination and thereby earned an exemption from the service obligation, thirteen members of the Chen family served in the army. Their native place was in Putian and they were originally conscripted to nearby Puxi Battalion. Under the rotation policy of 1394, their assignment was transferred to Tongshan Battalion far to the south, and that is where they served for the remainder of the 238 years in which they fulfilled their military household obligations. Though the patriarch returned in old age to his ancestral home, his descendants settled in Tongshan, forming what would become a great lineage there.

By the seventh generation, they numbered over a hundred members, and it was time to compile a genealogy. The compiler was not much concerned with the family's history of military service. His account does not make for riveting reading. It tells us only:

> In the eighth month of 1396, [second-generation ancestor] Deguang died. Chen Zongji replaced him; [he served until he] died.
>
> Chen Bangtian replaced him; [he served until he] died.
>
> Chen Shou replaced him; [he served until he] died.
>
> Chen Daying replaced him; [he served until he] died.
>
> Chen Yuan replaced him; [he served until he was incapacitated due to] illness.
>
> Chen Hua replaced him; [he served until he was incapacitated due to] illness.

and so on.[4] The sole moment of drama occurred around 1590, when Hua withdrew from his post due to illness and was replaced by Keqi. But then an officer learned that Hua was malingering, and he was ordered back into the army.

The Chen genealogy does not explain how the family made decisions about who should serve. Nor can we tell from the structure of the family tree (see figure 3.1; the numbers indicate serving soldiers and the sequence in which they served). Beginning in the second generation, the lineage was divided into two main branches, each descended from one of the patriarch's two sons. Nine of the twelve individuals who served came from the senior branch. Probably the senior branch had accepted hereditary responsibility, by the fifth generation if not earlier, and members of the second branch served only when there was no suitable candidate in the senior branch. This family thus effectively behaved much like a composite military household, with the different branches of the lineage corresponding to the different families in an ordinary composite household. Most of its members were not soldiers; we will see below the sorts of occupations they pursued.

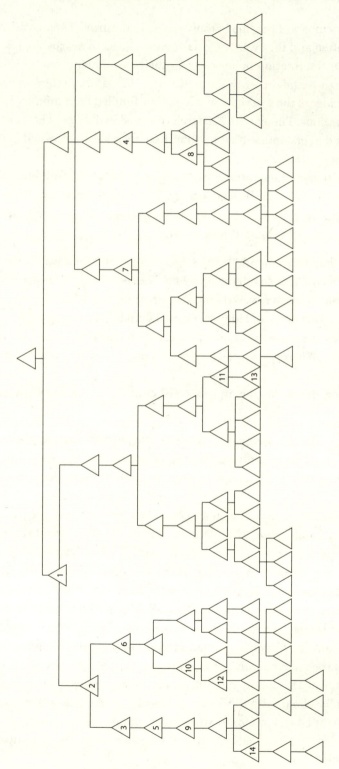

3.1. Family structure of the Chen of Tongshan

A Eunuch Admiral and the Dwarf Bandits

It was Zhou Dexing, later deified as the God of the Wall of Pinghai, who established the battalion at Tongshan where the Chen family would live for centuries, along with all the other Fujian garrisons in this book. Why did he choose to situate a battalion there? Like the other garrisons in this book, Tongshan was part of an empire-wide system of defense that would eventually grow to over five hundred guards and four hundred independent battalions. John Wong and I have plotted the five hundred guards on a map in order to analyze their geographic distribution. The results of this work show that the bases can be divided into five broad systems (figure 3.2). The highest concentration of units was on the northern frontier and in the capital region. The southwestern frontier was next. A third system consists of units stationed to defend and maintain the Grand Canal. The

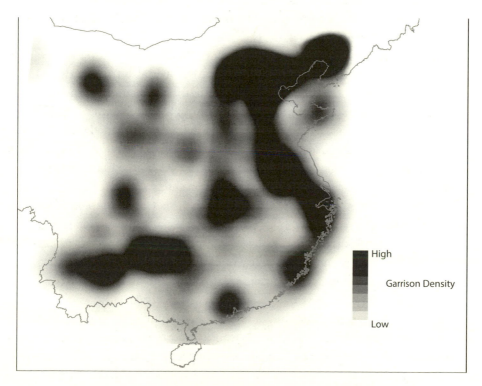

3.2. Heatmap of garrison distribution at the end of the Ming
The data for this map was prepared by John Wong, based on information
in Liew Fong Ming, *The Treatises on Military Affairs of the Ming
Dynastic History (1368–1644)*. The data is available for download at
https://www.fas.harvard.edu/~chgis/data/chgis/downloads/v4/datasets
/ming_garrison_pts.html

guards distributed lightly throughout the interior make up a fourth system. The fifth system, our subject here, followed the coast. The overall distribution pattern offers a concise summary of Ming priorities and perceptions of security threats: the dangers of border tribes and foreign states on the peripheries; the need to guarantee security of the imperial family; the importance of reliable streams of tax revenue along the canal; domestic stability maintenance; and, on the southeast coast, the need to control piracy and smuggling on the maritime frontier.

In China today, the military history of the maritime frontier is bound up with the story of a fifteenth-century eunuch admiral. Every schoolchild in China learns about Zheng He's amazing voyages to Southeast Asia, the Middle East, and possibly as far as the coast of Africa.[5] (One of the participants in his voyages was Pu Manu, who returned from the expeditions to a promotion to company commander, and whose military registration file we explored in chapter 1.) The Zheng He voyages are usually seen as the high point in China's engagement with the maritime world, after which Ming China turned its back on the outside world. It is true that soon after his journeys the court shifted back to its more conventional strategic priorities in the north and northwest. But it is also true that state-sponsored voyages are only part of China's maritime history. By the time the Ming was founded in 1368, a centuries-old trading tradition linked the south China coast, Japan, and Southeast Asia. Sophisticated maritime technology—in other words big, fast, and nimble ships—allowed ocean-going merchants to satisfy the global demand for Chinese manufactured goods and the Chinese demand for tropical products and silver.

Zhu Yuanzhang did not wish to eliminate this trade completely but rather to regulate and restrict it. Commerce, especially international commerce, could only disrupt his idealized self-sufficient rural order, stimulating acquisitiveness and encouraging mobility. Zhu also associated maritime trade and foreign states with more direct threats to his rule. He had some reason for thinking this way. A number of his rivals in the wars leading up to the dynastic founding had used powerful navies to resist him, and he wanted to ensure such threats would never recur. But his reasoning tended to the paranoiac. In 1380, he launched a massive purge of officialdom to root out a conspiracy by his chief minister, among whose supposed crimes were secret alliances with foreign enemies.

Zhu's foreign trade policy had three main elements. First, he restricted inbound foreign trade to the sidelines of official tribute missions.[6] Second, he prohibited outbound foreign trade. Chinese merchants were forbidden from going to sea to trade. Neither of these two measures ever worked quite as they were supposed to. Foreigners arrived at China's ports claiming to be official tribute missions far in excess of the authorized frequency. Coastal residents continued to trade overseas, often under the pretext of fishing, which local officials knew they could not ban without destroying the coastal economy. Already when Zheng He traveled to Southeast Asia in the early fifteenth century, he found communities of Fujian merchants in its port cities. Merchant bands made up of Japanese, Chinese, and Southeast Asians continued to ply the waters of China. Local officials mostly turned a blind eye to private trade, and there was an ongoing debate at court about how best to reconcile the tension between imperial principle and commercial reality.[7]

The third element of Zhu Yuanzhang's foreign trade policy, the main focus of this book, was the coastal garrison system. It was intended to enforce the first two elements and keep the Ming maritime order. The southeast coast presented a distinctive set of military challenges. Military units stationed there did not, as they did in the north, expect to face powerful military forces keen to seize control of Ming territory. Nor, unlike their colleagues in the southwest, did they need to keep unruly tribes from causing havoc. Their basic military task was to patrol the seas to limit illegal trade.

The duties of soldiers in the garrison revolved around this objective. The garrisons provided manpower to the maritime forts (*shuizhai*) that were the front line of the system. (The front-line units also included police offices (*xunjiansi*), but these were typically staffed by the county government and were part of a different administrative system.) Soldiers of coastal garrisons rotated periodically into active duty in the forts. Jinmen Battalion—today known as *Jinmencheng* (Jinmen walled town) is among the best preserved of the coastal garrisons today. Architectural historian Jiang Bowei has been able to use the surviving structures to reconstruct the layout of the community when Ni Wulang and his family lived there (figure 3.3).

Tongshan soldiers were assigned to nearby Tongshan Fort, where they served with soldiers from Liu'ao and Zhenhai. While stationed in the fort, they were responsible for patrolling the nearby waters and, twice a year, anchoring offshore in forward positions to deter smugglers and pirates from coming ashore. When not on patrol duty, soldiers in the guard were mainly occupied with drill. Some guards had their own shipyards to provide the patrol vessels; in these guards soldiers were also occupied with shipbuilding.

Life was not easy in the guards. Rations frequently went unpaid due to corruption by officers, and riots like the one in Panshi were not unusual.

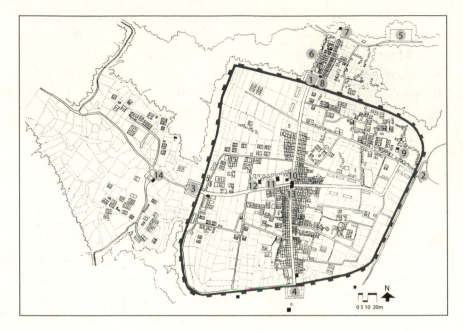

3.3. Jinmen Battalion

1. North Gate
2. East Gate
3. West Gate
4. South Gate
5. Military parade ground
6. Ming market
7. Temple to Wang gong

8. Temple to Yudiye
9. Shao ancestral hall
10. Shrine to Yu Dayou
11. Battalion office
12. God of the Wall
13. Temple to Guandi
14. Ancestral home of the Xin surname

There are many accounts of officers abusing their power to compel ordinary soldier households to provide labor, sometimes for official needs but often also for the personal interests of the officer. Desertion was frequent, increasing the burden on those who remained.[8] Then in the mid-sixteenth century, the situation took a turn for the worse.

With little warning, the seas off southeast China turned violent. Bands of marauders sailed up and down the coast and laid waste to villages, and eventually to towns and cities and even guards. The local folklore in many coastal guards is rich in stories both of heroic defense against the marauders and of the terrible suffering when defenses failed. The people of the former Puxi Battalion tell the story that their God of the Wall wore a special yellow robe bestowed by the emperor because the battalion had resisted effectively when other nearby garrisons fell to the sword. The people in some of the surrounding villages tell a more tragic story. They do not raise dogs—apparently even to the present day—because a barking dog once betrayed their ancestors' hiding spot to the marauders, leading to a bloodbath.[9]

Zhu Wan (1494–1550), the official first appointed to deal with the problem of the coastal unrest, made a good start at restoring order. But he antagonized powerful local interests who were themselves secretly involved in maritime trade. One of these was Lin Xiyuan (ca.1480—1560), a member of a military household from Tong'an, who Zhu Wan singled out as the worst of the Fujian literati in league with pirates and smugglers. (According to Zhu, Lin's family operated a huge fleet of ships engaged in the Southeast Asia trade; they avoided the prohibition against maritime trade by pretending the ships were local ferryboats.)[10] After exceeding his authority and executing captives, Zhu was demoted and committed suicide in disgrace. Raids by pirate groups spread up and down the coast. Some launched large-scale attacks in which major cities, and several coastal guards and battalions, fell to the sword.

Eventually the violence was suppressed under the leadership of competent generals who applied new tactics using mostly mercenary forces. Among them was Yu Dayou (1503–79), scion of a prominent military household from Jinjiang and commander of Jinmen Battalion. Together with the famous general Qi Jiguang, Yu and his forces won a great victory over the pirates in the waters off Pinghai Guard in 1563. But the ultimate solution to the problem lay in relaxing the Ming founder's restrictions on private trade. In 1567, a new licensing system was created, allowing Chinese merchants to travel legally to the Western Oceans (Southeast Asia) and the Eastern Oceans (northeast Asia).[11] The violence finally subsided.

The Chinese term for the perpetrators of these raids is *wokou*, Japanese (literally dwarf) bandits. A century ago, historians in China interpreted the *wokou* raids as a Japanese war on China—obviously they were drawing parallels with their own time. After 1949, scholars in the PRC recast the violence as class warfare, an attack by an emergent merchant class on the feudal political order. Neither of these explanations for the upsurge in violence seems very persuasive today, but no consensus has replaced them. Some scholars blame the Ming failure to maintain a sufficiently strong navy for the rise in violence; others cite a breakdown in the balance of power between the various parties to the trade. Recent interest in global history has led to the argument that it was the arrival of Europeans with their superior firearms in the region that destabilized the informal commercial order.[12]

Who were the *wokou*? In most of the historical sources, there is a simple, unambiguous answer: the Japanese dwarf bandits. This terminology is an attempt to resolve ambiguity by ethnicizing the problem, imposing solid categories onto fluid groups and shifting behaviors. But even at the time, local knowledge pointed out again and again that this was not accurate. One local official estimated that of the people who were labeled foreign bandits, actual foreigners accounted for fewer than one in ten, with perhaps another 20% coming from Okinawa, at the time a Ming tributary. Sacrificing strict mathematical accuracy to make his point, he continued that half of all foreign bandits were from the Zhejiang coast and fully 90% from the three large coastal prefectures of Fujian—Zhangzhou, Quanzhou, and Fuzhou. "Though they are called foreign bandits, in fact most are ordinary people who belong to registered households."[13]

Recognizing that many of the "Japanese bandits" were really coastal Chinese is only part of the solution to the challenge of categorizing the people involved. For the issue is not just ethnicity but behavior. Any attempt to draw clear lines between smugglers, traders, and pirates is undermined by the reality that the same people engaged in all three activities. As one Ming observer put it, "the pirates and the merchants alike are men. When trade is permitted, the pirates become merchants. When trade is prohibited, the merchants become pirates."[14] The distinction between trader and smuggler is constructed by policy not by people. Many of the famous pirates of the age were primarily engaged in illegal long-distance overseas trade, so they were also smugglers. In the lawless state of nature of the South China Sea, military capacity was crucial to commercial success, even to survival, so whether their trade was licit or illicit, merchants or smugglers had to be armed.[15] When the incentives changed, crews easily shifted from trade to plunder, of one another and of communities on the coast. (Issues of translation further complicate the question. Anthony Reid points out that the very category of "pirate" is a product of the European experience; it is used to subsume a broad continuum of terms in Chinese. The *wokou* are often called pirates, but their primary activity was never raids on legitimate shipping as the English word "pirate" implies. Rather, they were seaborne raiders who came ashore to plunder and take captives for ransom, and then fled back to the seas and offshore islands.)[16]

Depending on circumstances, the very same people labeled as pirates could either be an alternative to state authority or an element of state authority. Ming officials sometimes tried to "pacify" (*zhaofu*) piracy, that is, convince the leaders of maritime bands—traders and pirates alike—to submit to the throne and accept a commission to suppress piracy.[17] So some of them, some of the time, became state agents.

Furthermore, smugglers, pirates, and honest traders alike were fully embedded in the society of the coastal region. As the early pirate suppression official Zhu Wan noted, maritime trade was crucial to the well-being of its communities, such that "even a small child three feet tall looks upon the pirates as providing for their daily needs like a parent."[18] Coastal people from virtually every social status imaginable, from poor fishermen to salt traders to literati elites like Lin Xiyuan, were involved in illicit maritime commerce in some way.

As the Jiajing emperor learned in 1529 and again in 1547, so were the soldiers and officers of the coastal garrisons. Dozens of entries in the *Veritable Records*, spanning the whole of the dynasty, demonstrate this. In some records, soldiers are described as part of a general problem of illegal maritime activity. Official documents in the court annals frequently blame "soldiers and civilians" (*junmin*) for illegal trade. In 1525, the Regional Inspector of Zhejiang memorialized that "in Zhangzhou and Quanzhou, cunning soldiers and civilians have privately constructed large two-masted vessels in which they go to sea. Claiming to be engaged in [domestic] trade, at times they go out to raid and plunder."[19]

But not all of the complaints are generic. The *Veritable Records* also identify specific military men as smugglers. Since legal trade was only permitted by foreign tributary missions, soldiers who engaged in trade were smugglers by definition. There were many of them. In the very first years of the dynasty, "because the sea routes can be used to reach foreign lands, We [the emperor] have forbidden them to be used. We have heard that Li Xiang and Li Chun, officers of Xinghua Guard in Fujian, have themselves sent men overseas to engage in trade." Several decades later, the *Veritable Records* tell of Zhang Yu, assistant military commissioner of Fujian who, "being poor, sold foreign goods in violation of law." In 1434, a commander of Zhangzhou Guard was found to have traveled abroad to engage in trade, then bribed his superiors with the goods he brought back.[20]

Soldiers sometimes joined the very smuggling gangs they were supposed to suppress. Zhu Wan reports on two soldiers from Shaoxing Guard who "illegally went to sea and submitted to treasonous bandit Feng Zigui (still at large). They managed affairs aboard his ships, and planned with him to submit to the foreigners and guide them in their plundering."[21] Even after the sixteenth-century violence subsided and licensed trading was allowed, persons with ties to the military continued to engage in trade. A personnel assessment from the 1620s accuses an officer stationed on the island of Penghu of purchasing livestock and iron tools and then dispatching two of the boats under his command on the pretext of maritime patrols. In fact he had charged them to trade these goods with the Dutch on Taiwan. The same official is said to have invited a gang of pirates to feast with him, and later sent them oil, rice, and an actor as a gift.[22]

Even where soldiers on the coast were not themselves engaged in piracy or smuggling, troop deployment patterns meant they often had social ties to people who did. At the height of the campaign to suppress piracy in the mid-sixteenth century, four soldiers from Zhangzhou secretly entered into a surrounded pirate camp and agreed to let fellow Zhangzhou natives among the pirates escape the siege in exchange for a bribe. Two of the battalions of the region even appear on a list of "pirate lairs" compiled by naval commander Wang Yu (1507–60): Jinmen—home of the Ni family from chapter 1—and Chongwu—just to the north.[23]

Soldiers engaged in smuggling, trade with foreigners, and piracy over the course of the Ming. They played a variety of roles, as facilitators and as direct participants. Their officers were also involved, turning a blind eye in exchange for bribes. To appear in the historical record, these men had to have been caught, and to have been caught by superiors who chose to deal with them formally, through bureaucratic mechanisms. Besides those who turn up in the records, there were surely many more who were never caught, and many more who were caught but who managed to stay out of the records.

Why did soldiers engage in smuggling and piracy? Probably they smuggled for the same reasons that other people smuggled, in Fujian as in other times and places. They smuggled out of poverty, ambition, and opportunity. But members of military households in the Ming also faced distinctive pressures, distinctive incentives, and distinctive advantages that impelled them into these lines of work. These factors were a direct product of the evolution of the military institutions set up in the early Ming.

A crucial long-term change was demographic. Prior to the localization policy that encouraged soldiers to settle in the garrison, the number of adult males in each guard would in theory have remained constant. Every time a soldier retired from service, he would return to his native place and a replacement would be sent from his native place to the garrison. Desertion, which officials were already noticing in the early years of the dynasty, might cause a temporary drop in the number of men in the garrison. But this too would be made up as soon as a replacement was conscripted. After localization, the garrison became home to the soldier as well as to his immediate family, and eventually to his descendants. Natural increase meant that a single soldier in the early Ming might over time come to be the progenitor of a sizable group. Even desertion would not necessarily lead to a decrease in population unless everyone descended from the original serving soldier disappeared at the same time. The old problem of camp followers was bound to recur. Officials at the center recognized this, writing that "every one or two soldiers in the garrison has five or six or even as many as twenty or thirty dependents, young and old."[24] Local people saw this too. A late Ming literatus wrote of Wan'an Battalion in Fuqing (near the home of the Ye and Guo families in the previous chapter): "Every military household at first [provided] only one person to serve in the military. Afterwards the descendants became numerous."[25]

The clearest evidence for the demographic shift comes from the published genealogies that military households in the garrison compiled later. A single serving soldier in the late fourteenth century could eventually have descendants whose family tree fills volume after genealogical volume. The Chen of Tongshan discussed above numbered almost thirty members by the eighth generation, and the numbers continued to grow. Within a few generations, the numbers of military kin grew far beyond what the designers of the Ming military institutions had anticipated, and far beyond the capacities of the system.

For even as the actual population in a guard kept growing, there was no institutional mechanism to adjust to or even to record this change. From a fiscal perspective, the population remained unchanged: a battalion with 1,120 soldiers still had 1,120 soldiers. The "official" population actually tended to decrease because not all desertions and retirements were resolved—reports from the mid-Ming distinguish the "original" number of soldiers from the "actual" number. No matter how numerous the descendants of each original serving soldier became, they remained registered as a single household, providing a single soldier, and therefore entitled to a single salary.[26]

Moreover, as we have seen already with the Panshi riots, even this initial fiscal burden proved to be a problem in many places. We don't know why the commander of Panshi was not paying his troops. It may have been a problem of supply. The military colonies that were supposed to pay for the troops' rations were being sold off or seized illegally, or were falling out of cultivation due to desertion (see chapter 5). Or it may have been a problem of the institutions and individuals that intervened between the production of the salary rice and its delivery to the soldiers. Officials in the southeast and elsewhere were constantly being accused of embezzling rations, withholding them from the soldiers, and various other misdeeds with soldiers' salaries.[27] But even if a soldier did receive his due rations, this did not solve the problem for his cousins. They had to eat too.

The demographic changes created an impossible situation, one that Ming authorities could not help but be aware of. They repeatedly issued orders that military kin should be given land and become ordinary farmers.[28] People's own responses to the problem were not that different from the government response. Military kin found their own ways to make a living. They diversified. Some residents of Fuquan became fishermen, as we know from an account of a soldier fishing up a valuable Song inkstone in his nets (or perhaps he was using fishing as a pretext for trading in antiquities).[29] Just across the water in Jinmen, supernumerary Yang Tingshu and his family "were poor and made a living from fishing." Yang died at sea, leaving behind a young widow who mourned for him on the shore for three days and then killed herself.[30]

Naval strategist Tan Lun, in an essay on the declining quality of coastal garrison troops, outlines the range of occupations that soldiers and military kin got up to. He was interested in the question because he thought occupational diversification was behind declining military capabilities.

> Not only are the officers and soldiers of the garrison unable to kill pirates, they can't even defend themselves. The blame for this is generally laid on the depletion of their units . . . But in the coastal garrisons of Ningbo, Shaoxing, Wenzhou and Taizhou in central Zhejiang, there is not a single civilian living within the walls of the fort. The [military households'] homes are lined up side by side. Who could [the residents] be if not men of the garrison?
>
> But those who actually serve in the ranks are all the old, the weak, and the sick. They are stubborn and uncooperative. What is the cause of the problem? The better-off ones purchase positions as government clerks. Or they bribe the officers to let them go out and engage in commerce. Some learn a trade; some serve as mercenaries; some fulfill corvée labor [i.e., they hired themselves out to local taxpayers to fulfill their labor service obligations]. Some perform as actors. Those who are literate [forge documents?] and return to their native place.[31]

The Spanish Jesuit Adriano de las Cortes, shipwrecked off the China coast in 1625 while en route from Manila to Macao, wrote of the soldiers of Pengzhou Battalion: "besides being soldiers, they all have another job— what they make is used to supplement their income and help them feed their wife and children. They are for example porters, cobblers, or tailors, or do other jobs of this sort."[32] Some soldiers and supernumeraries diversified into banditry. As one official report puts it, "in the coastal garrisons, officers have embezzled rations, creating hardship for the troops. Some have gathered into groups to become bandits."[33] These sorts of behaviors were of course nothing more than a garrison-based twist on the diversification strategies of military households discussed in chapter 1, which are in turn just a military twist on more broadly distributed diversification strategies.

But demographic pressure and resulting diversification cannot be the whole of the explanation for soldiers' involvement of smuggling, since the phenomenon recurred throughout the dynasty. Another factor that mattered across the whole dynasty is that members of military households on the southeast coast, including both serving soldiers and military kin, had a number of attributes that drove them more strongly than others into the maritime world. In other words, they enjoyed a competitive advantage in the smuggling and piracy business.

First, they had easy access to ships and maritime technology. While most of the military households we have encountered so far were recruited through Zhou Dexing's or Tang He's general draft, some of the people conscripted early in the dynasty had longstanding connections to the sea. Conscription of the navies of Zhu's defeated rival Fang Guozhen (1319–74) brought many families with a long history of maritime activity under military registration.[34] So too did a 1382 decision to bring boat-dwelling people of Guangdong (danmin) under military registration. The officer who proposed the move noted that these people living on coastal islands were extremely difficult to administer. "When they encounter government soldiers they claim to be fishing; when they encounter foreign bandits they collude with them to engage in piracy and theft." Not only did these people traditionally specialize in seafaring, they even specialized in fooling the authorities by pretending to be engaged in legitimate business.[35] Conscription into the military would not have eliminated these longstanding family traditions and expertise.

Eventually family traditions of seafaring might dissolve. But the garrisons to which these families were assigned remained centers of naval technology. Privileged access to technology was the source of another kind of competitive advantage. For much of the Ming, the guards were the only places where construction of large ocean-going ships was legal.[36] Xuanzhong Battalion in southern Fujian had a reputation for specializing in construction of cargo ships.[37] Even the warships of the garrison were used for illegal trade. In the mid-fifteenth century, a commander of Yongning Garrison used "the ocean-going vessels under his command to engage in

trade in pursuit of profit." He was only found out when several of his soldiers died at sea, prompting an investigation.[38] There was also the advantage of location. The garrisons had quite deliberately been situated on
key harbors and traditional trading hubs. This created opportunities for
soldiers to impose informal tolls on passing trade and advantages in trading themselves.

Another source of competitive advantage for officers was the social
networks they formed with local elite families. They could be a source of
capital for mercantile activities. In 1530, literatus Zheng Xiao (1499–1566)
was approached by "two commanders from Haining Guard [who] told
him that there were foreign ships at sea with many rare goods. If he were
to lend them two hundred piculs of rice, then the next day he could earn
a 300% profit." Zheng reported the officers to their superior and to the
local magistrate, but nothing was done.[39] Zheng spurned this particular
offer, but that it was made at all suggests that other local literati were not
so scrupulous.

On the other hand, pressure from powerful local families who were
themselves engaged in illicit trade could make it difficult for military officials to do their duty, and could encourage them to turn a blind eye to
smugglers. "Government soldiers capture pirates and their vessels and send
them to the officials. . . . Prominent local families then go to the official and
say that these are family retainers named so-and-so who were sent out to
such-and-such a place on such-and-such a date to buy grain, or lumber,
or cloth, with a certain amount of money on their person that the soldiers
have taken . . . [The pirates are released and] the soldiers end up in jail."
In the long run, soldiers became resigned to collusion with smugglers. "It
comes to the point that the soldiers do not make arrests when they go out to
sea, but rather accept goods in return for giving free rein to the pirates."[40]

The most compelling competitive advantage that military households
enjoyed lay in the fact that it was they and their own kin who were responsible for controlling and suppressing maritime trade. There are repeated
hints of this point in official prohibitions. A 1433 report mentions that
in recent years people "not knowing to respect the law have repeatedly
constructed sea-going boats themselves and, claiming to be on state business, gone to sea to trade." Anyone who informed on such people would
receive half the property of the criminal. But "if the responsible officers
of the guard release or do not prevent [the offenders from trading], they
are to receive the same punishment."[41] The local garrisons were charged
with controlling the trade, but they obviously had a certain discretion in
practice.

Naval officers looked the other way to allow their own soldiers to trade—perhaps because such trade was seen as a perk of the job, perhaps because they hoped to use their laxness to gain support from their men, perhaps because trade by ordinary soldiers was inseparable from their own involvement in the illegal trade. In 1469, Fujian assistant commander Wang Xiong was found to have taken bribes from his subordinates, "allowing them to engage in trade with evil rascals on foreign islands. While leading troops at sea [he ordered them] to take evasive action when they encountered foreign ships."[42] Ming soldiers were the only group in coastal regions with a legitimate reason to go to sea, to conduct their patrols. But, as a late Ming policy statement warned, unless officers were vigilant, "the soldiers may use the pretext of going out on patrol to engage in plunder, and their commander is unaware. If he learns of it, he tends to conceal it, in order to avoid problems."[43] Having information about the routes and timings of coastal patrols, and confidence that if intercepted one could find a close personal connection, even a kinship connection, with the patrollers, is a strong advantage in illegal trade. But being personally responsible for the patrols must have been even more advantageous.

It certainly gave soldiers an edge when it came to intelligence. As the late Ming author of a gazetteer wrote of his friend, the former squad leader (*bazong*) of Wuyu Fort, "he knew all the dealings of the people on the coast, their comings and goings, what goods they were moving, what goods they had stored to take to which foreign markets." Once he brought them under his control, "he could use them as his eyes and ears."[44]

Officers also took advantage of their role in supervising the legal trade associated with tribute missions. When a Javanese mission arrived in Guangdong in 1465, a Chinese merchant who was himself a smuggler ("he frequently went to sea in pursuit of illicit profits") arranged to trade for the private goods carried by the ambassador. He then led the vessel to Chaozhou, where his associate served as commander. It was the commander's job to seal up the tribute in the hold for inspection, but he took advantage of the opportunity to take a quantity of valuable tortoise shell for himself.[45]

The arguments that military households and their kin had competitive advantage in illicit trade due to their access to maritime technology and their social networks converge in an exasperated but rhetorical question from Wang Zaijin (*jinshi* 1592), a late Ming expert on coastal defense. "The work of constructing [an ocean-going merchant vessel] is not something that can be accomplished in ten days. When at anchor in port it must attract attention. How can the local [people] not report it? How can the officials not prohibit it?"[46] The reterritorialization of soldiers and their families, their creation of new social relations in the localities around their bases, undermined the very goals for which the army had moved them around in the first place. Their privileged political status as agents of the state gave them strong advantages in smuggling and worse.

Jiang Jishi Raids a Pirate Camp and Returns with a Beautiful Prize

So far, I have told a story based on official reports and histories, which are uniformly critical of soldiers who sidelined in smuggling and piracy. If we go to the communities involved and study their genealogies carefully, we can also tell the story from the perspective of the participants. Jiang Jishi was a battalion commander in Fuquan. So far as I can tell, his name appears nowhere in the surviving official archive. But we can read about him in his family's genealogy. His story is so remarkable that it is worth spending a few moments discussing the source in which it is found. The *Genealogy of the Northern Mansion of the Fourth Branch of the Jiang Surname of Fuquan* is a handwritten work, first compiled in the mid-seventeenth century and edited most recently in 1958 to add the names of newly born members. It is a different *type* of source from a printed genealogy. A printed genealogy is a testimony to the power and prestige of the lineage, intended at least in part for outsiders. The Jiang genealogy, with its tales of adultery and illegitimacy, is clearly not for public consumption. It is a draft, a collection of preliminary material that was written down by ordinary family members probably with the expectation that it would ultimately be reworked into a proper genealogy, a hidden transcript of family history. It therefore serves as a reminder to scholars to keep in mind that there may be multiple versions of a single family's genealogy in circulation at any given time. Joseph Dennis has shown that the notion of the local gazetteer as a stable text is problematic. The same is also true of genealogies.[47]

The founding ancestor of the Jiang of Fuquan was a native of Fengyang in modern Anhui province, like Zhu Yuanzhang himself. While the accounts of recruitment in genealogies of ordinary soldiers are often frustratingly brief, the Jiang were officers, and so the genealogy provides more detail. The compilers have even recopied the family's copy of their personnel file from the archives into the genealogy. Jiang's ancestor joined Zhu Yuanzhang's forces in 1354 and fought on many campaigns. In 1363, he became a company commander and rose further up the ranks until he retired due to age in 1392. Shortly before his retirement, he was promoted to the rank of battalion commander (*qianhu*) and assigned to Fuquan, newly staffed with draftees from the Fuzhou area.[48]

His descendants served for generation after generation as Fuquan battalion commander, most of them with competence and a few with distinction. Jiang Jishi, the founder's seventh generation descendant, succeeded to the post in 1522, having inherited it from a cousin. Jishi's main official responsibility, like his ancestors and his descendants, was to defend the coast from the *wokou* raids. The leading bandit chief in the area was one Li Wenxin—a suspiciously Chinese-sounding name for a "Japanese bandit." Jiang had good intelligence about Li's activities; one of his most daring exploits was an attack on the bandit leader while he and his men were enjoying a feast. Jiang was able to capture Li, his wife, and his sister, and bring them back to his base. The raid also yielded a booty of "foreign trade goods." His fellow officers, jealous of this triumph, spread rumours that he had made a "blood bond" with the pirate chief's sister and accepted gifts of jewels, gold, and fragrant oils from her family. Angered, Jiang Jishi allowed Li Wenxin to escape. But rumours of his dalliance with the sister persisted. Eventually he had no choice but to "hand over all that he had received" to his superiors—which suggests that this was not his original plan. Still the rumors did not go away. People said that he kept the sister as a hostage, hoping to extract more trade goods from the pirate chief.

The pirate's sister makes another appearance later in his biography. But this mention is subtly different. Previously she has been part of the "rumors" that other people told in order to slander Jiang Jishi. But there seems to have been something to the rumor, for the author of the text, another member of the family, criticizes Jiang for his "fondness for women/sex" (*haose*), the evidence being that "after his victory he paraded the pirate chief's sister into the fort to the beat of foreign drums."

Another anecdote in the genealogy tells of how Jiang defeated a "pirate band," capturing two vessels laden with a cargo of porcelain. The "pirate chief" refused to accept defeat, chased after Jiang's forces, and intercepted the ships with grappling irons. Jiang then instructed his men to defend themselves by hurling the porcelain at the attackers. The porcelain shattered into shards on impact, "so that the pirates had nowhere to place their feet." The account may seem comical to us, but the original text is in earnest. Jiang defeated the pirate counterattack, captured the chief, and distributed the booty to his troops.[49]

Jiang's biography suggests a military world that is very different from the one portrayed in most official sources. Jiang Jishi was blood brother to Yu Dayou, the Jinjiang native and commander of Jinmen, and good friends with many local literati. But he also had a complex relationship with the region's leading pirate, not to mention his sister. The pirate ship he attacked, loaded high with stacked porcelain, was clearly not a man-of-war the sight of which put fear into local populations. It was more like a cargo vessel or a barge. Like all good pirate stories, Jiang's stories feature treasure. But this was not treasure stolen from its rightful owners by cruel pirates and returned by the hero. Both upstream and downstream from Jiang were more complex commodity flows. Perhaps some were gifts from the Li family; perhaps some was a ransom for freeing the sister. After it passed into his hands, the booty was neither returned nor added to the state treasury. Jiang disposed of it by giving it to his superiors or distributing to his troops. For this treasure, which took the form of "foreign trade goods," to have been useful to the people who received them, be they superior officers or subordinate soldiers, they must have been able to move them on the market. So the necessary market institutions must have been available for them.

We often think of illegality as something that happens most where the state is weak. But recent work by David Robinson on violence and by Eric Tagliacozzo on smuggling suggests this is an oversimplification.[50] There is little money to be made from brigandage in remote and lightly populated places. The wealth and power of cities creates opportunities in which men of violence can flourish. Local nodes of state administration can also be promising sites for criminality. Places where multiple administrative systems overlap create spaces in which illicit activity can occur, cracks through which it can fall unnoticed. For the smuggler, the presence of state officials creates the possibilities for corruption. Corrupt officials can actually reduce uncertainty for the smuggler by ensuring that the organs of the state "look the other way" at crucial moments.

Squad leader Zhang Siwei was even more brazen than Jiang Jishi. He became an ally of one of the most famous pirate leaders of the sixteenth century, Wang Zhi. He once gave Wang a belt of jade, "prostrated himself, kowtowed and willingly became his servant. He dispatched goods on his behalf. With one call [from Wang], Zhang would come, considering it an honor." As the author of this account put it, behavior like this showed "no distinction between obedience [to the throne] and rebellion."[51]

It was precisely their own position within the system that made the exploits of people like Jiang and Zhang possible. The schemes of officers who were simultaneously smugglers depended not on successfully evading the state but on taking advantage of their connections to it. Jiang and his ilk leveraged their proximity to the state, their position in the military, to reduce the costs and uncertainty of smuggling and piracy. The evolution of the Ming military system created strong incentives and gave them strong competitive advantage to operate in the latter sphere.

A Late Ming Judge Shirks a Risky Assignment

The death of the Jiajing emperor in 1567 created the opening for a policy shift to deal with the pirate threat once and for all. The new emperor agreed to ease the restrictions on maritime trade and to establish a customs office to licence and tax merchants.[52] Peace was restored. Manila soon emerged as a major entrepôt, with Portuguese traders serving as key intermediaries in the growing trade. But this does not seem to have meant the end of the special competitive advantage that soldiers in the coastal garrison enjoyed.

By the time Yan Junyan served as prefectural judge in Guangdong in the 1620s, the licencing system had long been in place and the ban on overseas trade was a thing of the distant past. Even more than before, the line between smuggling and trading was now defined not by what goods were being moved but by who was doing the moving. This issue lay behind one of the most complex cases in Yan's published casebook. Local officials reported that a large ocean-going vessel had put in to Humen, near Guangzhou, claiming to have been blown off course. The response from higher up in the hierarchy reminded the officials that "suspicious vessels" must be investigated and warned that officials who did not perform such investigation diligently would be punished according to the statutes on "weighty crimes." As an intermediary official noted, "Matters of border security are no child's game." Yan wanted no part in such a tricky matter. Instead he sent excuse after excuse that he was ill, too ill to get involved, and tried to compensate for his absence by making various suggestions to his superiors about what they should tell every one else to do. Yan may truly have been at death's door; it is more likely that he recognized the case was a minefield and tried to stay as far away from it as he possibly could.

The captain of the vessel, one Huang Zhen, initially claimed to be on an official mission to the Portuguese. He was carrying what he said was an official instruction from the grand coordinator (*xunfu*) of Fujian to conduct coastal patrols. But many things about his story did not add up. His vessel carried more than two hundred men, far more than would be needed for either a diplomatic mission or a coastal patrol. The ship's rich cargo of trade goods was so densely packed that one of the investigating magistrates said it could take weeks to do a full accounting. The official instruction, whether it was real or fake, said nothing about engaging in trade. Under interrogation, Huang claimed that he had loaded the ship with cargo with the intention of trading to meet expenses such as rations for the crew and repairs to the ship. But as the interrogating official noted, military regulations clearly specified that soldiers were to be paid from the treasury; there was nothing in these regulations about officers engaging in foreign trade in order to pay their wages. There was another complication. Despite Huang's claims to have been blown off course, when the ship arrived on the coast, "residents of Guangdong had rushed to meet it, and set up to receive the goods." Neither of Huang's explanations seemed to fit the facts—the ship was clearly not on an official mission, nor was it engaged in coastal patrols.

Some officials argued that the case fell under the jurisdiction of the Fujian authorities and called for the ship and its crew to be transferred there. Others called for the investigation to proceed in Guangdong. All urged for a combination of speed and caution. The longer the case dragged on, the more likely it was that the evidence would simply disappear. The crew would find ways to trade off the cargo. Or the soldiers charged with guarding the ship would find ways to broker the goods themselves. "Even if the soldiers are given strict orders, how can it be that they would see the opportunity to profit and not act?" Or, as indeed later happened, the crew would claim to have run out of food and request permission to trade their goods in the local market to buy supplies. "Don't listen," wrote Yan, "to the argument that they are dying of hunger, and don't listen to the arguments of evil-doers who claim to be coming to their aid." (The problem with Yan's position, of course, was that if the sailors were not allowed to trade, then the local officials would have to supply them with food. Presumably the local magistrate did not much appreciate Yan's suggestion that he pay for the privilege of hosting the suspects from his own pocket.) If the ship were to be transferred to Fujian, it would be completely empty by the time it arrived. If the crew themselves did not trade the goods, then the soldiers guarding them would.

Inspecting the cargo was the first priority. Yamen underlings found vast quantities of pepper and fragrant oils—trade goods from Southeast Asia. The inspection also allowed the officials to reach a key judgement. "This is a military vessel. The people aboard are all soldiers. Not one is a merchant." This made the resolution easy: "Guilty!" Huang Zhen and another man were sentenced to conscription at a distant garrison, and the other members of the crew were given a beating.[53]

The case is complex, and there is no reason to think that officials fully grasped the situation or even that Yan's is an accurate reflection of how the case transpired. It matters little. What is most interesting are the various assumptions the officials involved hold and the possibilities they consider. A ship is blown ashore on the coast—perhaps it is a merchant vessel; perhaps a navy ship. If the latter, then perhaps it is simply following its mission. But perhaps it is following its mission while doing a little private trading on the side. Or perhaps it is using its mission as a ruse to engage in trade, possibly with the connivance of the senior official who issued the orders. Or perhaps the mission is simply invented, the orders faked in anticipation of possible apprehension. To the officials, all of these possibilities are plausible. Investigators assume that virtually all of the parties involved—the crew itself, the soldiers sent to guard the ship, porters sent to offload the cargo so it can be investigated, even the residents of the locale where the ship happened to come ashore—have the wherewithal, the skills, the capital, the market knowledge, to deal in foreign trade goods. Despite the official efforts to categorize those involved, in the maritime world of the early seventeenth century, the line between merchant, smuggler, and soldier could be very thin.

In 1529, in the story with which I opened this chapter, word reached the emperor that his officers were engaged in smuggling in the aftermath of a riot over unpaid wages. A century later, the two issues were juxtaposed once again in a report to the last emperor of the dynasty. Two vessels carrying trade goods were intercepted off the coast. Investigation revealed that two local military officers were behind the smuggling. While the goods were being held, relatives of the men arranged for soldiers of the garrison to make trouble over unpaid rations. While the soldiers rioted, a squad leader burst into the commander's chambers and seized his official seal and the trade goods. The next day, the crews of the two ships sailed away with their recovered goods, beating drums to celebrate their victory.[54]

The Spanish Jesuit de las Cortes, writing only a few years before this incident, records that the soldiers "who are sent aboard the war fleet to protect and clear the coast attack the coastal villages, killing and stealing from the poor Chinese peasants." They seized any vessels they could find, claiming they belonged to "enemy pirates." In the Macao region, de las Cortes continues, an encounter with the Chinese navy was often fatal; the soldiers killing everyone aboard and pretending that the victims were pirates and thieves. "They can easily satisfy the officials, to whom they give a portion of the booty."[55]

Over the entire course of the Ming, military men used their proximity to the coastal defense system to their benefit, smuggling with varying degrees of brazenness. The whole period was not of a piece; there had been the upsurge of pirate violence in the middle of the dynasty and the subsequent changes to the rules governing trade. The arrival of the Europeans complicated the story. But one thing was consistent—officers and their men took advantage of their privileged status in one regulatory system— the army—to gain benefits in another—the international trade regime. The primary military function of the soldiers of the southeast coast was to maintain maritime order and prevent smuggling and piracy. Their job was to suppress the dreaded "dwarf bandits." At least some of them were themselves dwarf bandits.

Conclusions

Many soldiers and their families on the southeast coast exploited their connections to the military to get rich through smuggling and piracy. Of course not all soldiers were smugglers, nor all smugglers soldiers. Rather the point is that illegal behavior was not a straightforward function of separation and distance from enforcement and regulatory mechanisms. On the contrary, soldiers, officers and their kin were able to profit from illegal trade precisely because of their proximity to the state. Their actions fall further along the axes from compliance to resistance than the optimization strategies discussed in previous chapters. But terms like resistance or misconduct still fail to describe this behavior fully because they fail to capture that it was only possible because of the ways households were embedded in these institutions. Military households could do the things they did because they engaged with state systems in particular ways. In chapter 1, we saw them attempting to calculate the costs of service and find ways to minimize or redistribute those costs. In this chapter, we see them calculating, though less explicitly, the advantages that can be gained by continuing to bear the cost of service. The consequences of their calibration undermined the purpose of the very institution in which they served, but this does not seem to have been of much concern to the men involved.

The social networks in which military households were embedded at the moment of their conscription help explain why Zhu Yuanzhang and his successors were keen to deterritorialize the army. Troops had to be relocated from their native place not only for reasons of military operations but also because leaving them where they were made it easier for them to undermine military objectives. Nowhere is this more evident than in the southeast, where longstanding illicit trade networks were an important part of the local economy. But the rotation of assignments did not solve this problem permanently. Even as the troops settled in their new assignment, they began to reterritorialize, to form new social networks that facilitated precisely the same consequences. By the mid-sixteenth century, families like the Jiang of Fuquan were embedded in a new set of networks with which they managed to undermine the very institution they were supposed to serve.

Ming officials frequently tried to convince leaders of maritime bands, traders and pirates alike, to submit to the throne and become loyal subjects. This pacification (*zhaofu*) policy and the behaviors discussed here are two sides of the same coin. Both are products of the ill fit between the ambiguous status of people in coastal regions and the hard categories into which state policy sought to fit them. Both pirates and soldiers could exploit this ambiguity when it served their purposes. According to Cai Jiude, when pirates raided the coast in the 1550s, "they imitated the clothing of local people or *the uniforms of our troops*. The confusion made it impossible to distinguish them and so they were often victorious."[56] Other sources make the same claim. An account of a battle in this period reads: "The pirates then disguised themselves in the uniform of our troops, circled around . . . and attacked from behind."[57] (One wonders where the pirates obtained their disguises. Could it be that they wore their own some-time uniforms, that the clothes were uniforms when they were behaving like soldiers and disguises when they were in league with the pirates?) Brave squad leader Zhang Wanji of Tongshan used disguise to the opposite effect. On foggy days, he would pretend to be a pirate and go out in a small boat, bearing a sword. When other pirates approached, he would attack.[58]

Given their close connections to maritime trade, it only stands to reason that members of military households would have been involved in the early movements of Chinese people across the maritime frontier. It comes as no surprise that Jiang Jishi's genealogy records several relatives who crossed over to the frontier zone of Taiwan. Other family members ventured even further, settling among the Overseas Chinese communities of Southeast Asia. The descendants of a cousin of Jiang Jishi "went to the Eastern Ocean as merchants to making a living, and prospered." Li Boyan, a ninth-generation descendant of a military household stationed in Yongning, moved to Luzon in the late sixteenth century.[59] Were the descendants of Ming military households from Fujian among the first Chinese to settle abroad? I should not overstate the case—the genealogies of ordinary civilian households in the region record hundreds of thousands, perhaps millions, of members who migrated abroad. But it is still intriguing to think that members of Ming military households might have been some of the earliest Overseas Chinese. Perhaps even more than the enormous treasure ships of Zheng He, this would be a fitting symbol of China's history as a maritime power and of the ties between the Ming military and China's position in global history. The very Ming institutions that were intended to limit China's economic interaction with the rest of the world actually played a crucial role in structuring that interaction. Families strategizing about how to work within those very military institutions, working the system to their advantage, making decisions about the degree to which they would or would not be incorporated by the Chinese state, played an important role in the development of China's diaspora and its global trade linkages.

CHAPTER FOUR

An Officer Founds a School

NEW SOCIAL RELATIONS IN THE GUARDS

THOUGH HE WAS ONLY A LOW-RANKING OFFICER, Chen Yongzhi has become one of Yongning Guard's most honored sons. Troubled by his fellows' disregard for education, Chen went from household to household to hector the youth of the guard and their fathers. Or at least so the story goes. "Even when they were out on a campaign," Chen told the young men of the guard, "the ancients did not neglect poetry, reading, and the arts. In the human world, this spirit is the one thing that cannot be absent." It would take more than skills of persuasion for the residents of Yongning to devote themselves to learning. So in the mid-fifteenth century, Chen decided to establish the guard's first school. (Probably what this really means is that he secured permission and funding from higher-ups.) He recruited a local scholar to teach there. Then he managed to convince local education administrators that the youth of Yongning should be treated the same as civilian students in ordinary Confucian schools. Those who passed a qualifying exam could be admitted to the prefectural academy in Quanzhou and receive a stipend. Thanks to Yongzhi's efforts, "the spirit of culture in Yongning advanced daily."[1]

In Qing times, the scholars of Yongning erected a shrine where offerings could be made to Yongzhi's spirit. The shrine no longer survives, but Chen Yongzhi is not forgotten. Though he has no descendants in Yongning today to offer sacrifice to his spirit, another prominent Chen family, many of whose sons attended the school he founded, has placed a tablet to him in their own ancestral hall.

Neither victorious general nor heroic footsoldier, Chen Yongzhi might seem an odd choice to receive such commemoration in a military base.

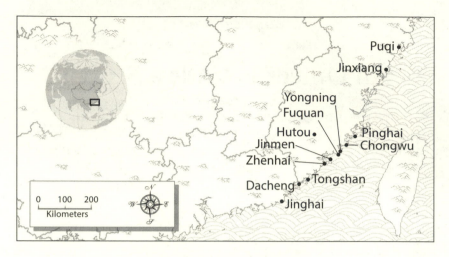

4.1. Key places mentioned in the text

But Yongning was more than simply a military base. It was also a community, and Chen Yongzhi is celebrated because of his contributions to that community.

Wherever Zhou Dexing ordered the construction of a garrison in the late fourteenth century, he created a new community, of which the soldiers of the garrison and their families became part. This was true in places like Pinghai, already the location of a village even before the guard was established, and also in places like Pumen, eventually abandoned by the army but today the site of a village that grew up in its ruins. With one significant interruption—discussed in chapter 7—these communities have survived ever since. Guard communities developed as an unintended consequence of military policy decisions. How did they transcend the limits of their foundation?

New social relations were an unanticipated by-product of the workings of Ming military institutions. This chapter traces the development of some of these social relations—in particular those based on marriages, temples, and schools—and shows how they could endure even after the institutions that gave rise to them were long gone. It explores some of the ways soldiers assigned to the garrisons and their families created, reproduced, and maintained their community and how they integrated into the larger society around them. This chapter is thus about another kind of everyday politics, the politics of communities and community formation.

As we saw in part 1, the initial assignment of soldiers to a guard was de-territorializing. It lifted soldiers out of their familiar context and set them down in a new place according to military requirements. But the policy that encouraged soldiers to settle in their guard spawned a reterritorializing response, as soldiers and their familes became embedded in this new context. The new social relations that they created, different expressions of reterritorialization, were unintended but were among the most enduring consequences of Zhou's founding of the guards in the fourteenth century.

Commander He Peng Takes a Wife: Guard Soldiers and Their Marriage Networks

He Peng (1517–77) inherited the position of battalion commander of Puqi in the fall of 1531, when he was only fourteen in Western reckoning (Puqi was an independent battalion under the jurisdiction of Panshi, whose rioting soldiers we met in chapter 3). He was the eighth member of the family to hold the position. If the timing is any indication, his appointment sparked a decision in his family to arrange his marriage. Who should he marry? His great-grandfather, his grandfather, and his uncle had all taken wives from within the battalion; each had married the daughter of another commander. Peng's father, though, had married a woman, Peng's mother, from a prominent local literati family.[2] Peng's matchmaker proposed that he too should take a wife from outside the battalion. A year older than he, his bride was descended from a prominent local family like his mother. Peng was a military man through and through. He fought with distinction, even participating in one of the greatest battles of the anti-pirate campaigns, the 1548 attack on the pirate lair at Shuangyu. He received several awards of silver for bravery, the Ming equivalent of being mentioned in dispatches.[3] But his social network extended well beyond his military colleagues. Through his mother's and his wife's connections, he and his family became part of the local elite society of southern Zhejiang.

Arranging a marriage for one's child would have been part of the experience of almost every parent in late imperial China. Marriage itself was of course not an everyday but an exceptional affair. But the long-term process of calculation, planning, and negotiation that went into making a marriage was very much part of everyday politics. This may have been especially true of military households. Though female marriage was basically universal in premodern Chinese society (polygyny and concubinage mean the same cannot be said of male marriage), military families often ran into difficulties arranging marriages for their daughters. Potential partners worried about the possible consequences of marrying into such a family. If a military household had no son, would the obligations fall on the son-in-law? Such fears of entanglement were not baseless according to Zheng Ji, the Putian literatus we met in chapter 2. In his litany of complaints about a conscription official, he wrote of "households of old men and women who had no adult males able to serve in the army. Their sons-in-law were made to report [for service]. These were called soldiers by virtue of being a son-in-law (*nüxu jun*)."[4]

In some places, fear of becoming entangled with military registration could distort the entire marriage market. In the Hunan county where Hong Zongzai (*jinshi* 1397) served as magistrate, the problem of military households being unable to make marriages reached crisis levels. "Civilians worried that if they intermarried with [military households], the burden [of service] would fall on them. There were men and women who had reached the age of forty and had still not married."[5]

The challenge of arranging a marriage did not disappear after recruits settled in the garrison. If anything it might have become worse. Not only would potential matches worry about getting dragged into military service, but also the pool of potential matches must have been very small. In the early years of their assignment, military households were strangers in the locality, with no history of marriage alliances to build on, and no local social network. It stands to reason that they would have made marriages for the most part with other military households. And this is exactly what the sources show.

Three types of sources can help us learn about marriage patterns for soldiers and their families in the garrisons. We can use the small number of genealogies that include detailed marriage information to do intensive research; we can extract information more extensively from biographies and general comments in gazetteers; and we can mine written sources more broadly for anecdotes involving marriage and military households. Only a few genealogies include much useful information for this task, and those that do tend to be genealogies of officers. This makes sense, because officers were the elite of the garrison, so their marriage networks were more likely to be a source of prestige. (This is not to say that marriages of ordinary soldiers were not made strategically, but only that those strategies, like so many other aspects of life in the guards, tend not to be recorded.) Some compilers of genealogies of ordinary soldiers did include details about the wives of lineage men and the families into which lineage daughters married. But even for the most diligent of such compilers—like the authors of the Meihua Lin genealogy—the registration status of sons-in-law and daughters-in-law was not something they thought to include.

The genealogy of He Peng's family, the He lineage of Puqi, is unusual because it includes information about both sons' and daughters' marriages (though there is still more information about sons than about daughters). This lets us trace the changing marriage patterns of the lineage as a whole. He Peng's experience was shared with kin near and distant. The He patriarch had been an early supporter of Zhu Yuanzhang, and his descendants were rewarded with a hereditary position as battalion commander. It was the patriarch's son who was assigned to Puqi. So it must have been the patriarch's grandsons, the members of the third generation, who first had marriages arranged there. Over the course of the Ming, sixteen sons of the lineage married daughters of other commanders. Descendants who served as commander themselves were the most likely to marry daughters of fellow officers; three of eight successive commanders took the daughter of a commander as their wife. But with each passing generation, the likelihood that a He, serving officer or not, would marry a commander's daughter declined. Two of three members of the fifth generation married a commander's daughter; so did six of seven members of the sixth generation, and six of fifteen in the seventh. Two members of the much larger eighth generation married the daughter of a commander; thereafter the number falls to zero. Not a single one of the twenty-five members of the ninth generation took a wife from the family of a fellow commander (figure 4.2).

Roughly the same pattern holds true for the daughters of the lineage. The likelihood that one of them would marry a commander declined with every passing generation. A total of six of the thirty-four daughters of the lineage for whom we have information married either a serving commander, a man who would later become a commander, or the son of a commander. But all of them were concentrated in the early Ming. Both of the sixth-generation daughters for whom there is information married commanders. By the ninth generation, not a single one of the eight daughters for whom we have information married a commander.[6]

The genealogy says nothing about the logic of marriage-making, but the obvious explanation is that the network of possible affines for the He grew over the course of the Ming. Increasingly they married with other families living in the surrounding area, regardless of registration. In other words, their marriage behavior increasingly came to resemble that of the area as a whole. Over time their behavior shed its distinctiveness from the civilian families around them. A family with hereditary entitlement to the position of commander is unusual, but there is no reason to think that the same basic pattern of gradual reterritorialization did not apply to officer and ordinary soldier households alike.[7]

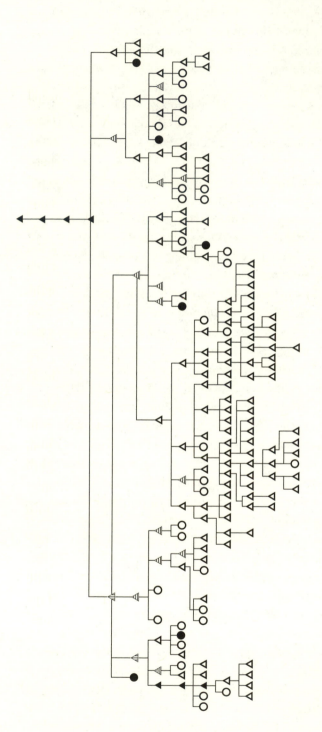

- ▲ Commander
- ● married a Commander
- ⟁ married Commander's daughter
- ⟐ Commander, married the daughter of a Commander

4.2. Marriages of the He family of Puqi

Genealogies allow us to look intensively at the marriage networks of a single family. If we examine the issue extensively using gazetteers we get similar results. The section on exemplary women in a late Ming gazetteer-style account of Jinmen includes five biographies where either wife or husband has a clear connection to the garrison. In two of the five, both husband and wife are from the garrison, that is, these are cases of military households making marriages with other military households. Li Jin-niang was the "daughter of a soldier in the battalion." She was betrothed while still a child to a battalion supernumerary, the relative of a serving soldier. From our perspective their tale was not a happy one. The fiancé's parents died when he too was still young, so he was raised by her parents. Although he was a supernumerary, and an educated man, he was conscripted. Probably he was a victim of one of the periodic campaigns to fill ranks that had been emptied by desertion. Wealthy families were able to bribe their way out of the situation, but "because he was poor, he had to fulfill his military service." He soon fell ill and died, whereupon Li Jin-niang also killed herself.

Three of the five biographies show that, by the late Ming, military households were also making at least some marriages across the civilian-military divide. Lady Zhao of Pubian village married Wang Rusheng "of the battalion." Lady Xiao of Shawei village also married a soldier. After she was widowed at the age of twenty-four, she raised her son to be a successful scholar. When her son too died in the capital, she took charge of raising her grandson. She lived to be eighty and was said to be respected by all the officers of the battalion. Qiu Yinniang, daughter of a poor local family, married a man of the battalion. He must have been a serving soldier because he was transferred to some distant place on campaign. She served her in-laws faithfully until news came of her husband's execution for some unknown offense, whereupon she too hanged herself.[8] The military households of Jinmen, like the family of He Peng, gradually became integrated into the communities around them by marrying their sons and daughters to the daughters and sons of civilian families.

The challenges that military households faced in making marriages may help us to make sense of two anecdotes recorded in another gazetteer. Born on the coastal island of Haitan in the early Ming, Pan Siniang was betrothed to the son of a family of good reputation. But before the marriage could be finalized, their community was thrown into turmoil by the new policies on coastal defense. Pan's father, like so many others we have encountered, was conscripted and her family registered as a hereditary military household, assigned to serve in Yongning Guard.

At that time, Siniang was already of an age where there could be no delay [that is, it was time for her to marry]. But she reflected that her parents had together gone through so many hardships and survived so many dangers. She could not bear to leave them or let them be destitute. Nor was she willing to alter her course due to hardship [that is, having been betrothed already to one man, to marry another would be unchaste]. So she took an orphan from Beigong to raise as a son [and remained unmarried].[9]

Was Pan Siniang making a virtue of necessity in the face of the obstacles to making a good marriage after the family's registration and transfer?

The miraculous story of Hu Xianying is recorded both in the gazetteer of Anxi county as well as in the Hu's own genealogy. The Hu were conscripted together with two other local families to fill a slot in the Nanjing Garrison in 1376. On her wedding night Hu Xianying, the daughter of founder of the lineage, disappeared. Later, she appeared in the sky over Houshan hill. (In the more dramatic version of the story, she disappeared while she was being taken to the wedding and was actually seen to fly up into the sky.) The local people worshipped her as the "Dragon Immortal" (*longxian*), carving an image and erecting a temple. She continues to be venerated up to the present day. Could the legend of Hu Xianying be a story of a marriage contract broken because of the bride's family's registration status?[10]

Finally, after two stories of marriages that did not happen, we have an account of one marriage that did. A stone inscription in Yongning Guard records that an early Ming commander lacked a son. He arranged an uxorilocal marriage for his daughter with a man from a local family. The son-in-law eventually inherited his official position, linking the two families together forever.[11] Here too we see a marriage across the military-civil divide solving a pressing problem for an officer household.

Most of the discussion in this book is about men, for the simple reason that the institution that the book is about was an institution that concerned itself with men. But attention to the issue of marriages showed that women in military households also played an important role in family strategies. As the historical and anthropological literature shows already, it was women who through their marriages tied families and lineages together. The military households of Ming Fujian were no exception; indeed, because of the challenges they faced both making marriages due to their registration status and integrating into local society because of their transfer, this role for women may have been even more important than for civilian households. Daughters and daughters-in-law played a significant role in the reterritorialization of military households in the communities to which they were assigned.

Pan Hai'an Carries the Incense Fire to His New Post: Temples in the Guard

The founding ancestor of the Pan family of Jinxiang Guard was a native of Ningbo who was awarded a hereditary officer's position in the guard as a reward for military service in the early Ming. Among his many contributions to local life was to introduce to the town the protective spirits who to this day watch over the residents. "He brought with him the incense fires of the Brave and Meritorious Emperor, the equal of Heaven, and Marshall Yan. Up to the present day the descendants have installed the incense burner of the gods in their central hall. They are the gods of this family." The reference to carrying the incense fire is not metaphorical—it means that Pan carried with him ashes from an existing temple or shrine dedicated to these deities and installed the ashes in the incense burner of a new shrine in the guard, thereby establishing the gods' presence in the family's new home. This practice of "division of incense" (*fenxiang*) is the common method even today of establishing an affiliation between an old temple and a new one.[12]

Intermarriage with locals was one way soldiers and their families responded to the effects of deterritorialization. Village temples were another. Like the towns and villages around them, a single guard or battalion today typically has many different temples, ranging from simple roadside shrines to massive stone structures with exquisite carved stone and murals. Tongshan, for example, had several dozen shrines and temples before 1949; more than a dozen have been rebuilt since the 1980s. To a first-time visitor, the temples of Tongshan, like the whole of the southeast China region, might seem largely identical to one another, even generic. Each typically has an image of the main god on a central altar, an incense burner resting on a table in front of the altar, and perhaps minor deities on either side or a commemorative plaque donated by a worshipper overhead. But through their iconography, their rituals, their legends of miracles past and present, each of these temples tells its own story. These temples are not, or not only, expressions of eternal, universal cultural principles and structures. They are also the product of concrete historical processes. The temples in the guards were not only places of worship and interaction with the gods but also venues for management of local affairs, assertions of leadership, negotiation of interests, and resolution of conflict. As Barend ter Haar writes, cults and their rituals played an integrative function for virtually all local social groups in premodern China.[13] Which gods are worshipped in a community, when temples are built or restored and by whom, and how ritual networks are constituted and reshaped over time can all serve as markers of inclusion and exclusion, important aspects of how communities create and reproduce themselves. In a sense, temples and their cults are the very site of local politics.

The soldiers in Tongshan participated in at least three different types of religious organizations: cults they or their ancestors brought with them to Tongshan, cults native to the locality, and officially mandated cults.[14] The Sages of Nine Carp Lake (*Jiulihu xiangong*) is an example of the first type. The cult, to the spirits of nine brothers said to have lived in Putian in the Han dynasty, had one of the largest temples in Tongshan before the destruction of the Maoist era.[15] The cult remains very popular in Putian but is virtually unknown elsewhere—except in parts of Southeast Asia where there are communities of Putian emigrants. Tongshan is the only place in southern Fujian where the cult of the Sages is found. It can only have been brought there by the soldiers who were transferred there in the early Ming as a result of the troop rotation policy. Like the port cities of Southeast Asia, Tongshan too was a community of Putian emigrants. But it was a community created not by voluntary overseas migration but by government fiat.[16]

Soldiers and their families also joined in the cults of deities local to the region. The Kings of the Three Mountains (*Sanshan guowang*), a cult prominent in the Chaozhou region just to the south of Tongshan, is an example of this type. The Kings were originally mountain spirits who had been protecting local people from natural disasters since at least the Tang dynasty.[17] We do not know when the cult first spread from Chaozhou to Tongshan, but it was already part of religious life in the surrounding area well before the battalion was first established in the early Ming. Soldiers, their families, and their descendants, as well as the other residents of the battalion, must have taken to worship there in the generations after they arrived.[18]

One also finds in Tongshan officially mandated cults. The temple to Lord Guan in Tongshan is an example of this type. Lord Guan, later known as Emperor Guan or Guandi, is the apotheosis of the Three Kingdoms hero Guan Yu and an important spirit in the Chinese pantheon. Because of his connection to military concerns, cults to the god were mandated for all guards. Tongshan's temple was first built in 1388 by the commanding officer. A successor rebuilt it a century later. The god remained important to the soldiers. His assistance was credited repeatedly in the defeat of pirates in the fifteenth century. But his efficacy made his popularity grow beyond the garrison officers and soldiers. A reconstruction effort in the sixteenth century was led by a man not from Tongshan itself but from nearby Yunxiao county.[19] By the late Ming, the temple had emerged as the main temple for the people of Tongshan and thus a symbol of the corporate identity of the town that had grown up around the Ming military unit. We will see its enduring legacy in chapter 7.

A second official cult found in Tongshan was *Chenghuang*, the God of the Wall.[20] Temples to the God of the Wall, who was simultaneously a protective deity for the inhabitants of the city, the administrator of the local spirit world, and judge of the underworld, were a universal feature of walled cities in late imperial China. (As I noted in the introduction, the conventional translation for *Chenghuang* is City God, but since the guards were not cities, a more literal translation makes more sense.) On Zhu Yuanzhang's orders, in early Ming the God of the Wall temple was incorporated into the official ritual system: each county seat was required to establish a temple, and the magistrate required to worship there. Temples to the God of the Wall were ubiquitous in the military system. Every rural guard and battalion in Fujian had (and in most cases still has) a temple.[21] "Where there is a guard there is a wall, a moat, and a god who oversees them. This is why the temple is built."[22]

Temples to the God of the Wall were common in the market towns of the lower Yangtze's Jiangnan region. Strictly speaking these temples, many built during the height of mid-Ming economic prosperity, violated Ming regulations, for their builders were usurping the privileges restricted to government centers. But as Hamashima Atsutoshi's research shows, their elite patrons found ways to get around the rules. Rather than choosing their own God of the Wall, they *invited* the legitimate God of the Wall from the nearest county to take up residence in their town. This allowed them to assert their status as a place of importance without openly transgressing state regulations about administrative and ritual hierarchy. But, concludes Hamashima in a gesture to Weber, this meant that the God of the Wall in these market towns could never serve as the locus of a new urban identity.[23]

In a few coastal battalions, the God of the Wall resembles those Hamashima found in market towns, that is, his identity is the same as that of the god in the nearby administrative town. The people of Fuquan, for example, worship the God of the Wall of Anxi.[24] But in most garrisons, the god has a distinctive identity, one that affirms not the place of the community in the local civilian administrative hierarchy but rather its distinctiveness and difference. Nowhere is this more evident than in those former guards where the people venerate a god who is the apotheosis of a human being who was (and still is today) despised by the people of the surrounding communities.

As we saw in the introduction, in Pinghai the God of the Wall is none other than Zhou Dexing, the senior officer who built the coastal defense system in the late fourteenth century. The people of Quanzhou have never forgiven Zhou for this; even today he is a reviled figure. Folklore from villages all over the region tells of how he deliberately destroyed the local geomancy. Quanzhou's physical features had once been so auspicious that in the natural course of events the area might have produced an emperor. Out of loyalty to Zhu Yuanzhang, Zhou made sure this would never happen. Everywhere villagers can point to what they say are the ruins of pagodas that he tore down, streams that he dammed, dikes that he had destroyed. They also tell stories of how their ancestors secretly mocked and eventually outwitted him. Wang Mingming argues that such stories simultaneously reflect the imperial state's political domination of local space and local people's critical reflections on the imperial presence.[25]

But in Pinghai itself, Zhou Dexing has a very different reputation. For the residents of the former guard, Zhou Dexing is both founder and eternal protector. This is why he is venerated with such devotion at the annual temple festival in the new year. Local farmers tell a story of how Zhou's men tore up the great sea dike at Huangshi, to the great suffering of their ancestors. But residents of the guard tell a different version of the same story, in which the stones provide the foundation for the Pinghai wall that protected their ancestors from pirate raids in the sixteenth century. The wall itself is now gone, but villagers can still point to the spot where Zhou's spirit appeared on the wall and drove off the Japanese bombers during the Second World War.[26]

In some communities, the God of the Wall is even more one of their own, the spirit of a member of a local military household. The God of the Wall of Jinxiang for example is the apotheosis of Wang Taigong, founding ancestor of the Wang lineage.[27] One of his two wives also has a connection to a local family. A spirit medium was recently possessed by the wife, who revealed herself to be the daughter of the local Li lineage. She committed suicide after the death of her human betrothed and subsequently married Wang in the afterlife. In Jinghai and Dacheng too, local lore is that the wife of the God of the Wall is the daughter of a local lineage. These female deities play a similar role in the supernatural world to that played by their human counterparts in the world of the living. Their heavenly marriages are the supernatural equivalent of reterritorialization through marriage. They confirm the integration of the military households into the larger population around them.

The particular configuration of cults that emerged in each place was a function of local history. The presence of each kind of cult is probably at least in part a legacy of patterns of troop assignment in the early Ming. Where many soldiers from one native place were assigned to a single garrison, they were more likely to continue to worship familiar gods. But where soldiers found themselves relatively isolated, their old gods were less likely to survive as objects of communal worship.

In communities like Pinghai where the God of the Wall is the apotheosis of an early Ming commander or the member of a military household, the temple festival of the god is, among other things, a reminder of the community's difference from the villages around it, an annual symbolic expression that even centuries after the guard ceased to exist, the descendants of the soldiers who lived in it have never been entirely reterritorialized. Difference created by state policy in the early Ming—and social responses to it—persist, in different forms, even up to the present.

Guard Schools

While almost everyone in a guard married and almost everyone worshipped at local temples, only a small percentage of the residents of a guard ever aspired to participate in the civil service examinations. But the social relations generated by the examination system could be just as important to the history of guard society as marriage patterns or temple organizations. Guard schools (*weixue*) like the one founded by Chen Yongzhi played a crucial though also unanticipated role in the history of the guards as communities.

Guard schools were not military academies; they were simply Confucian schools located in guards to educate students from the registered military households. Their original raison d'être was to prepare students for the civil service examinations, but like other state schools they eventually ceased to offer actual instruction directly and became simply "quota-based way stations" for students who studied on their own.[28] That is, an aspiring scholar had to be registered in a school in order to be eligible to participate in higher-level examinations or to receive a state stipend. Unlike civilian schools, guard schools initially had no quota for stipendiary, or tribute, students. This institutional discrimination was addressed right around the time Chen Yongzhi was active, in the mid-fifeenth century, when guard schools received their own quota.[29] This had dramatic consequences for the schools themselves, for the students who studied in them, and, as we shall see, for the guard communities as a whole.

If a guard had no school of its own, aspiring candidates from military households in the guard generally returned to their native place to register and participate in the examinations. Zhou Ying, for example, was born in Zhenhai Guard before it had its own school. So when it came time for him to take the examinations, he had no choice but to go back to his family's ancestral home in Putian to register and sit for the examination there.[30] His intellectual life was centered on Putian rather than Zhenhai.

Once a school was established within the guard, promising students could remain in the guard. This was more than just a matter of convenience. Like their civilian counterparts, the chief ambition of scholars in military households was to serve in government. Like their civilian counterparts the odds were against them, for there were far more aspirants than positions available. Like their civilian counterparts, the many scholars who did not realize their ambition to become an official found a variety of ways to reconcile the ill fit between their self-image and the reality, some through continued diligent study, others through abandonment to aesthetic and other pleasures, and still others through devotion to Buddhism. One common reaction was to assert leadership in local affairs, to take charge of efforts to fund, build, and manage public works projects—temples, schools, bridges; to organize local charitable works; and to lead the construction of lineage institutions and the activities that went along with lineages—genealogies, ancestral halls, and ritual observances.

So the creation of a school in a guard often had a powerful side effect. It encouraged the growth of a community of locally engaged, locally committed elites. This was an important element in the organic development of the guards into communities. The transplanted origins of the military households and the transient, contingent element of their association faded into the background, replaced by a sense of permanence and communal life. In the long run, guard schools, and the local literati elites whose formation they encouraged, were thus a powerful force for the reterritorialization of the military households.

Conversely, the establishment of schools could also work to strengthen ties between households in the guard and their kinfolk in the original native place, though again in a way that no one would have expected. We have already seen many cases of soldiers in the guard who maintained ties with their kin in the hope of securing material support, and of military household members in the ancestral home who maintained ties with their kin in the guard so as to be able to verify that the household as a whole was fulfilling its obligations. The quota for tribute students in guard schools created a new reason for people in the ancestral home to want to stay in touch with their kin in the guard. Xu Wenzhang belonged to a military household registered in Zhejiang. Their family's military assignment was to a guard in Guizhou in the distant southwest. Xu lived in Zhejiang, but he went to Guizhou and registered for the examinations through the guard school. He passed the lower-level examinations and became an official. His son followed in his father's footsteps, also registering at the guard school, also taking and passing the examination in Guizhou. Their successes caused an uproar among the actual residents of the guard, who no doubt objected to a form of regulatory arbitrage that hurt rather than helped their own sons' chances.[31]

Xu and his kin in Guizhou, like the families we met in chapter 2, maintained a social relationship over long distances and generations at least in part because that relationship could be turned to their advantage. The famed integrity of Chinese patrilineal kinship groups has sometimes been seen as a product of the need for self-protection in the absence of the state. The strategies that families developed to maximize their chances of success in the civil examinations are just one more example of how, in the aggregate, it was the Chinese state itself that could provide a powerful stimulus for patrilineal unity.

Two other guards along the Fujian coast built schools besides Yongning (there may well have been others that do not survive in the records). Pinghai's school was the first of the three to be built, and it produced the most successful alumni. Over the course of the dynasty, a total of sixty-four provincial graduates and thirteen metropolitan graduates were registered at the school. The school was established in 1442 or 1443 at the behest of the commanding officer. Three decades later, at the request of a local scholar, local civilians became eligible for admission as school students because the existing schools were inadequate. In 1562, the school was destroyed, along with the rest of the town, when Pinghai fell to pirates. The school had obviously come to be seen as part of the fabric of local society, for it was soon rebuilt not by guard commanders but by local civilian officials. Another reconstruction followed in the early seventeenth century, again sponsored by the local prefect, after the buildings were damaged. Other local officials donated funds for the reconstruction of the Confucian temple at the heart of the campus and arranged for the transfer of lands belonging to a nearby Buddhist temple to become a permanent endow-ment for the school.[32]

In Yongning too, the guard school first built by Chen Yongzhi outlived the dynasty that created it. It was destroyed, along with much of the guard, in the turmoil of the mid-seventeenth century. When order was restored in the early Qing, the guard itself was dissolved (see chapter 7). But local elites decided on their own initiative to rebuild their school, even though the guard that housed it no longer existed. The school now became a pri-vate academy.[33] It had become a wholly local institution, a part of commu-nity life. It operated over the whole course of the Qing and even beyond. The former guard school housed offices for the Yongning primary school until 2005.

Guard officers had to be creative in finding funding for a guard school. Officers in Zhenhai and Taicang, two guards in the Suzhou region, received permission to build a school in the mid-fifteenth century. They turned to the grand coordinator (*xunfu*), effectively the provincial governor in the Ming administration, for help. He could not spare them any funds, but he proposed a creative alternative. Local soldiers, probably supernumeraries, were renting civilian land near the guards. The tax on this land was paid to a tax-collection station far away; the surtax to cover the cost of transport-ing the tax was as much as the tax itself. So the governor transferred the tax obligation to a depot that was closer by. He then applied the former transport surtax to meet the expenses of the school.[34]

The administration and financing of guard schools tied guard affairs more closely to the responsibilities of officials in the civilian administrative hierarchy. More importantly, schools fostered a community of elites who saw the guard as more than just a temporary assignment but also as the main local arena for their ambitions and their activities. As the schools opened up to local civilians, they tied elites from the military households to elite families in the surrounding area. All of this further laid the founda-tions for community formation in the guards.

In all three Guards, the construction of a school and the establish-ment of a stipend quota in the sixteenth century had a clear impact on local identity. Local literati soon petitioned and received permission to construct a Shrine to Local Worthies, including those who had devoted themselves to the school. This then became an important locus of elite communal activity. This emergence of the guard as a site for collective action and source of collective identity was not planned; it was guard of-ficers, trying to do their job well, and guard families, pursuing their own interests and strategies, who led these changes. By the late Ming, men in these families began to refer to themselves in their essays as "Men of the Guard" (*weiren*); they continued to do so into the Qing when the guard no longer existed.[35]

Conclusions

One of the great joys of the research for this project has been the chance to sit with elderly villagers, drinking tea or sweet potato liquor, and talking about the Ming dynasty. Their tales of ancestors who bravely fought pirates and outwitted government tax collectors are a source of much local pride. In the past few years, lineage activists have begun retracing connections to the places whence their ancestors were conscripted and compiling genealogies together with their distant kin in these places. But these ancestral places are not home. Home is where they live now, the coastal community that grew up around the Ming garrison. (Whether this will also be true of their children, who study and work in cities like Xiamen or Shenzhen, is another question.) How did these communities come to be home? They came to be home as soldiers and their families intermarried with one another and with other local residents. They came to be home as schools were built, and these schools then fostered a sense of literati identity that then spread among the rest of society. They came to be home as villagers used the organizational, social, and cultural resources available to them to create their own venues for managing local affairs.

In some places, garrisons have become all but indistinguishable from the communities around them. But in others, time has not effaced all the distinctive features of a guard. In some parts of China, former guards are even today linguistic islands, whose people speak a distinctive dialect, typically known as "soldier dialect" (*junhua*), that is different from the communities around them.[36] A few coastal garrisons were still linguistic islands as late as the end of the Ming, and local linguists insist that minor differences in vocabulary and intonation still persist between guards and the surrounding countryside.[37] It would be striking enough for distinctive linguistic, culural, social, or religious elements to have survived more than six hundred years since the creation of the garrison. But it is even more striking because more than three hundred years have passed since the garrisons were dissolved in the early Qing. These legacies must therefore be a product of how new social relations developed after the establishment of each garrison.

Even two garrisons located very near to one another could have different types of relationships with the communities around them. Fuquan and

Chongwu Battalions are about thirty miles apart; both fell under the jurisdiction of the same guard, Yongning, to which they lie on either side, one to the south and the other to the north along the coast. Fuquan is today indistinguishable from the surrounding villages; it participates in the same ritual networks and its youth intermarry with those nearby. Chongwu remains distinctive in many ways from the surrounding area. The low level of intermarriage between Chongwu and the surrounding area has already been mentioned. Some widely shared customs in Hui'an county, in which Chongwu is physically located, are completely absent from the town. Prevailing social practices in rural Hui'an, such as delayed transfer marriage, whereby women remain in their natal home for some time after marriage before moving to their husband's house, are unknown in Chongwu. A woman wearing the distinctive Hui'an costume of headscarf, short jacket, and wide black pants inside the walls of Chongwu immediately reveals herself as a visitor from outside.[38] Chongwu has remained a "marriage island" for centuries after it ceased to house a battalion.

Contingencies large and small help explain the variation. Having an official school was important to the formation of a local literati elite in each guard and therefore probably encouraged the emergence of a sense of guard identity. Where an area came under direct attack from the pirate scourge and the guard served as a haven for nearby residents who fled into it, relations between a guard and the surrounding area are typically closer even up to the present day.

Processes of reterritorialization varied not just between guards but within guards. For households with hereditary standing as officers, maintaining the right to inherit their position, with its stipend, status, and opportunities for further advancement, was a paramount concern. Members of such households had perks associated with their special status, and more ways to leverage that status, so they were probably more likely to maintain their distinctiveness and remain relatively less embedded in their community. For households of ordinary soldiers, evading the responsibility of service could be more attractive. Disappearing into local society was more of an option for them. This also explains why households of officers appear disproportionately in the historical archive, both the official archive and the local one. Genealogies of officer households are naturally much more likely to mention the military household status of the family than those of ordinary soldier households (and indeed officer households are more likely to have genealogies than ordinary soldiers). Where local gazetteers mention that only a few dozen soldiers remain in service in a garrison to which hundreds or even thousands had been assigned, it is safe to assume that these dozens are officers rather than ordinary soldiers. Within individual households, the serving soldiers and officers must have been relatively more fully captured by the military administrative system, so that it would have been supernumeraries and housemen who were more likely to become more fully embedded in the broader locale.

When sons and daughters of the guard married, both to fellow military households and to other local families, they created new social networks that territorialized military household families in the locale. As the communities in the garrison grew in population and in complexity, they exceeded the organizational capacity of the guard to manage them. Communities had to find new ways to manage themselves, using the political and cultural resources available to them. Their efforts, whether to found schools or to build temples, had a host of unanticipated consequences for the community. Just as in other towns and villages in late imperial China, temples often served as the main venue for local management, the site where conflicts and tensions were worked out. Because the residents of the guards often worshipped different gods from the people around them, this could be another source of enduring distinctiveness. In general, official military cults tended to be gradually displaced by popular gods, both those that soldiers brought with them from their own native places and those that were already worshipped in the area. When the garrisons were dissolved as administrative units in the early Qing, the temples to these gods effectively replaced them as the basic structuring unit for local life. Tracing the history of these temples forward to the Qing and beyond, as we shall continue to do in chapters 6 and 7, allows us to see the legacies—profound, lingering, and unanticipated—that Ming state institutions could produce. In some places temples effectively became the sites of local self-government, a function they continued to fill until modern attacks on popular religion in the late nineteenth and early twentieth centuries.

PART III

In the Military Colony

CHAPTER FIVE

A Soldier Curses a Clerk

REGULATORY ARBITRAGE STRATEGIES
IN THE MILITARY COLONIES

EVEN TOLD THROUGH THE GENRE OF GENEALOGY, with its endless descent-line charts and formulaic biographies, the story of the Yan family of Linyang is a dramatic one. Indeed, parts of it seem hardly credible. The tale begins with a devastating blow to a promising family. This turns out to be only the beginning of their suffering, the first in a series of tragedies that follow one after the other relentlessly until it seems the family can endure no more. But eventually the few survivors recover and ultimately even triumph over their adversities. To tell their story we must move to another part of the Ming military institution: the farms that fed the soldiers of the garrison.

The Yan call their early Ming patriarch Master Jinhua (*Jinhua gong*) because, they say, he once held an official position in that Zhejiang prefecture. This was where disaster first struck. The only official in the region able to deal successfully with its endemic banditry, he became the target of envy by his colleagues who ganged up and slandered him. He was impeached and convicted of a trumped-up charge, and sentenced to hereditary conscription. Perhaps it was a blessing that Master Jinhua died just as the family set off for their new assignment. He was a good man, done wrong.

Master Jinhua left behind his widow and three sons. They were "entered into the registers as a military household" assigned to Yanping Guard, upriver from Fuzhou.[1] In 1404, they were sent to nearby Yongtai county and assigned to farm an allotment of land that belonged to the guard (figure 5.1). Misfortune continued to stalk the family. Master Jinhua's eldest son Fazhen had a fierce temper and got into a serious quarrel

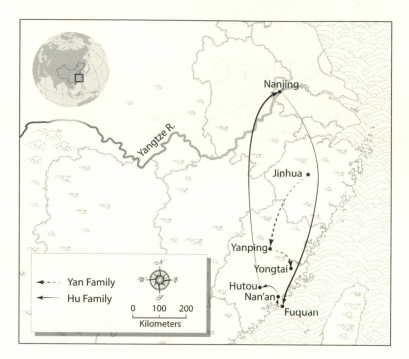

5.1. The stories of the Yan and Hu families

with two other men. Unfortunately for him, his adversaries were powerful men in local society. Members of military households themselves, they worked as clerks who administered the allotments of farmland. Fazhen's enemies nursed their grudge and waited for the right time to gain revenge. That chance came in 1447, during an uprising known, after its leader, as the Deng Maoqi rebellion. The clerks charged Yan Fazhen with being in league with Deng's rebels.

The officer responsible for handling the case only made things worse. He offered to make the problem go away in exchange for a bribe. Little did he know that Fazhen like his father was righteous through and through. Fazhen refused the offer, and was tried and sentenced to death. Vowing to bring a lawsuit against his tormenters in the afterlife, he went willingly to his execution.[2]

Fazhen's crime was no ordinary one. Involvement in rebellion was one of the Ten Abominations, the most serious crimes in the entire Ming code. The death sentence applied not only to Fazhen himself but to his entire extended family. Dozens of Master Jinhua's kin were killed. Only a few managed to escape. One youngster briefly found protection in a nearby city; he was concealed by a family who then sold him into servitude.

Eventually the family's fortunes turned around. According to the genealogy, it was filial piety that saved them. Fazhen's nephew Xuan, the only member of the third generation to survive the imperial fury, intended to flee far away. But his wife pleaded with him to reconsider. It might seem, she warned, that saving their own lives was the most important thing. But if this meant neglecting their ancestors' graves, then the price was too high. Convinced by her reasoning, he took refuge instead with her family and survived.[3]

Several years later, the false conviction against Fazhen was overturned. The survivors were able to return to Yongtai. There they resumed their position in the military registers. Xuan "recovered the old property" (*fu guye*), the very allotment that Fazhen had been assigned to farm. Having fallen so low, the family now enjoyed a meteoric rise in their fortune. Xuan's son, born during the period of troubles, became a merchant and grew rich. So did one of his cousins, another grandson of Fazhen. Their descendants would go on to become scholars and officials.

What of Fazhen's dying curse? He must have carried through on his threat to bring a lawsuit in the courts of the afterworld (this sort of posthumous litigation is a common element in Chinese popular religion). And he clearly won. For, according to the compiler of the genealogy writing about a century later, "Our posterity has been transmitted up to the present day, but the three men [the two clerks plus the officer who solicited the bribe] have no descendants." Fazhen's posthumous vengeance was even more terrible than this. The officer had a handicapped brother, who after the officer's death was reduced to begging, eventually lived off the Yans's charity, and also died without a son to carry on the family line.[4]

Is the Yan tale plausible? Inflated or even entirely fictional accounts of distant ancestors are not uncommon in genealogies. But they tend to be conventionally positive; tales of disgrace, even undeserved, are unusual. So perhaps there is something to this particular story. On the other hand, I have not found a single piece of corroborating evidence.[5] But even if we dismiss the episodes concerning Master Jinhua and Heaven's vengeance on Fazhen's enemies, we are still left with a plausible core story of military registration, misadventure, and recovery. Whatever their origins, whether they were an elite family laid low or came from more humble beginnings and were simply routinely conscripted, assignment to Fujian was profoundly deterritorializing for the Yan. It lifted them out of the contexts they knew and placed them in new and difficult ones. But deterritorialization also generated a territorializing counterforce; the family developed new relationships in the next context. Some were cordial; others, such as with the two clerks, were not.

While the family might seem to us to be strong candidates for desertion and disappearance from the military system entirely, this is *not* how they saw things. As soon as their troubles were over, surviving family members returned to their allotted fields and their alloted roles in the military institution. In spite of their earlier mistreatment at the hands of state officials, the family maintained its registration as a military household. The later chapters of the Yan story are an elaboration of the very same strategies that we saw in chapter 1. Family members sought to distribute the benefits of military registration as widely as possible while limiting the burdens as narrowly as possible. They obviously thought there were advantages to remaining inside the military registration system. They were apparently still fulfilling their obligations to the military when the Ming dynasty came to an end centuries later.[6]

Institutions

Most of the soldiers in the Ming army were not actually soldiers at all—at least not as we usually think of the term—but farmers. Even in early Ming, only a minority of the serving soldiers in each guard actually spent their days doing the sorts of things that we think of as a soldier's work—weapons training, drilling, patrolling, or on rare occasions fighting in battle. The rest of the soldiers of the guard were, like the civilians with whom they are usually but inaccurately contrasted, farmers who worked the land.

To make sense of this apparent paradox, we must go back to the founding emperor. Just as a newly founded state chooses from a range of options about how to staff its military, it also makes choices about military finance and supply. At one extreme are conquest states in which booty is the main or even sole source of army revenue. More elaborate state formations typically collect taxes from civilians to pay for military expenses.[7]

Zhu Yuanzhang's approach to the issue is captured by his celebrated though probably apocryphal remark that "We maintain a million soldiers without costing the people a single grain of rice."[8] The hereditary military system was designed to ensure a constant supply of manpower to fill army ranks. The military logistics and supply system was designed to ensure the army would be self-supporting. The two approaches were two parts of a single project with a consistent logic. Zhu Yuanzhang wanted his army to be a self-sustaining closed system, requiring neither inputs of labor power nor inputs of food to support that labor power. An army that could feed itself was necessarily an army in which soldiers were also farmers.

To achieve military self-sufficiency, the early Ming state revived an institution with a long history, the *tuntian* or military colony system. The core meaning of the term *tuntian* is land reclaimed and farmed by soldiers. In late Ming perhaps 10–15% of all arable land was military colony land.[9] In every guard some soldiers worked military colony land to provide for their colleagues who did the real soldiering. These farmer-soldiers lived outside the guard garrisons, in the countryside among other rural folk. Their social world was very different from that of their colleagues within the fortified walls of a guard or battalion. They developed their own strategies to maximize their interests within the microecology of the colony and its surroundings.

To get a better understanding of how the military colony institution worked in practice, let us first turn again to the experience of a single household. Like the Ni family in chapter 1, they are not an invented family but a real one, who lived in Fujian in the Ming and whose descendants still live there today. In the early Ming, the Hu family lived outside the town of Hutou in Anxi county. Like the Ni, we don't know a great deal about the Hu. They were recruited in 1376, caught up in Zhou Dexing's province-wide draft, and registered as a hereditary military household under the name Hu Liuzai (Hu Number Six). Like some other families we have encountered, the Hu formed part of a composite military household made up of three families, the Hu, the Wang, and the Lin. The Hu genealogy takes pains to identify the different status of each family because each status implied a slightly different obligation. Certain obligations associated with the registration fell to the Wang; the Lin and Hu became liable if the Wang were unable to fulfill these obligations. Other obligations defaulted to the Lin; the Hu became liable only if neither the Wang nor Lin could meet their obligations.[10]

In early Ming, the three families provided a serving soldier in rotation.[11] Hu Yizai, the first serving soldier from the Hu family, was assigned to a guard in Nanjing. In 1428, their assignment was transferred back to Fuquan, the same battalion where a member of the Jiang family (who we met in chapter 3) was in command. This transfer must have been part of the voluntary disclosure policy that sent Yan Kuimei's relative—who we met in the introduction—back to Fujian. They did not stay long in Fuquan. Soon afterwards the household was transferred again. But this was a different kind of transfer. They were not transferred to a different battalion or a different guard; they remained assigned to Fuquan battalion. Rather, this transfer was functional. They were now given the job of supplying food to the battalion by farming.

The transfer brought the Hu into the military colony system. Every guard unit in the empire was assigned arable lands; a certain proportion of the men in each unit were sent out to farm these fields. The proportion varied according to local conditions, both the strategic significance of the unit and the fertility of the land in the surrounding area. Where military threats were more pressing, more soldiers were assigned to defense; where the land was poor, more soldiers were assigned to farming. On the frontier, 70% of soldiers were typically farmers; in the interior the proportion rose to 80%.[12]

Some of Fuquan's farmland was located in Nan'an county, and this is where the Hu family was sent. Hu Yizai (or whoever was the actual serving soldier at the time of the transfer) received an allotment of land in Nan'an (figure 5.1). Allotment sizes varied by local conditions; thirty *mu*—approximately two hectares or the size of two football fields—was the official standard in Fujian. Because each allotment was assigned to a specific soldier, these allotments are sometimes also described as a "share" (*fen*) of military fields or one "name" (*ming*) of fields. They were recorded in registers that were the military equivalent of the "fish-scale registers" that civilian officials used to keep track of civilian land.

Regardless of whether a family was assigned to the garrison or to the military fields, the core principles of the hereditary military household system still applied. Each household was nominally required to provide one man to the military farms—this was the name listed on the register. When he grew old or died, a replacement was sought from his household. The allotment was transferred from the original soldier to the replacement, whose name was then added to the register. So over time the colony register, like the personnel register, also came to resemble a genealogy, a genealogy of service to the Ming state. But there was an important difference. Whereas the serving soldier in the guard was normally the only member of the household expected to soldier, the serving soldier in the colony did not actually do all of the farming of the allotment by himself. Like farm households throughout Chinese history, he worked the land together with his immediate family.

Using the same rough figures for yield as in chapter 1, an allotment of thirty mu should have produced a harvest of around sixty bushels of rice. In the early decades of the dynasty, colony soldiers in Fujian were expected to deliver twenty-four bushels, a little under half the total harvest, to the authorities each year. Half that amount was then issued back to the farming soldier as his monthly ration. This amount was called the "basic tax" (*zhengliang*). The other half was shipped to the garrison to feed the soldiers and officers there. This was called the "surplus tax" (*yuliang*). A soldier's ration was supposed to be one bushel of rice per month, so in theory a colony soldier received the same ration as his colleague in the guard. In 1422, the surplus tax obligation was cut in half in the hope of encouraging compliance, bringing the total annual payment down to eighteen bushels. Officers also realized that the whole arrangement was needlessly complicated. Rather than collecting the soldier's harvest and returning it back to him month by month, it made more sense just to let the soldier look after himself. The basic tax was eliminated, and each soldier was made responsible simply for a payment of six bushels. Confusingly for us, this residual obligation was still called the "surplus tax" even though the payment to which it was "surplus" no longer existed. By the mid-fifteenth century, the main obligation on the farming soldiers of Fujian was thus a payment of six bushels per year, perhaps 10% of average yields on the land to which they were assigned.[13]

The genealogy does not say how Hu Yizai and the other two families negotiated their shared responsibility at first. But a century later, in 1535, they came to an agreement that "each [family] would collect the rent and submit [the surplus tax] for a period of ten years in rotation." In other words, they applied the same principles to handle their obligation to supply grain as families in the guard used to negotiate their obligation to supply labor. By this time the descendants of the original three households were not farming the land themselves but renting it out to tenants. The Hu family had even moved back to their old home in Anxi. But just as conscription officials cared that a slot was filled, not who filled, it, the chief concern of colony officers was that the allotment surplus tax was being paid; keeping control of the physical location of the serving "soldier," or even ensuring who was actually farming the land, was secondary.

The Hu family continued to value their access to military colony allotments and to take seriously the rules and procedures of the regulatory system. We know this because they included in their genealogy two "forms" (*tie*), dated 1570, recording their acquisition of rights to the allotments of two dead soldiers. Probably the dead soldiers had no living relatives; rather than trying to conscript replacements, the guard officers had transferred the land to the Hu family in exchange for a commitment to pay the surplus tax. A 1584 land survey produced another document recording one of their allotments. The Hu first copied this document into their genealogy almost five hundred years ago and they have recopied it into every subsequent edition. Their conscientiousness makes it possible for us to read an official document from a local Ming archive, even though neither the document itself nor the archive that contained it survive. The modern reprint has been typeset, so we can't directly see what the original document looked like. But we can guess at the original format from the contents. The document probably looked similar to a modern-day form, with a printed section at the head followed by a body that was filled out by hand. The printed header explains the purpose of the document and gives instructions on how to complete it. It consists of an order from the commander of Yongning Guard to survey colony lands. Below the header is the main content, which would originally have been filled out by hand, recording the results of the survey:

> *Wang Bingzai, a soldier of Fuquan Battalion, a colony soldier under the command of Company Commander Liu Shufang of that battalion*

has taken over one allotment of military fields previously assigned to Ni Zongxian, deceased soldier, located in Sector 9/10 of Nan'an county.

The form then lists the location and dimensions of the seven plots of land that make up the allotment. As we would expect, they total thirty mu in area and the total tax burden is six bushels. Because some of the land had been damaged by flooding, the tax assessment has been slightly reduced.[14]

The Hu family was first conscripted and became part of the military system in the 1370s. In the 1420s they became farming soldiers and were assigned an allotment. They were still paying the tax on the allotment land in the 1580s and indeed had taken responsibility for further allotments. In fact, their connection to this land would endure past the end of the dynasty. For as we shall see in chapter 7, Hu Yizai's descendants were still paying taxes associated with the military colony system until well into the eighteenth century, long after the hereditary military system itself had disappeared.

Most official sources give a more negative account of the institution. Senior officials were already complaining about its decline as early as the 1420s. "The Guards do not respect the old regulations," wrote Board of Revenue president Guo Dun (1370–1431) in a memorial. "The term military colony still exists, but the reality does not." The colonies were falling behind on their tax receipts, and this meant a shortfall in the supply of grain to the garrison. A few years later, another official reported that fewer than 1% of farming soldiers could actually be located.[15] While this figure is surely exaggerated, there was certainly a problem. Some colony soldiers had been conscripted for military service and never replaced. Others had deserted, or been forced to provide labor to officers and other officials. Colony lands had gone fallow or been seized illegally by other people.

In a pattern common to tax deficits, not just in China, this created a vicious cycle of further shortfalls. Quanzhou native Zhu Jian (1390–1477) described the problem in a memorial requesting tax relief. Officers anxious to meet their tax targets pressed hard on the colony soldiers who remained, so hard that some were "forced to sell their wives and children." This led to further desertion, making the burden on those who remained even heavier. Officers responded to the shortfall by redistributing tax obligations to the soldiers underneath them regardless of how much land they were allotted. The result was that some soldiers who no longer had the use of their land still remained responsible for tax payments on it.[16]

In the hope of ensuring tax receipts, local officers sought replacements to farm the fallow fields. There was potentially a ready source of replacements in the family members and kin of the soldiers who had deserted, the supernumeraries. (Recall that this term refers to military kin, members of military households who were not themselves serving soldiers). Officials began to allow or even to compel the supernumeraries to work the fields. This was called "substituting as the cultivator" (*dingzhong*). This was how the household denoted by Wang Bingzai came to take over the allotment assigned to Ni Zongxian.

As revenue flows from the colonies declined, they became inadequate to meet the needs of the guards. In some parts of Ming China, the shortfall in military supply was addressed through the *kaizhong* system, whereby merchants were required to ship grain to the frontier in exchange for licences to trade salt.[17] Officials in Fujian experimented with variations on this system—at one point troops were actually paid in salt—but their chief solution was to siphon off civilian tax revenues. A more direct violation of the dynastic founder's intentions would be hard to imagine, but officials agreed there was no alternative. Civilians were instructed to deliver a portion of their taxes to nearby guards. Already by 1425 Zhendong Guard was receiving contributions from civilian taxpayers of Fuqing county. Eventually the magistrate insisted that the guard granary be relocated to his county seat, to spare his people the inconvenience of having to deliver taxes to the guard. Over time, civilian and military systems became increasingly intertwined, and just as civilian taxes were increasingly commuted to silver, so too was the colony "surplus tax."[18]

On the northern frontier, military fields were often created by reclaiming wasteland; each allotment consisted of a single plot, and the allotments under a single military unit were contiguous with one another. Fujian was a different kind of frontier. There were no vast tracts of land waiting to be reclaimed, no frontier that could be pushed outward. In Fujian, colony allotments were mostly pieced together out of land that had been abandoned during the wars of the Yuan-Ming transition and land seized from Buddhist monasteries at the start of the dynasty. So a typical allotment might consist of multiple plots of land interspersed with ordinary civilian land.[19] Land had to be found where it was available, so a given unit's land might be located far from the garrison itself, often in another county or even in another prefecture. Many of the colonies belonging to coastal guards were located in the upland interior (figure 5.2). "The land assigned to the soldiers is all in the deep mountains," wrote Zhu Jian. "The *qi* is noxious, causing many soldiers as well as civilians to die. For this reason they are afraid to go. Many farm soldiers prefer to remain in the garrison rather than relocate to their assigned fields."[20] Their reluctance was due to more than just miasmic *qi*. The colony soldiers had been drafted from the coastal communities. They lacked skills to cultivate the high mountain lands. And even if they or their descendants acquired these skills, it was still a tough environment. Tools, seed, fertilizer, and in some cases even water all had to be carried up by hand. (This was brought home to me when I talked to an elderly resident of Yongchun, a descendent of colony soldiers, who helped me to locate allotments mentioned in a late Ming will. He could still identify most of the plots and showed me where they were by raising his arm and pointing this way and that, far up into the surrounding hills, where narrow steeply-stacked terraced fields could be glimpsed in the mist.)

There is some justification for telling the history of the military colony system as a story of decay and failure; over the long term the institution did indeed fail to accomplish fully its intended purpose of maintaining the self-sufficiency of guard forces. But here we are not interested in the reasons for or processes of decline for their own sake, any more than the purpose of the book as a whole is to show the failures of the Ming military system. Rather my interest is in showing how people worked in and around the institution as it evolved over time, turning its specific features to their advantage and minimizing its costs to them wherever they could. And even if the system did not fulfill its intended purpose, its impact on the lives of ordinary people, both military households and local civilians, could be enormous.

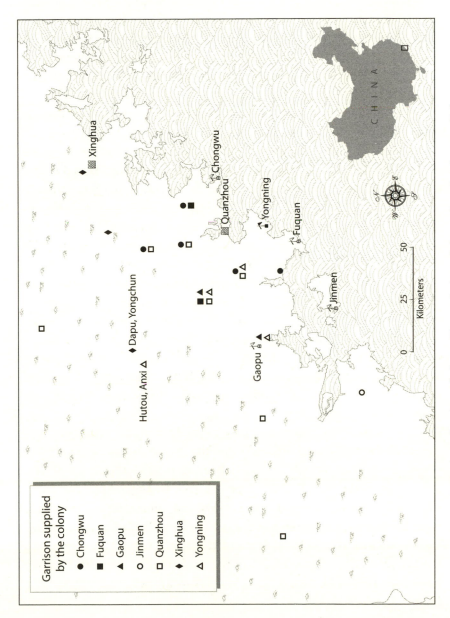

5.2. Approximate locations of select military colonies and the garrison that they supplied

Xu Shisheng Accuses the Colony Clerks

Surviving records of land claims and disputes can help us understand how the descendants of military colonists first registered in the fourteenth century interacted with the institutional legacies of the system and how they found their own ways to work the system by making use of it even as they got around it. Like the optimization strategies discussed in chapter 1, we can recover these family strategies because they were recorded. Thus I do not deal here with many other behaviors that must also have been part of the operation of the system—theft, shirking, and so on. Some of the relevant documentation, such as registration and tax forms, was produced by encounters with the colony system administration; other materials were produced by encounters with the legal system. Settling land disputes through the legal system was not unusual in late imperial China; there is a rich historical record of families devoting time and energy to jurisprudence. Military households in Fujian were no exception. Soldiers and their families copied the documents produced by these encounters into their local genealogies. Sometimes they even carved them onto stone. Another source of information are the casebooks of local judges. Two prominent judicial officials in the region published casebooks that include summaries of disputes involving colony lands. We have met these judges already: Yan Junyan, the shirking Guangdong judge from chapter 3, and Qi Biaojia (1602–45), who handled the case of the visitor from Sichuan in chapter 2. Because the summaries describe both what litigants are said to have done and how they justified their conduct, they can help us to uncover the motivations of the participants.

From these various sources, I have located twenty-six separate documents dealing with land disputes in military colonies on the southeast coast, most from the late sixteenth and early seventeenth centuries. Twenty-three are from Fujian; three are from Guangdong.[21] The documents often provide considerable background information—land deeds trace the history of ownership of the land; effective adjudication of a lawsuit requires that the judge understand the history behind the dispute. So the twenty-six documents actually provide information going back to long before the time they were written and cover far more than the specific issue at hand.

In the documents land is bought and sold, mortgaged, or inherited. But land is also embezzled, illegally occupied, or registered under false pretenses. Rights to land are sometimes secured, reinforced, or challenged by registering or otherwise submitting paperwork to the authorities. The

Table 5.1. Examples of land transfer events involving colony allotments

Identifier	Event	Source	
1/5/01	Xu Jun'ai (and brother Jundao) sell allotment to Wang Erguan for sixty-seven taels	Qi Biaojia, *Puyang yandu*, 107	prior to ca. 1624–28
1/5/02	Wang Erguan registers, obtains certificate	Qi Biaojia, *Puyang yandu*, 107	prior to ca. 1624–28
1/5/03	Judge allows Jun'ai to redeem on payment of additional twenty-five taels	Qi Biaojia, *Puyang yandu*, 107	prior to ca. 1624–28
2/21/01	Allotment assigned to Huang Jianshao	Yan Junyan, *Mengshuizhai cundu*, 537	prior to ca. 1630
2/21/02	Huang Jianshao leases allotment to Li Daisi and Wu Shimao	Yan Junyan, *Mengshuizhai cundu*, 537	ca. 1630
2/21/03	Huang's allotment transferred to Ren De	Yan Junyan, *Mengshuizhai cundu*, 537	ca. 1630
2/21/04	Huang Jianshao seeks to redeem allotment from Ren De	Yan Junyan, *Mengshuizhai cundu*, 537	ca. 1630
4/24/02	Allotment assigned to Ni Zongxian	"Zutun," in Anxi Hushi zupu, 1417-18	early Ming (?)
4/24/03	Ni's allotment transferred to Wang Bingzai	"Zutun," in Anxi Hushi zupu, 1417-18	prior to 1584

parties involved in these various developments are not always willing participants; sometimes they are not even aware of what has happened to their rights until after the fact. The term "transaction" does not cover all these possibilities. So instead I use the less-intuitive term land transfer "event" to describe both transfers involving rights of ownership or use of land and the making of claims about such rights or usage. In all, the twenty-six documents provide information on eighty-one events, examples of which are illustrated in table 5.1. Taken together these eighty-one events allow us to piece together a picture of the interaction of people, land, and institutions in the military colonies of the region.

The different documents belong to different genres, each created for different purposes and intended to support particular positions. Nothing in them is disinterested. The casebook accounts may relate the facts of the cases, but they were written primarily as testimony to the investigative perspicacity and wise judgement of their authors. When a family erected a stone inscription recording an official judgement, they were making a public statement of support for a particular understanding of an event. The documents include among other things accusations, claims, and interpretations. But as with many of the sources in this book, we do not need to accept these accusations, claims, or interpretations at face value for them to be useful. Even if the specific people named in a suit did not do the specific things they are said to have done, the plaintiffs thought that accusing them of doing these things was likely to result in a favorable judgement. Whether or not the accusations in a lawsuit were true, they were all more or less plausible.

Qi Biaojia was prefectural judge of Xinghua, the civilian jurisdiction in which Pinghai Guard and Puxi Battalion were located, from 1624 to 1628; he was also often called upon to render verdicts in other Fujian jurisdictions. One of his most complex cases arose when a poor military colony soldier named Xu Shisheng brought a lawsuit against two clerks responsible for maintaining records (they had the same job as Yan Fazhen's tormentors). The single suit involves thirteen separate allegations. Judge Qi investigates. The clerks offer innocent explanations for each allegation, but it certainly seems that something fishy is going on. Qi ultimately concludes that the lawsuit is the ill-conceived result of a grudge Xu had nursed against the clerks since losing his own allotment. He rejects every allegation and finds for the clerks on every count. But if we set aside the question of who is in the wrong and who is in the right, Qi's investigation and analysis of each specific allegation can tell us a great deal about how the military colony system operated in Fujian in the late Ming and how people strategized within the system.

First, though officials had long decried the decline of the military colony institution, Qi takes for granted that the core of the system is still functioning even in the very last years of the Ming. Allotments are still assigned to individual registered households; the serving soldier responsible for the allotment is still updated in the register with each passing generation. The surplus tax is still being collected, at least on some allotments, and when it is not, someone notices. Clerks copy and update records; Qi is able to consult the "military colony record" (tunzhi) to clarify the muddy history of one allotment. When allotments are transferred, the transfer is registered on forms—like the one in the Hu genealogy—that are completed in multiple copies. Allotment holders are expected to have a copy of the form in their possession to demonstrate that they are the legitimate occupier; Qi dismisses one of Xu's allegations because this form is missing. In another case, a soldier shows Qi both an outdated form and the revised form that was supposed to have replaced it. The very fact that Qi sees both versions enters into his deliberation, for the soldier could easily have produced only the version that was more favorable to him and concealed the other version. Why would he show both versions and open himself up to the possibility of a problem unless he was simply telling the truth? He "might be dumb, but he is not so dumb as this."[22] Colony functionaries are in place and, at least sometimes, doing their jobs. To get to the bottom of another allegation, Qi interviews the relevant headman (*xiaojia*), the man responsible for pressing the allotment holders for payment of the surplus tax. The continued functioning of the system, albeit in a degraded fashion, created all manner of strategic opportunities for the people involved, and this is at the core of Xu Shisheng's accusations.

But even if the overall system has survived, clearly some things have changed. One obvious change is demographic. Just as the households of soldiers in the guard faced the challenge of making a living as the number of members grew over time, many of the households out in the colonies also grew larger over the centuries. State officials were aware that the growing number of men associated with each military registration, both in the guard and in the colonies, was a problem.[23] The issue had after all inspired the whole debate around whether or not to simply send soldiers' dependents back to their ancestral native place. Unlike in the guard, where there was no obvious solution to the employment problem, there was an obvious path forward in the colonies. Families who remained in the system could take over the allotments of families who had deserted, failed to pay their surplus tax, or were in financial distress. They could do this in different ways, by registering officially for allotments, by purchasing the right to use allotments, or by subterfuge.

People had been taking matters into their own hands since the very start of the dynasty. In Sichuan and other remote places, where the land was insufficient to sustain the population of the guard, some members of colony households had registered with the civilian authorities. This practice was called "attaching registration" (*fuji*) or "temporary registration" (*jiji*) to convey that it did not constitute a violation of the rules against military households dividing up. While perhaps not technically legal, the arrangement seemed to make the best of a difficult situation.[24]

If a family continued to grow, then even if some of its members registered as civilians, the problem would recur over time. Qi's investigation of colony records made it impossible to ignore the reality that a single registered household might now include dozens of able-bodied men. In other words, each of the individual households assigned to a colony in the early

Ming had now grown into a large lineage with many members. Under these circumstances, it made no sense to stick to the original limit that each military household should have a single allotment. Qi repeatedly ignores the limit. A single household having ten or more allotments did not strike him as unreasonable. Yan Junyan mentions one registered colony household that had eighteen.[25] The judges recognized that the system had to adapt to a changing reality.

A second development evident in the casebooks was that the distinction between military colony land and private land had become muddied. Colony land was treated in many respects as if it were private land. The terms "bought" and "sold" are generally not used in the deeds themselves—because officially the land still belongs to the guard—but land usage rights are clearly being transferred between different parties. In one of Qi's cases, rights to an allotment had effectively been sold twice before the case even arose. The second purchaser mortgaged his rights to the allotment in exchange for a loan; the lender gained temporary rights to the use of the land and was therefore entitled to collect the rental income from the tenants.[26] The possibility of transfer of rights of usage and ownership to colony allotments was what created the space for arbitrage strategy, and members of military households proved themselves expert at exploiting this space.

There was however still a crucial difference between colony land and ordinary land. When disputes over colony land arose, all else being equal, judges favored registered colony soldiers over civilians *because* they were colony soldiers. In the case above, Li (A), a colony soldier, sold usage rights to Lin (B). Lin then sold the rights to Liu (C). Liu then used the rights to the land as collateral to obtain a loan from Guo (D). According to the terms of the agreement between Guo (D) and Liu (C), Guo (D) would gain permanent ownership of the land if the loan was not repaid on time. But despite the terms of the contract, the judge decides that Li's (A) descendants were entitled to recover the land. That is, they retained certain rights to the land even after they had sold it and even after multiple subsequent transfers.

Xue Liangyan Reports for Duty

Xue Liangyan's ancestor was a colony farmer who had deserted and returned to his native place during the years of pirate turmoil. His allotment had gone fallow. Later a supernumerary named Zhang San spent a considerable sum to rehabilitate the land. In 1619, he had registered his occupancy of the allotment with the colony clerks and received a registration document, confirming both his use of the land and his liability for the surplus tax. Armed with this documentation, he had rented the land out to tenants. They knew nothing of the situation and simply assumed the land belonged to him. They had been paying him rent for years without incident.

Now Xue Liangyan turns up and demands control of the land, on the grounds that the allotment was assigned to his household. He sues Zhang San (or perhaps the other way round) to recover his rightful inheritance. The case eventually makes its way to Qi Biaojia's court. Qi investigates and learns that back when the original soldier, Liangyan's ancestor, had deserted, an order had been duly issued to conscript a replacement. Had Liangyan done his duty and presented himself at that time, he would have received the allotment and there would have been no issue. But Liangyan and his family had willfully defied the conscription order for years, refusing to report. Qi suspects that Liangyan must be in cahoots with the local commander, who for years had done nothing to track Liangyan down. Now suddenly, "since there is profit to be made," Liangyan has reported for duty.

Qi reckons that Zhang San's investment has raised the value of the land and that Liangyan wants to take advantage of the situation. His solution, a judicial parallel to the solutions hit upon by military households in dealing with their own service obligations, is to quantify or monetize Xue Liangyan's special claim. He allows Zhang San to keep the land but orders him to pay Xue Liangyan compensation. While this seems unfair to Zhang San, Qi thinks it necessary to uphold the overall integrity of the system.

Several events in the casebooks share the same basic narrative as the struggle between Xue Liangyan and Zhang San. A colony soldier has transferred his rights to an allotment to some other party at some time in the past. Now he wants it back. Xu Shisheng, the instigator of the complex lawsuit against the two colony clerks, claims he had in the past transferred a colony allotment to a third party. That person had then developed the land and transferred it onward to one of the clerks for a higher sum. Xu says that the land had become infertile due to salt deposits and that he now wants it back so he can repair the damage. But it is obvious to Judge Qi that Xu hoped to gain some benefit from the increase in the value of the land.[27]

Huang Jianshao was a military colony soldier who had previously leased one of his multiple allotments to two tenants for a three-year term. The tenants then sublet the land to a fourth man. Huang brings suit against them, demanding that the lease be cancelled. Why would he do this? The only plausible explanation is that the land had risen in value, which explains why his tenants had tried to sublet it in the first place.[28]

Owning land was a stable, low-risk investment. This created possibilities for strategizing. As we have already seen, military households who had been given allotments of land might later lose the usage rights for their allotments for any one of a number of reasons. Their members deserted to avoid the tax burden or they were transferred to new operational deployments. Or they sold or transferred the land willingly in exchange for cash. If the value of the land rose, they tried to recover it so that they could profit from the increase in price. They did so by asserting their special claims within the distinctive regulatory system, by arbitraging the ways in which military colony land was not exactly the same as ordinary private land.

These practices resemble in some ways the widespread institution of conditional or live sale (*huomai*). In land transactions in Ming and Qing China, the seller often received less than the full market value of the land and retained for some specified period the right to return the purchase price and regain rights to the land. To obtain full control of the land, the buyer would have to make additional payment or payments, the amount to be negotiated. Thomas Buoye argues that at least until the eighteenth century judges and litigants alike retained a certain sense of land inherited from ancestors as inalienable patrimony, as different from an ordinary commodity. It followed therefore that sellers should be allowed to redeem their land indefinitely. Buoye sees this lingering sense that land was not just an ordinary commodity as a sort of last-ditch response to commercialization or a survival of a moral economy under threat.[29]

But there is a crucial difference between transactions involving allotments and ordinary conditional sale. Efforts by military households to recover lost military colony allotments were an attempt to treat land as something other than a commodity subject to pure market forces. But in this case, the "other" is not a set of norms shared by the community. It is the fact that these lands were under the jurisdiction of a separate regulatory regime from the one that applied to civilian land. The contrast in the military colonies was not between market and moral economies but between official and market economies. Our two judges recognized this, pointing out repeatedly that colony land was not the same as ordinary land. "Military colony land is not the same as civilian land," wrote Qi, and so it had to be handled differently.[30] Litigants appealed to the official economy to gain advantage in the market economy.

Where there is doubt about who has the right to use an allotment, both judges show a preference for assigning it to members of military households. There are a total of six cases in the two casebooks where the parties to a dispute over colony land are unambiguously a civilian household and a military household.[31] In two cases, the judge simply returns the land to the military household. In two, he allows or requires the military household to redeem the land by repayment of the original price. In one case, he confiscates the land and returns it to the colony authorities to reallocate to another military household. In only one case—that of Xue Liangyan—does the judge allow the land to remain in the control of a civilian household, and even in this case he orders the civilian to pay compensation to the military household's representative. The size of the sample is small, but the implication is strong. Judges sought to keep colony lands within the system as much as possible. Ming judges, like their successors in Qing, may well have recognized the subsistence rights of poor peasants; they may well have held land transactions that would threaten a family's livelihood to a different standard. But whether or not they had some sense of what scholars call a moral economy is not the issue in our sources. Rather, judges held that a colony soldier retained a residual claim to his allotment even after he sold off the rights to it, because the regulatory system had allotted him, or his ancestor, the land. Despite all the changes to the larger political economy of Ming Fujian, there remained limits on the transferability of land rights of military colony allotment holders. Members of military colony households used this judicial preference to their advantage.

This special right is most evident in a case where a colony soldier pursued a scheme that, at least as the judge presents it, is almost laughably egregious. Chen Jin, an officer in the Guangzhou Guard, had sold the long-term rights to use a plot of military farm to one Ju Zhaojue.[32] Later Chen Jin conspired with his relative Yuanyue to throw Ju off the land. The relative claimed that he was a newly conscripted military colony soldier to whom the land had been allotted. Ju therefore had to leave. Jin and Yuanyue hoped to force Ju from the land but keep his money. As the judge sighed in exasperation, "How could [Ju] have accepted this?" Jin had transferred the land to Ju under the terms of one regulatory regime and then tried to expel him from the land under the terms of another. Under the regulatory regime that applied to ordinary land, there was no reason he could not transfer the land. But he and Chen Yuanyue then turned around and argued that the military colony regime applied, and therefore Ju's claims to the land were trumped by the assignment of the land to Jin's relative.[33]

Civilians too could seek advantage by exploiting the differences between two regulatory systems. Su Xiangwu was a civilian whose land was located up in the hills, where it adjoined the allotment assigned to soldier Cai Ruzhong. Su came up with a scheme to seize the allotment. He went to the county yamen and reported that he had reclaimed land that had been allotted to Cai but that had been abandoned. He seems to have been hoping that Cai Ruzhong lacked the documentation to confirm his allotment. But Su was disappointed. Cai was able to produce his registration document. His tenants, the very people who Su had said he had hired to reclaim the land, confirmed the story. The judge considered but dismissed the possibility that the tenants might have had a grudge against Su or been partial to Cai. Since Cai was collecting unusually high rents, it would have made no sense for the tenants to side with him unless his rights to the land were genuine. Qi saw through Su's schemes to take advantage of bad record keeping in the military colony in order to transfer the land into the civilian registration system illicitly. "This land already has a proprietor. How can it be 'reclaimed?'"[34]

Two men reclaim thirty mu of land, which happened to be the exact size of a standard colony allotment. One of the men registers the land with the civilian authorities and assumes the tax obligation. Now a third man, a colony soldier, tries to take over the lands, claiming they were actually an allotment that had been assigned to him in 1617. But the earliest document he could produce was a register dated 1625. Qi concludes that the register was a forgery (or rather that it was not legitimate. It could well have been a genuine document that had been obtained through bribery). He orders the fields returned to the two men who had reclaimed them. The status of the land was ambiguous. It was registered as civilian land but looked suspiciously like military colony land. This made it potentially subject to two distinct regulatory regimes. The soldier was trying to use his position in one of those regimes to take advantage of the situation. Qi would have none of it: military households might have a special claim on colony allotments, but not on land that they falsely claimed was an allotment.[35]

An allotment carried benefits—the right to farm the land or earn rent from it—as well as obligations—the burden of paying the surplus tax. Some strategies sought advantage by unbundling the two. This is the background to an inscription in the village of Maluan, near Xiamen. It was composed by Lin Xiyuan for the Du family, to celebrate (and secure) their triumph over adversity. We have met Lin several times already. Though never a regular, he belonged to a military household from Tong'an. He was the man anti-pirate commander Zhu Wan called the very worst of the Fujian literati who were in league with pirates and smugglers.[36]

The Du were registered as a military household in the early Ming and assigned to a colony in Dehua county. In 1518, they received an additional allotment, substituting for another military household that had died out.

They had subsequently lost the use of both of these allotments. They claimed the lands had been taken over by local bullies; it is also possible that they had sold the rights. But the tax liability had not disappeared with the usage rights; the Du remained liable for the tax on both allotments. They pleaded with colony clerks to be relieved of the obligation, to no avail. So the members of the lineage, for by this time the descendants had multiplied considerably, set up an internal mechanism to distribute the taxes amongst themselves. But that did not mean they were happy about the situation. In 1540, an elder decided that something had to be done. "Why," he demanded to know, "should the laws of the state apply only to the descendants of our Du family?" The Du raised funds and launched a suit. Their opponents hatched all sorts of nefarious schemes to hold up the matter. The case dragged on and on; officials from multiple jurisdictions had to get involved. But eventually the family was partially successful in their bid. The land was ordered returned to them, "so our lineage need no longer worry about being unable to bear the burden of the tax."[37]

The Du of Maluan worked within the military colony system in order to relieve themselves of what they saw as an unfair obligation. The obligation arose because the tax levy on the farms had been separated from the right to use the land. One might ask why they did not appeal for relief, or ask that the tax be transferred to the current occupant. It is easy to see why this would not have worked. The local colony officers would have been concerned only that their tax collection quota be met. They had no incentive to relieve the Du's obligation, since that would only oblige them to make up the shortfall somewhere else. So the only way to appeal to their interests was for the Du to suggest that they were in such difficult straits that they could not be confident that the tax would be paid. This then gave the officials a strong incentive to return the land use rights to the Du, in order to make it more likely that the tax would be paid in future.

One possibility is that the Du were simply not telling the truth—at some previous date they had sold the land while retaining the tax obligation—this would have enabled them to get a higher price for the sale. But assuming that the Du account is accurate, which we have no reason not to, we can guess what the other party, the "local bullies," might have been thinking. For anyone in the market for illegal land seizure in the Ming, military colony land would have been highly desirable. Because it was not included on the civilian land registers, the "fish-scale registers" of the county authorities, the embezzlement may have been less likely to be exposed by the regular updating of the records. There is another, perhaps even more compelling reason. As we saw in chapter 2, hereditary military households were eligible for an exemption from corvée, on the principle that their members fulfilled their labor duty to the state through the provision of a soldier. In law, the exemption had limits—when reporting their corvée liability military households reduced the number of eligible males by one— but in practice military households had long succeeded in avoiding corvée entirely. This exemption was maintained even after the corvée became attached as a surcharge to the land tax. Since the households that farmed military colony land were not liable for corvée, this meant that military colony land did not bear a corvée surcharge. Corvée surcharges grew and grew over the course of the Ming, so exemptions became more and more valuable.

It would be a mistake to think that families always acted in concert, putting collective interest first in their dealings with the military colony system. One case in Qi's casebook shows individuals within a household trying to work the system to their own advantage at the expense of their kin. Yi Guoqi adopted Zheng Yuanhui when he married the boy's widowed mother. Zheng had come to control three allotments. Now he had died. Guoqi's natural-born son Wenxue thought he was entitled to all of the allotments. His family disagreed (figure 5.3). They decided that the allotments should be divided evenly among the descent lines of Guoqi and his two brothers, with each line receiving the rights to one allotment. Despite some murkiness about how Zheng had acquired the land, Wenxue had no qualms taking the issue to the magistrate. In fact he had done so not just once but twice. Qi found Wenxue's complaints tedious. "The lineage members had resolved this and expressed it clearly," wrote Qi of this disposition. "This accords both with the particularities and with principle" (*qingli zhi dangran*). He ordered Wenxue be fined for bringing a frivolous lawsuit.

The efforts of lineage members of the lineage to resolve their dispute through informal and internal mediation calls to mind the work of Philip Huang which shows that there was a complex relationship between informal mediation and formal legal action. Magistrates often tried to push cases back into the informal sector; people used the threat of formal action to obtain desired results in informal mediation. This was probably what happened here. Wenxue was unhappy with the results of the informal mediation and hoped to bring his kin round to his point of view by threatening to go to the magistrate. When they did not, he carried out his threat, but it ended up backfiring.[38]

Though Qi's account of the case is almost telegraphically concise, it is adequate to get a sense of the arguments that were made. The Yi family must themselves have been registered as a military household, for Wenxue

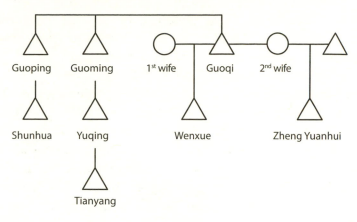

5.3. The Yi family

went to court apparently unconcerned about any risk that the allotments would be confiscated. Wenxue argued in support of the basic algorithm of soldier selection. He had inherited the position of serving soldier from his adopted brother, and therefore he should inherit the rights and obligations of the position. His relatives disagreed with this application of the algorithm. They may have argued that the rights to the allotment were part of the patrimonial estate of Yi Guoqi's father, to be divided evenly and fairly among his heirs. Or they may have considered the matter in light of the regulations on military farm allotments, whereby supernumeraries who were without allotments were entitled to receive them so long as they took on the corresponding tax obligation. Perhaps they tried both lines of argument. What united all the parties was their desire to use the rules of the system, and the way military colony land was similar to but not quite the same as private land, to their advantage. It was impossible for both sides to succeed, but both sides certainly tried.

Two documents from the early seventeenth century, found by Li Ren-yuan tucked into a genealogy, show deliberate efforts to use administrative adjustments to gain advantage. The core strategy rests on confidence in officials' preference to assign allotments to people with some connection to the military colony system, either actual serving soldiers or supernumeraries. The first document, issued in 1606 by the commander of the military colony for Jianning Left Guard, concerns an allotment in Gutian county, just upriver from Fuzhou. The allotment had once been assigned to a colony soldier named Gao Xing. On his death it had been transferred to Gao Hu'er, probably his son. But Hu'er had "for a long time" been remiss in paying the surplus tax. So Xu Yuanzhao, himself a colony soldier, had "substituted as cultivator" (*dingzhong*) for the Gao family. In other words, the allotment had been rescinded and transferred to Xu.

At some point the surplus tax on this allotment had come to be collected by the Gutian county offices (as we saw previously, this was not uncommon once civilian magistrates began to cover the revenue shortfalls of nearby guards). Xu himself lived closer to the guard in Jianning. Clearly he was not farming the land himself. He was in Jianning; the allotment was in Gutian. Rather, he was managing it, presumably renting it out to tenants. The document is his petition that he be allowed to submit the surplus tax owing directly to the guard. Xu was asking to return to the original spirit of the military colony system, submitting his taxes directly to the guard where they could be used to support the serving troops, rather than paying them in a roundabout way through the local county government.

The complexities of collecting colony taxes and financing the guards had led to the emergence of two overlapping tax systems. There was the original system in which colony taxes went directly to their guard, and there was a mixed system in which colony taxes were collected by civilian administrators and then blended with their subsidy to the guard. Xu wanted his own tax obligation to be transferred from the second system back to the first, because it saved him time and money. He wanted to use one regulatory system rather than another in order to reduce his costs. One could not ask for a more clear demonstration of regulatory arbitrage. The request was granted—from the perspective of the guard the important thing was that the surplus tax was paid, not where it was paid—but he was told he had to fill out the necessary paperwork.

Twenty-four years later, Xu was back at the yamen. He had decided that even with the tax issue solved it was inconvenient to manage the property at such a distance. Now he wanted to relinquish his claim on the property by transferring it to someone else. Not coincidentally, the someone else was a supernumerary. The document recording this transfer superficially resembles an ordinary land deed, but there are a few interesting differences. The term "sale" does not appear anywhere in the document. Ordinary land deeds typically explain how the vendor has come to own the land, through inheritance, purchase, or some other means. So does this document. Xu explains that he has acquired the land through "substitution as cultivator," and the purchaser now "succeeds to the substitution" (*chengding*) in exchange for a payment. This language was a gesture to the ways in which military colony land was *not* ordinary private land. It remained subject to a different administrative system, with its own bureaucratic requirements. While it could not legally be bought and sold, in practice this was precisely what was happening.[39]

Not all of the cases warrant the term regulatory arbitrage. Sometimes, what happened is better described with the simple term corruption. Just as military households were registered in special archives, military colony lands were recorded in archives of their own. The existence of these documents is part of what kept the system operational and also created vested interests among clerks and other functionaries. Bradly Reed's study of the Baxian archives in Sichuan first brought into the light these shadowy figures who actually produced much of the documentary record on which we now rely. His study is based mainly on nineteenth-century cases. But in Qi's casebook, one such figure makes a rare appearance three hundred years earlier. Lin Jie, a colony soldier in Yongchun county, had acquired a new allotment. But he had not registered this acquisition with the authorities. He never filled out the paperwork. A clerk in the county office accused him of occupying the land illicitly. Lin launched a countersuit accusing the clerk of some other impropriety. The matter was easily resolved, since Qi saw through the issues immediately. The clerk was trying to extract fees for registering the transfer and Lin Jie refused to pay. Qi told Lin he had to file the necessary paperwork and sentenced the clerk to a beating. The clerk turned out to be a repeat offender. He was known to collect the registration fees but then never issue the actual document. Evidently his position was lucrative enough to justify the repeated beatings.[40]

But maintaining the paperwork of the system was not just something that clerks and officials imposed on an unwilling populace and from which they could seek rents. Compliance with the rules of the system obviously had its benefits in strengthening the owner's claims on the property, making it less likely that a magistrate would reject those claims in the future. The registration system served to authorize people's claims to property, so people saw value in keeping their paperwork up to date.

Conclusions

Tens of thousands of families were relocated into the newly established guards and battalions when the coastal defense system was first established in the early Ming. The creation of colonies to support these garrisons meant the further relocation of tens of thousands of these families into the surrounding hinterland. Unlike on China's other frontiers, colonists on the southeast coast could not simply reclaim empty land; the settlers were assigned land that was confiscated or abandoned, and that was interspersed with civilian lands. There they had to deal with their surroundings and try to build a life. The challenges they faced and their relationship with nearby civilian populations was a problem created by high-level institutions. It was resolved by everyday politics. Both the existing residents and the new arrivals, civilians and soldiers, took advantage of regulatory overlap and loopholes to pursue advantage in the local economy.

Regulatory arbitrage, recall, means to take advantage of differences between one's real situation and how one is perceived by a regulatory regime, or of the differences between multiple regulatory systems. In this chapter, we have explored several examples of both types. Qi Biaojia's adjudication of the case of Xue Liangyan, the descendant of a colony soldier who tries to recover his ancestor's abandoned allotment, suggests that he *himself* understood Xue's actions to be regulatory arbitrage. Xue had stayed outside the colony regulatory system when it was to his advantage; now he wanted back in because there was a benefit in doing so. Qi worried that if the land were returned to Liangyan, he might change his mind in the future and try to step out of the system again. Nor did it seem right to ignore the interests of Zhang San, who had incurred expenses in reclaiming the land and had faithfully paid the taxes. Qi's judgement sought to prevent the plaintiff from using regulatory arbitrage to take advantage of the benefits of his military household status while avoiding the burdens, while at the same time recognizing and even quantifying the special rights that Liangyan had due to his status.

Officials like Qi Biaojia and the military farm administrator who authorized Xu's deeds recognized that military colony lands had increasingly come to resemble private lands, but still they maintained that the two were not entirely the same and were subject to different regulatory systems. They accepted that military households had special claims on these lands. They were fighting a rearguard action against the normalization of colony land, and this is what created the possibility of regulatory arbitrage. Members of military households were aware of the situation and sought to use it to their advantage. Over and over again in the documents, we see members of military households seeking to assert special claims whenever it was in their interest to do so. Qi was suspicious of such claims and at times he ruled against them. But the fact that such claims arose shows that regulatory arbitrage was seen as a viable and legal strategy and was widely used.

After the fall of the Ming, in his magisterial yet wistful summary of historical geography, Gu Yanwu summarized the various problems of the military colony system in Fujian in the later years of the dynasty, "There were cases where the land was extant but there was no soldier [to farm it], and cases where a soldier [was assigned to] but there was no land." Clearly Gu does not mean that lands or soldiers have actually disappeared. He is using the language of the scholar-official to point to the distinction between reality and regulatory position. Regulatory position is simply another way of saying how reality appears to regulators. Gu is pointing out that there is a difference between this version of reality and everyday reality. He continues, "There were cases where a single soldier controlled three or four allotments of military colony land, and cases where a single allotment of land was shared by three or four soldiers."[41] For all the dramatic changes of the Ming economy, the regulatory system that had been created at the start of the dynasty continued to shape the working of the economy even to the end.

The distinctive system of registration meant that even as colony land was increasingly privatized, it remained distinct from ordinary private land. Members of military households often tried to take advantage of their special claims to such land. They sold allotments off to civilians as if they were private and then tried to recover them for free on the basis of their status. Or they tried to recover the land by refunding the original sale price even though the land had risen in value. Or they sought to profit by separating the income from the land from its tax obligations. Such efforts were part of a larger pattern of responding to rising prices by seeking redemption of land that had been sold conditionally; they were distinctive—and they represent a form of arbitrage—because they sought to take advantage of the regulatory reality that *all* sales of military colony land were conditional. The common feature of these strategies was that they exploited the gaps and loopholes created by the multiple overlapping regimes by which the Ming state regulated land ownership and use. These strategies show regulatory arbitrage to be a recurrent feature of the social landscape of southeast China in Ming.

These strategies also help explain why it is that while many people deserted, many others chose to remain within the system. According to the genealogy of the Li of Taiping, they hailed originally from distant Sichuan. The founding ancestor of the lineage was the younger brother of a distinguished supporter of the founding emperor, a fellow campaigner (*congzheng*). Having inherited a junior officer position on the death of his brother, this man had been assigned initially to Fuzhou Guard and then, in the reorganization of the military colonies of the early fifteenth century, transferred to Yongchun county. There he served as a minor official in the military colony system, while also farming his own allotment. His son, grandson, and great-grandson each "inherited the task of administering the military colony." By the time of the great-grandson, the family had become hugely wealthy. This great-grandson built an estate of almost five thousand *mu*, enough to set aside significant income for ancestral sacrifice and to support the education of descendants. The first members of the lineage to succeed in the civil service examinations would appear within a few generations.[42]

Economic historians have shown that people in China used land rights as a vehicle to maintain and improve their status. Rural people developed strategies to "financialize" their land-use rights in ways that resemble contemporary financial instruments.[43] Military households on colony lands took the process one step further. Not only did they make use of their land use rights, they took advantage of ambiguities in the rights that accrued to particular lands and particular households in service of their interests. They arbitraged the distinct but overlapping regulatory regimes that applied to civilian lands and military colony lands

Despite their special privileges, members of military households faced huge challenges. They had to address the larger question of how they would integrate into the existing communities around them, how they would make a future for themselves and their descendants in a new and sometimes hostile environment. They used a variety of approaches and methods, sometimes infiltrating and taking over existing community organizations such as temples and thereby developing and maintaining a separate communal identity within the larger society, sometimes integrating as individuals and families with that society and blending into it. These strategies are the subject of chapter 6.

CHAPTER SIX

A Temple with Two Gods

MANAGING SOCIAL RELATIONS BETWEEN
SOLDIER-FARMERS AND LOCAL CIVILIANS

A SMALL AND REMOTE TEMPLE and an even more remote upland village might seem odd places to look today for clues about the lives of Ming soldiers. But the rituals of the Houshan temple in Hutou and the genealogies of the Lin of Dapu offer a window onto how Ming military institutions have shaped local social life over the centuries and how their legacies shape social relations even up to the present day.

We begin in Hutou, in the northeastern part of Anxi county, inland from the city of Quanzhou and the guard at Yongning. It is a round basin valley about six kilometers across, surrounded by steep hills, and bisected by a brook that flows down to Quanzhou and the sea. Hutou has long had a reputation as a prosperous place; its many famous literati sons included the Kangxi emperor's confidant Li Guangdi (1642–1718). We have come across several military households from the valley already. It was a branch of Li Guangdi's family who, in chapter 1, endowed an estate in response to a kinsman's pleas that "the road is far and the duties onerous, and [they lead] only to death in a distant place. Is there no one who can take my place?" Hutou was also the native place of the Hu Yizai, the colony soldier whose story was told in chapter 5.

Hutou was a place from which soldiers were conscripted; it was also a destination to which other soldiers were sent, for Hutou was also the location of one of Yongning Guard's military colonies. To learn about the history of this colony, the small temple at Houshan is actually our best historical source. Hutou is one of a few dozen villages in Laisu, the local term for the east side of the river; Ganhua is the name of the west side.

6.1. The Supreme Emperor of Houshan

On the sixth day of the lunar new year in early February 2014, in preparation for their annual procession festival, the images of the two gods of the Houshan temple, the King and the Emperor, are carried out of the temple and down to a temporary residence in Shangtian village. The King, whose full title is Venerated King of Heroic Martiality (*Yingwu zunwang*), is a fierce figure with full black beard and wild eyes. The Emperor carries a sword but he is otherwise less fear inspiring than his colleague, with his ivory-white skin, neatly trimmed beard, and hat of a government official. His full title is Supreme Emperor of the Dark Heavens (*Xuantian shangdi*) (figures 6.1–6.4).

Shangtian, a single-surname village whose male residents are all surnamed Li, is the village responsible for organizing the ritual this year; in the old days, the gods would have been housed in the Li ancestral hall on the first night of the festival.[1] But the hall was torn down long ago to build a primary school, so the gods spend the night instead in a warehouse owned by the head of the organizing committee for the festival. He also owns a fireworks factory.

The men of the village line up before dawn on the seventh day of the new year. In front are men dressed as Qing lictors, carrying the traditional symbols of a magistrate's authority, heavy wooden signs warning

6.2. The Venerated King of Houshan

6.3. Houshan Temple

6.4. Offerings at the Houshan procession festival

spectactors: "Be Silent!" and "Make Way!" To appeal to modern male sensibilities, they are joined by a troupe of heavily made-up young women in tight *qipao*. A parade of more than a hundred villagers follows, carrying lanterns, banners, parasols, drums, and gongs. Then come the hired performers: lion dancers, gymnasts, musicians, and motorized carts bearing teenage singers of *Nanguan*, the elegant local operatic tradition. Next come four village elders in beautiful embroidered gowns and the Daoist priests who have been hired to perform rituals at the festival. Behind them follow the statues of the deities, loaded into the back of a truck. At the very rear of the procession is another modern variant on traditional practice, the mobile artillery (*paoche*), a pickup truck mounted with a noisemaker cannon. It sets off bursts of firepower so that even if the firecrackers run out there will still be noise, flame, and smoke—the essential elements of a festival.

The first stop on the procession is a temple about six miles away in Pumei, where the gods pay their respects to Emperor Guan in a ritual called "collecting the [incense] fire" (*xiehuo*). The temple is too small to accommodate the whole procession, so only the image of the King and a small core group from the procession enter. They are welcomed by the temple-keeper, an "incense and flower" (*xianghua*) Buddhist.[2] His

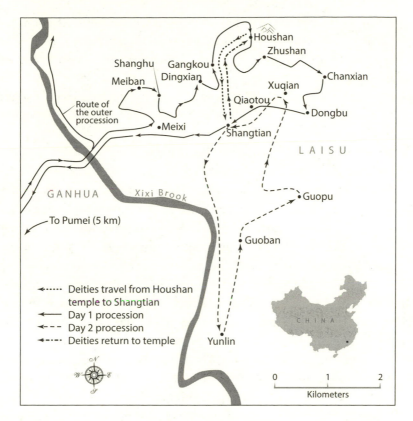

6.5. Hutou procession map

wife—for incense and flower Buddhists may marry—assists with the ritual, preparing a coal lantern while her husband recites sutras. She grumbles about the early hour—complaining that when one emperor pays a call on another emperor, there is no need to show respect by arriving before dawn. The coal fire is transferred to an incense burner and fanned into a great flame; the ritual is complete. The procession sets off back to Hutou.

At dawn the marchers divide into two groups, the "outer" and the "inner" procession. The outer parade traces the edge of the Hutou plain; its participants will walk for hours over the next two days to visit its more distant villages. The core of the procession remains in Laisu, following a prescribed route from village to village (figure 6.5). Even as virtual participants, we can only be in one place at at time, so let us follow the "inner" procession. One of the first stops is the village of Meixi. In a large open space, ordinarily used for drying and threshing rice, the gods are placed at the head of a row of tables, on which every family of the village has placed its own sacrificial offerings. This is the first time that village women appear in the festival, for it is they who bring the offerings. Each household lays out its plates of food and there is good-natured scrambling to get the best spot.[3] This is also the first appearance of outward signs of personal devotion to the gods. The women bow down fervently; they reach forward to touch the chairs of the gods. Placing their own lit incense sticks in the burners, they use their open palms to sweep the smoke from the burners over their faces.

At each subsequent stop the routine is the same. The Daoists set up a simple altar and perform sequences of chanting, bowing, offering and ritual dance with musical accompaniment. The performance is elaborate but the core of their ritual is simple. They consecrate the offering, identify the donors, and ask for the gods' protection. Then the men who are carrying the gods in their heavy sedan chairs race around the circle in a competitive display. They leap over the lit firecrackers and burning piles of incense ash and paper money. Around and around they go in an intense spectacle. As the men of the previous village drop out, sweaty and exhaused, men of the next village jump in and take over the task of carrying the chairs. The hosts try to run their visitors into the ground. Then the procession forms up again and continues on its way. The offerings, having been consumed by the gods, are gathered up quickly and taken home, where they will soon be transformed into feasts for the gods' human devotees.

This sequence is repeated a dozen times as the procession wends its way for the next two days through the villages of Laisu. On the third day, the gods return to Shangtian, where the villagers have laid out even more impressive offerings in the schoolyard, including a whole pig from each family. After a day-long liturgical sequence, there is a final burst of fireworks, and the Daoists pronounce the festival complete. Quickly, the villagers recover their offerings and return home. Soon the schoolyard is all but deserted. When night falls, the gods are carried back to their temple. The festival is over.

Like the temples that house the gods, much about this festival appears to be generic, and would be familiar to anyone who has spent time in rural south China in the last twenty years. But in fact the specifics of this ritual have a history. The ritual we can see today is in many respects an artifact of the new social relations created by Ming military institutions. Though the institutions have been gone for centuries, the rituals endure and today provide a way for us to better understand the everyday politics of that time. They constitute a different sort of archive of local politics.

This chapter uses two stories—an account in a genealogy of a mysterious man of ambiguous background who turns up one day in a former colony and the story of the Hutou temple—to explore the social lives of the military families in the colonies. The point of the first story is to show how military households in the colonies worked with and manipulated Ming systems of registration; the second shows how they sought to integrate themselves into the communities in which they were settled. The two stories might seem to be connected by little more than geographic proximity; in fact, they each show different facets of everyday politics in the military colonies and their legacies. In the colonies as in the guards, soldiers and their families had to come to terms with the society around them and construct new communities. This was a complex process involving different kinds of everyday politics that leave only subtle traces in the historical record. The two stories in this chapter illustrate two forms this politics could take.

A Stranger Appears in Dapu

One day in the mid-sixteenth century, a young stranger appeared in Dapu, just to the northwest of Hutou in the neighboring county of Yongchun. He arrived in the company of two brothers who were well-known to the villagers. They explained that the stranger was in fact their long-lost nephew Chunzhai. Late in his life, their father Fosheng had unexpectedly had a fourth son. This fourth son had died young, but not before leaving behind his own son, Chunzhai. (As is typical in genealogies, the son is called by various names in different documents. For the sake of simplicity I will stick with this one name.) His widow had taken the boy away with her when she remarried and contact had been lost. Now the brothers had taken it upon themselves to find their nephew and bring him home.

This heartwarming story appears in the nineteenth-century genealogy of the family, compiled by descendant Lin Liangjun. Lin Liangjun of Dapu was confident that he had the early history of his family right because he relied on something called the "military service [register]" (junyao). This can mean only one thing. Liangjun had in his possession the family's own copy of its personnel file from the Ming dynasty, that is, their copy of the military register that had once been held in the central government archive.

According to this register, Lin explains, the family was originally conscripted from their home in Tong'an in 1387 and assigned to Yongning. Seven years later they were transferred to Xinghua as part of the interregional rotation. Already at that time they belonged to a company under the hereditary command of the Luo family. In 1404, the company, including

Commander Luo, the serving soldier of the Lin family, Weizai, and another soldier named Ma De, was sent to farm colony lands in Dapu.[4]

One of the techniques that I have used repeatedly in this book is to compare the general information in official sources with the specific information in genealogies. The families of Dapu present an unusually rich opportunity for this kind of comparison. Most of the families in this book are not mentioned in any surviving official source. But Commander Luo, Lin Weizai, and Ma De are. We can read about them not only in the genealogy but also in a Ming gazetteer of Yongchun county, compiled in the mid-sixteenth century by our old friend Lin Xiyuan. He writes:

> *Under the Rear Battalion of Xinghua Guard [there is] one colony*
> *under Hundred Commander Luo Guoyi.*
>
> *Located in township 9/10*

[There are] currently two allotments under cultivation

1. [the allotment originally assigned to] Ma De, now [held under the name] Ma Ciyi
2. [the allotment originally assigned to] Lin Weizai, now [held under the name] Lin Cong.[5]

The Lin family's own account of their history, apparently copied from their military registration into their genealogy in the nineteenth century, is thus consistent in every detail with an official gazetteer from the sixteenth century.

Cong was Weizai's grandson (or his great-great-grandson according to other editions of the genealogy). As serving soldier, he took over nominal responsibility for the household's military field allotment. He oversaw a considerable improvement in the family's fortunes. But he also made enemies with the Ma family. The Ma were not just fellow farmer-soldiers; they also held the minor post of banner-head (*qijia*), responsible for collecting the surplus tax from the allotment holders. Relations between the families were civil as late as 1515, when Ma Ciyi witnessed a document of household division (since the will touched on the disposition of their allotment, it may have needed the banner-head's signature to be valid). But the cordial relations did not last. Apparently Cong's continued success was the problem. "His enemy Ma was envious of him, and repeatedly made the situation uneasy for him."[6] Things came to a head in a dispute over a plot of land owned by some of Ma's relatives. Cong hoped to acquire the land to build an ancestral hall and arranged to trade it for another piece of property. Ma Ciyi objected and launched the first of many lawsuits. Cong eventually prevailed and the Lin ancestral hall was built on the site. As was common practice, the Lin made a copy of the judgement, so they could produce it if the issue ever came up again. They still had it in the early nineteenth century, when genealogy compiler Lin Liangjun was able to refer to it.

According to Liangjun, Cong decided to use the occasion of the updating of the population and tax registers to try to free the family of its ties to the Ma. Sometime around 1522, arguing that the death of Ma Ciyi's father had complicated the registers, Cong sought to "obtain entry into the [civilian] household registers and report his property." He "established a [civilian] household [registration] under the name of Lin An." Lin An was Lin Weizai's long-dead father and hence the effective founding ancestor of the Lin of Dapu.[7]

By the early sixteenth century, the Lin family had become unhappy with their official registration status as colony farm soldiers and was looking for a way out. They rejected desertion and flight as options; Lin Cong and his family had houses, lands, and even temples in Dapu. The solution Cong came up with was to register the family in the civilian registration system. Cong moved his family from one regulatory system to another because he thought it served their interests. There must have been another arrangement behind this agreement. To make the switch, Cong would have had to ensure that the family's military obligation, the payment of the surplus tax, was also being fulfilled, or that someone else had agreed to pay it. Otherwise the clerks would never have allowed the change. Local officials probably felt that so long as the tax obligation was clear it was better to accept such arrangements. As we saw in chapter 5, local officials were well aware of the demographic challenges in the colonies and were willing to acquiesce to informal arrangements so long as they did not interrupt the flow of tax.

Many military families in Ming Fujian came to arrangements like those of Lin Cong, often as soon as they could afford it. Two descendants of Fazhen, the colony soldier falsely accused of involvement with the Deng Maoqi rebellion in chapter 5, transferred their registration in this way. One of his grandsons went into trade, became a wealthy landowner, and then took advantage of the provisions on "attaching registration" to register his household with the local magistrate. So did another, even more successful grandson. The family's upward trajectory continued in the predictable way; the merchants converted their commercial capital into cultural capital and then into political capital by having their sons educated to succeed in the examination system.[8]

The genealogies portray the shift from one regulatory system to another either as an innocent move by law-abiding subjects or a reluctant response to evildoers in positions of power. But when officials investigated they sometimes found a different reality. In 1542, a Guangdong official was updating the tax registers in Longchuan county. There were complications. A wealthy battalion soldier lived in the county. He owned vast lands that ordinarily should have borne a huge corvée burden. But he had registered the lands under the name of his wife and other women in his family. Since he himself was exempt and there were no other adult males associated with the property, he hoped thereby to avoid the corvée obligations. The magistrate tried to pretend that the world was not so complicated. "Military households should be under the jurisdiction of guard officials, and civilian households under civilian officials."[9] But the reality was different. Families straddled both categories.

Circulating between the two regulatory positions was a strategy aimed at evading the obligations of both. A fifteenth-century official noted that some families who had taken out "attached registration" consisted of a dozen members. But only one or two of them were actually registered with the magistrate. "The rest are concealed." When civilian officials came to secure corvée labor, the family members reported that they were serving in the ranks and were therefore exempt. When guard officials sought to register them for possible future conscription, they reported that they had taken out a civilian registration and were already fulfilling their civilian labor obligations. When conscription officials threatened to expose them, they bribed clerks to confuse the situation, hoping the conscription officials would give up and go back to their family's original native place to seek a replacement.[10] This could be a textbook case of regulatory arbitrage.

We return now to the story of Lin Chunzhai's arrival in Dapu. Recall that Lin came to the village in the company of his uncles, brothers Lin Fa and Lin Weinü, who explained that the stranger was actually the grandson of their late father Fosheng. They had found him and brought him home. This is already a touching story of a family reunion. The story gets even better. Some years prior to Chunzhai's return, in 1522, Fosheng's three surviving sons had divided the estate they inherited from their father. There are different versions of the document of family division in the different editions of the genealogy. The version seen by Liangjun, the nineteenth-century genealogist, mentions only three sons, whose names match those in the genealogy, Cong, Fa and Weinü. But in another version of the same document, a portion of the estate is set aside for their nephew, the son of their deceased fourth brother, "because he may return home when he comes of age." Perhaps there is nothing sinister here, or nothing more sinister than a change of heart. The three brothers may not have intended to cut their nephew out of his inheritance; they may not even have known that he was still alive. But when they learned that he was, they revised the will to give him his share. Thus the young man who appeared in the village was returning not only to the warm embrace of his family but also to his rightful inheritance.

The happy story was complicated by matters concerning household registration. As we have already seen, Lin Cong by this time was no longer registered as a military household. He had purchased a civilian registration. But it seems that Chunzhai was not considered to belong to the newly registered civilian household. As far as the authorities were concerned, he was still registered as belonging to a military household, liable to fulfill military service obligations. We know this because decades later Chunzhai's own grandson Yuanying (1564–1621) himself purchased a separate civilian registration in order to gain exemption from military obligations for himself and his heirs. Yuanying must not have been part of the household for which Cong had acquired a civilian registration, which means that neither was his ancestor Chunzhai, which means he must still have been registered under a military household.[11] But if Chunzhai still belonged to a household registered as having military obligations, what household was it?

The Lin of Dapu today are proud of their connection to Lin Xiyuan of Tong'an. Who would not want to celebrate a kinship connection with such a distinguished and wealthy scholar-official? They know they are related because at some point in the Ming someone from Dapu visited Lin Xiyuan's home and "recognized [their common] ancestry" (renzu), confirming on the basis of genealogical evidence that they were descended from a common ancestor. Modern editors have copied into their own genealogy an essay that Lin Xiyuan wrote about his family without realizing that it actually casts doubt on their own claims. Lin Xiyuan's essay tells of a member of his lineage, a serving soldier, who deserted his post and fled to Dapu. For the reasons we explored in chapter 2, this must have raised the concern of the rest of the household. Xiyuan's own father, worried that if the desertion was noticed officials might come to conscript a replacement from his own family, tracked the deserter down but failed to persuade him to return to his post. Decades later, while he was in Yongchun compiling the county gazetteer at the request of the magistrate, Xiyuan tried to locate the deserter again. But this time there was no trace of him. Subsequently, however, the deserter's descendants returned to their ancestral home of their own volition, in order to "recognize [their common] ancestry."[12]

Given the timing, and the details common to both stories, including the "recognition of common ancestry," the deserter in Lin Xiyuan's account can only have been the man the villagers called Chunzhai. So who was this mysterious stranger who arrived in Dapu? Was he just a deserter who somehow found a way to inveigle himself into a respectable family? Was he really the fourth son of Fosheng, whose widow had remarried into Lin Xiyuan's military registered family and taken the boy to be raised by them? Perhaps Lin Xiyuan and his father had simply misunderstood the man's return to Dapu as desertion, when in fact he was just returning home. An intriguing possibility is that our sources actually provide an incomplete account of one of the strategies discussed in chapter 1. Perhaps Xiyuan's family had adopted Chunzhai with the intention that the orphan would fulfill their military obligations—we have seen other families use just this strategy. In their view he had a responsibility to serve, so from their perspective his return to Dapu was tantamount to desertion. Or perhaps the Lin of Dapu had arranged for Chunzhai to take on responsibility for their registration and compensated him with a portion of Fosheng's estate (if Chunzhai really was who they said he was, then this would be a concentration strategy; if he was an outsider then it would be a substitution strategy).[13]

Unfortunately we lack the evidence to decide from among the conflicting narratives. The identity of our Ming Martin Guerre must remain a mystery. But whatever the truth of the matter, the mystery itself shows Ming subjects using multiple types of household registration strategically to minimize the costs of their involvement in state registration systems. They made choices between two overlapping regulatory regimes, choosing to situate themselves under the regime that they thought most advantageous to their interests. This was another form of regulatory arbitrage, Ming-style.

Military Colonies as Communities

In chapter 5, we saw how military colonists devised and deployed strategies to get and keep land while acknowledging, limiting, or shirking tax obligations. The first part of this chapter showed them developing strategies to manage their registration status. These economic and administrative strategies are only part of their history. When Lin Weizai and his family were first sent to Dapu, together with their commander Luo Guoyi and fellow soldier Ma De, besides finding ways to manage the state systems in which they were embedded, they also had to find ways to get along with one another and also with the people already living in the area. The guard system moved people far from their homes, forcing them to create new lives, to forge new communities. Soldiers and their families in the colonies, where they were settled not within the walls of a largely homogenous community of soldiers but into already existing communities, had to create relationships with these communities and come to terms with their new neighbors. The military colony system thus generated new social relations.

The existing residents would not have welcomed the new arrivals. They would have seen them as a threat to limited resources. Their special status with the local institutions of the state gave them unfair advantages; they seemed subject to different rules than ordinary civilians. A genealogy from Putian laments the arrival of colony soldiers in early Ming. "Because they had long been living in the wilds, they had gradually become savage. They plundered the people's property and destroyed the people's homes. The officials could not restrain them." Eventually the lineage raised a militia and took up arms against the soldiers.[14] In some places tensions between soldiers and local residents persisted for centuries. According to Qi Biaojia, writing in the late Ming, "in Zhao'an county, the soldiers are arrogant and the civilians crafty. The Shen surname and the soldiers of Nanzhao Battalion had a small grievance that grew into a grudge and then into a feud. They fought and then dispersed, dispersed and then fought. This lasted three months. Finally they met at Shanchuan to fight to the death. The knives and arrows mustered; there would never again be peace in their world."[15]

Two Shattered Inscriptions at Houshan

There is nothing whatsoever in the official archive that speaks to the relationships between the soldiers transferred to Hutou and their neighbors, and for that matter there is little in the genealogical record either. But we can learn something about their interaction from the story of the Houshan temple. To put this another way, in the next section I hope to tell the history of this minor village temple not as the expression of the eternal, timeless spirit of Chinese religion but as the product of six centuries of local politics, of the interaction of the different constituencies who worshipped at the temple over those centuries and whose descendants perform rituals there even today.

Recovering this history requires the use of a distinctive type of archive, one produced by observation of contemporary ritual. Like most village temples of the region, the most important ritual of the Houshan temple is the annual procession festival of the deities. Prior to 1949, processions for the deities worshipped in village temples on the southeast coast were typically held in the first month of the lunar new year. In Taiwan these festivals have been going on more or less without interruption. On the mainland, they began to be revived in the 1980s. The scope of these processions varies. Some gods tour only their own village; others visit communities with which their village has a special relationship; still others have multiday procession festivals in which they tour dozens or even hundreds of villages in the surrounding area. This periodic movement of a deity across the landscape is not simply a reflection of some preexisting social structure. The procession festival is performative—it can create, reinforce, or challenge social relations. The route of any procession festival is the outcome of a process by which the community of worshippers of the deity has been defined and redefined. In other words, a temple festival is a product of local history. The route of the procession materializes a political imaginary.

Using a ritual performed in the early twenty-first century as a source to describe a centuries-long history is of course a risky enterprise. Contemporary rituals can all too easily be framed as "remnants or survivals of traditional, archaic, or premodern modes," ignoring both the contemporaneity and the historicity of ritual practices.[16] If ritual can serve as a venue for political or material competition between different individuals and groups in the community, it can reflect current dynamics as much as historical ones. There are other reasons that should caution us against assuming historical continuity. When villagers in China today conduct a ritual, they consciously frame the performance in relation to state policy. The ritual must be conducted in such a way that they can claim it is either "religious" (that is, conforming to a state definition of religion) or "an expression of cultural heritage." If they don't frame it this way, or don't do so persuasively, they run the risk that it will be framed for them, as "feudal superstition" or worse.

But on the other hand, traditionalism, the desire to perpetuate tradition, means that the organizers of a festival try to replicate as much as possible the ritual as they remember it. Ritual participants take the efficacy of the ritual seriously. We need not concern ourselves with specifying that efficacy—whether it is to secure the protection of the gods, or to reinforce the social order, or to challenge it—to recognize that efficacy is important, indeed critical, to the participants. So the codes that determine whether a ritual has been performed correctly, such matters as the rules of selecting leadership or limiting participation, or of the spaces through which a procession must pass and must not pass, are matters of great seriousness. They are not taken lightly, or changed carelessly.

By combining contemporary performance with other kinds of sources, such as folklore and records of donations to temple reconstruction, we can sometimes recover a sense of how these rules have changed over time. A temple's rituals are not just like a text that can be read and interpreted but also like an archeological site that can be excavated. Each layer of sediment is the product of a particular historical moment, and each moment becomes the substratum for subsequent ritual organizations and behavior. To study local history in this way, to reconstruct as much as possible the ritual's codes at different historical moments, is to recover a history of successive presents.

The people of Hutou might not find my approach surprising. They know how important ritual is to their lives. A verse of local doggerel collected by anthropologist Wang Mingming suggests something of the cultural geography of the area. "In Changkeng, [in the western part of the county, the people] hunt tiger, snake, deer and buffalo. Hutou has flowers, gongs, banners, drums and cannon. Lower Anxi [on the coast] has eels, fish, turtles and sea grubs."[17] It is little wonder that Hutou was defined by its rich ritual pageantry, since ritual was one of the chief means by which its different communities structured their relations with one another.

Our first task is to determine as best we can who the players involved at each phase were. When military colonies were set up in Hutou in the fourteenth century, it was not on an empty landscape. Several families who live in Hutou today are descended from ancestors who were already living there in the early Ming. Most were registered as civilians. Some were registered as military households. In the early Ming, a member of each such household would have been conscripted and transferred to his assigned garrison. Thereafter, as we have seen, his direct descendants fulfilled the household's military service obligations. So under normal circumstances, the rest of the family back in Hutou would over time have become more or less indistinguishable from civilian families (in Chinese scholarship, these people are referred to as "military households living in the original native place" (*yuanji junhu*)). For the sake of simplicity I will describe them here as civilians, in contrast to the military colonists who were assigned to the area.

The Hu family, who we encountered at the beginning of chapter 4 as an example of a colony soldier family, was one such household. We know they were already living in Hutou in the early Ming because that is where they were registered and conscripted from.[18]

The Lin family was another. Like the Hu, one of their members was conscripted, sent to Nanjing, and later reassigned to be a colony soldier in Nan'an, supporting Yongning Guard. The serving soldier had settled there and the genealogy records no further contact between him and his heirs and the family back in Houshan.[19] By the mid-Ming, when their genealogy was first compiled, they had lost track of their early origins, and the genealogy contains contradictory accounts of their arrival in the area.[20] But the sources all agree that the Lin descended from an ancestor who served long ago as an official in Quanzhou. The official's son, known as Eighth Gentleman (*Balang*), was no refined scholar but a man of violence. In his mid-thirties, he was appointed to lead a militia against another powerful bandit gang. He pursued the bandits inland to the slopes of Houshan in Hutou, where he engaged them in battle and was killed. His kinfolk found his corpse and buried it at a place called Rulin, then settled nearby.[21]

The story of Eighth Gentleman in the Rulin Lin genealogy contains one other important detail. When he came to Hutou to meet his heroic fate, "he carried with him the incense fires of Master Zhang (*Zhang gong*)." What this means in concrete terms is that, like Pan Hai'an in chapter 4, he carried with him ashes from an incense burner from a temple or shrine dedicated to a deity called Master Zhang. In more abstract terms, it means that he worshipped Master Zhang as his protective spirit.[22]

In Houshan, Master Zhang became known as the Venerated King of Heroic Martiality. A temple to him was first built some time after the death of Lin Balang by local residents including Lin's own descendants. Master Zhang's wild iconography matches the local legends that are told about him. Before his apotheosis he was a person of low status; his face is black and his demeanour rough because he earned his living making charcoal. Little else is known about him; the important thing is that he cultivated the Way and became a god. The fact that he is known as the Venerated King shows that after he was brought to Hutou by Eighth Gentleman he took on the role of tutelary deity, the god responsible for the well-being of the community. It may be that this was the first time the community had such a deity, or it may be that an existing, previously anonymous deity was now recognized to be Master Zhang. One can imagine villagers making offerings to the god to beseech his protection for their families and their fields, calling on him to bestow good fortune and protect the locality from evil influences. There would have been a festival to the god, probably in the first month of the new year, involving offerings, feasting, and perhaps a procession and theatre. Because of his special role in bringing Master Zhang to Hutou, Lin Balang was also given his own shrine in the temple. It was called the "ancestral altar." His descendants thus enjoyed a special position in the temple's organization.[23]

By the mid-fourteenth century, then, at least two families and perhaps others were already well established in the area.[24] They had been there for generations. They had ancestral tombs, farms, and other property. They were watched over by a protective deity who was housed in the temple they had built for him and in which they enjoyed special privileges.

The social composition of Laisu district changed dramatically in the early Ming. Much of the district was taken over by the guards, converted to military colony lands, and assigned to colonists and their families.[25] Unlike in nearby Dapu, there are no surviving government records to tell us who these people were. But here fieldwork can help. Several lineages today maintain written records that show that their ancestors were colony soldiers. According to the genealogy of the Yan of Yangtou their founding ancestor arrived in the early Ming; his great-great-grandson was conscripted and sent to Guangdong. The ancestor must have been a military colony soldier and the descendant a supernumerary. The Hong of Shangshi tell the same story; they too were a colony soldier household.[26]

Other lineages transmit oral migration legends that suggest their ancestors too were colony soldiers. The Dong of Chanxian pass on a story, relayed to me by the village's party-secretary, that long ago their ancestors moved from Shishi to Jinmen and then to Hutou. Shishi is the modern name for the former Yongning Guard, Jinmen a battalion under the administration of Yongning Guard, and Hutou one of Yongning's military colonies. This is a narrative about a series of military transfers.[27]

Genealogies of some other lineages assert early Ming arrival in Laisu district but do not mention military service. The Zhushan Lin claim their founding ancestor moved to Laisu district in the reign of Zhu Yuanzhang, and this is well supported by other material in the genealogy such as a 1426 deed for the purchase of a site for his tomb. As for why the ancestor settled here, the genealogy reports only that he came from the interior county of Longyan to Anxi for his studies.[28] This could possibly be a retrospective claim to shed a less distinguished narrative of origin, quite possibly a story of military service. The Zheng, another family living on the slopes of Houshan hill, have a very spare genealogy last compiled in 1941. The first person about whom the genealogy has any detail is a member of the fourth generation to live in the area, a man born in 1476.[29] This is not strong evidence of anything, to be sure, but not inconsistent with settlement in the area in the late fourteenth century.

Table 6.1. Registration status of Houshan lineages

Colonists	Possible Colonists	Civilians
Hong—Shangshi village (now incorporated into Shangtian) Dong—Chanxian village Yan—Yangtou village (now incorporated into Qiaotou)	Zhushan Lin—Houshan village Zheng—Zhushan village	Hu—Houshan village Rulin Lin—Zhushan village

We can thus come up with a rough list of colony soldier families in Hutou. They include the Hong, Dong, and Yan who were definitely colony households, and the Zhushan Lin and Zheng who might have been (table 6.1). This is only a partial list, comprising only those soldiers who were assigned to allotments in the district who have descendants living in the area and who have maintained genealogies. Other families have no doubt died out or moved away. Having traversed the whole district multiple times, I think it is close to a complete list of all the colony soldiers with descendants still living in the area.

No surviving source describes explicitly how the previous residents and the new arrivals interacted. There are no lawsuits from Laisu in the legal archives or casebooks. But the story reveals itself in the history of the Houshan temple. In a deserted outbuilding of the temple lie two stone inscriptions, each cracked into several pieces. The first inscription, dated 1621, was composed by a man named Zhuang Jichang (1577–1629) (figure 6.6). A native of nearby Yongchun, he was a man of national reputation, having placed first in the metropolitan exam of 1619. The name by which he calls the temple in his essay, "Temple of Perfected Martiality (*zhenwu*)," suggests that something important about the temple had changed since the time when it was first constructed. The Rulin Lin family called the temple by a different name. To them it was the Temple of Heroic Martiality (*yingwu*), in honor of Master Zhang. The distinction between two types of martiality, one "heroic" and one "perfected," seems trivial in English, but in the world of Chinese popular religion the difference could hardly be greater. For Perfected Martiality signifies not a minor local god like Master Zhang, but one of the most awesome deities in the entire pantheon, the Northern Emperor, Supreme Emperor of the Dark Heavens, patron of successive Ming emperors.[30] Zhenwu, to use the god's title as his name, had been worshipped since antiquity as the spirit of the stars in the northern sky. Anthropomorphized and incorporated into the Daoist pantheon as a cultivator of self and a martial demon-fighter, under the Ming his cult soared to the heights of imperial patronage. Though Zhenwu had been worshipped in a few places in southern China before the Ming, imperial patronage now led to the rapid spread of the cult.[31] Zhenwu temples sprang up in garrisons across China, often patronized by senior officers. One such temple was built in Yongning Guard, the garrison from which the military colonists were dispatched to Hutou.

There are two other important differences between the story told by the Lin family and the one recounted by Zhuang in his inscription. According to Zhuang, the Houshan temple was first built not by Lin Balang's descendants, but by Lin Balang himself. According to Zhuang, the temple had always been a temple to Zhenwu. Zhuang's inscription was commissioned to commemorate a reconstruction of the temple. The key figure in this project was Zheng Xianying, whose biography appears in the Zheng genealogy, a family we have identified as probably having been a colony household. Born in 1571, he was a rich and respected man of fifty when the temple was rebuilt. Taking charge of this project was but one of his many local good works. The biography confirms his leadership role: "At that time people in the community discussed rebuilding the temple to Zhenwu. This would have been difficult for the people [to do on their own]. He happily took on the management of the task," and contributed personally for the expansion of the temple and purchase of ritual implements. In gratitude for his efforts, the biography continues, he too was given a special place in the temple after his death in 1633. Every year at the time of the annual festival, an image of Zheng was placed in the temple. In temple reconstruction projects today, everyone involved wants their contribution recognized. Leadership roles are often divided to ensure there is enough credit to go around. It was probably much the same in the late Ming. So though it was Zheng Xianying who led the actual temple reconstruction, the stone inscription to commemorate the reconstruction was commissioned and paid for by two other local men from the Shangshi Hong family, a family that we know were colony soldiers. Of the three known leaders of the project, then, two certainly and the third probably belonged to colony soldier lineages.[32]

We can make sense of the discrepancies between the two accounts, one in the Lin genealogy and the other on the 1621 inscription, by relating them to the interaction of two groups: the original local residents and the incoming colonists. Just as it did elsewhere, the arrival of the latter must have thrown Hutou society into turmoil. One of the ways in which the newcomers made their presence felt seems to have been by changing the

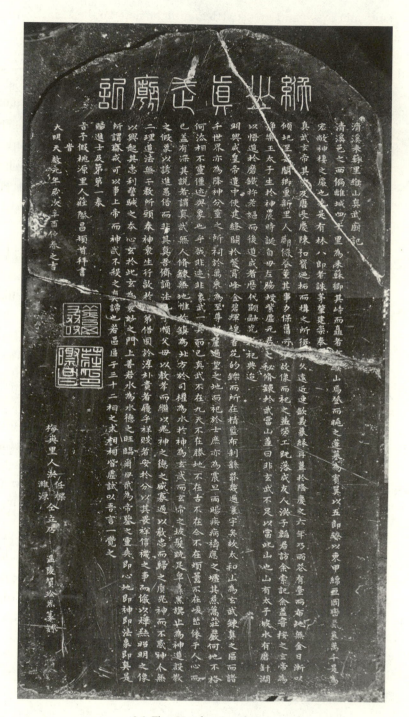

6.6. First Houshan inscription

6.7. Second Houshan inscription

character of the Houshan temple. They brought *their* god into the temple. We know this because by the time the temple was rebuilt by Zheng Xian-ying and the two Hong men, this new god was being worshipped beside Master Zhang. The temple had become a temple with two gods. The two gods were not equal; the new god's position in the pantheon was vastly higher than the old. He had no personal or prior connection to the community of Houshan; the stories and legends about him emphasize not local prosperity but martiality and ties to the imperial state. With his strong martial aspect, Zhenwu was the perfect vehicle for the soldiers of the Hutou military colony to assert themselves. The new god's symbolism was nothing more than an expression of the attributes of his patrons, the colony soldiers who had settled in the area.

Zhuang's inscription can thus be understood as part of an attempt to obfuscate the temple's origins. Its claim that the temple had always been dedicated to Zhenwu contradicts everything we know about the timing of the spread of Zhenwu worship in the region as well as the Lin family's own account. The inscription suggests that the temple had always housed two gods; the reality was that the second god, though he might have been the more powerful and the more widely recognized of the two, was an interloper, introduced only centuries after the temple was first built.

Local folklore supports this interpretation. As villagers today tell the story, long ago a statue of Zhenwu from some other place was being paraded around Hutou. When the procession arrived at the Houshan temple, the god so delighted in the virtues of the area that he refused to leave. His statue miraculously became so heavy that the men carrying his sedan chair could no longer lift it. But the local people did not want this outsider god to stay. After some negotiation, the Venerated King tried to play a trick on Zhenwu. He said that Zhenwu would be allowed to remain only if he could reverse the course of a nearby stream. The King had miscalculated; this was a simple matter for such a powerful deity. Zhenwu met the challenge. The King and the Lin family now had no choice but to allow Zhenwu to move into their temple, and they even yielded the place of honor to him.[33]

The traditions of the local Daoist masters also support this interpretation. The manuscript collection of one local Daoist contains a text called the *Various Talismans for the Rituals of Eliminating the Fetus and Gathering Clouds*. It includes the most extensive biography of the Venerated King. He was a man of humble origins, a charcoal-maker. He was killed in a fall into a gorge in the deep woods and subsequently became a deity. His incense burner flew to Houshan, so the local people built a temple for him. One day, an image of Zhenwu was brought to collect incense fire (just as he does at the Pumei temple at the start of the ritual today). The visiting god refused to leave. This made the local people angry. But the King, speaking through a medium, said that Zhenwu should be given a chance to indicate through divination whether he wanted to stay or return to his temple. The divination blocks were thrown; Zhenwu conveyed that he wished to stay. "So the main hall was yielded to the Great Emperor, and the King took the hall on the left."[34]

On this interpretation, the 1621 reconstruction was the concrete expression of the position of the immigrant military families in the power structure of the temple and the larger community. An image of Zheng Xianyang was now installed in the temple, just as Lin Balang's had been centuries earlier. According to the Lin genealogy, the shrine to Lin Balang was also refurbished by his descendants in 1621.[35] There was thus not one but two construction projects at the temple in 1621. A subtle sign of tension between the two groups is that the two projects occured adjacent and simultaneous to one another, and if the layout of the temple was then what it is now, they actually shared a wall. Both reconstructions produced a written record; neither even mentions the other.

To the Lin, their exclusion from the larger project must have made it seem as if leadership of the temple was now in the hands of the *arriviste* families whose ancestors had arrived in the early Ming as military colonists. The original deity of the temple, their Venerated King of Heroic Martiality, had been relegated to a subordinate position, and by extension so had his devotees. It was time for the original residents to respond. And this they did, by seeking an ally from the most powerful family in the whole area, the Li of Ganhua, on the other side of the river.

In the same abandoned shed in the temple complex where the Zhuang inscription lies is a second stone inscription, also broken into shards and lying on the ground. The text is in two parts (figure 6.7). The first part was composed in 1724 by Li Guangdi's nephew Zhongwang. Li Zhongwang's text commemorates yet another temple reconstruction, in the early eighteenth century. It describes a Houshan temple different yet again from its predecessors. Li calls the shrine "the Temple of Opening Up the Mountain" (*kaishan miao*). According to Li, the local villagers told him that the deity is "Lin Balang, who settled here. He was diligent in his life, and after he died people believed that he had attained the Way and therefore offered him sacrifice." The deity of the temple is "the Lord of the District. His responsibilities are to bestow prosperity, eliminate sickness, and control the winds and rain."

Some twenty years after the death of author Li Zhongwang, his sons were inspired by an extraordinary incident to revisit their father's text. In autumn 1748, the god himself "descended to communicate" (*jiangji*). What this means is that he possessed a medium and transmitted a message through spirit-writing, a common form of communication with the divine in China. In Hutou today, spirit-writing mediums draw characters on the ground or in a pan of sand using a forked stick (or sometimes a miniature sedan chair with a stylized brush pen suspended from it); a second specialist then interpets and transcribes the characters. In 1748, the god was moved to communicate in order to clarify some confusion on the part of Li Zhongwang. The god explained that Li Zhongwang had actually misunderstood his identity. He was not Lin Balang, as Li seemed to think, but Master Zhang, the Venerated King. He then gave yet another version of the early history of his temple. It had actually been built first in the Song, soon after his apotheosis, then destroyed in the turmoil in the late Song, then *rebuilt* by Lin Balang in the early Ming. Now the god had become even more numinous. "Tens of thousands know his power; it extends beyond the prefecture, even reaching to Taiwan and overseas."[36]

Through this series of revelations, the Venerated King of Heroic Martiality now reasserted himself as the god of the temple and bestower of good fortune to the community. This was a revival of a local tradition in the face of the power of the military colonists and their descendants. But it was too late for him to reclaim his primacy. It was one thing to clarify the origins of the temple, quite another to depose an important god like Zhenwu. So in the eighteenth century the temple remained a temple to two gods, each the representative of a different social constituency.

The configuration of deities in the temple has apparently not changed much since then. Master Zhang, the Venerated King of Heroic Martiality, sits in a shrine to the right-hand side of the temple. On the left is Lin Balang, restored to some measure of his earlier prominence. Today, as it has been since the early Ming, the central shrine is to Zhenwu, flanked by his various assistants. The centrality of the colony soldiers has been diminished by the elimination of their representative Zheng Xianyang from the temple, possibly as a consequence of the tensions during the later revelations.

Today the route of the temple's procession festival visits the villages that are home to the descendants of the two groups, performing communal solidarity in a community that had once been divided.[37] In other words, both the temple itself and the ritual as we see it today represent a kind of compromise in a centuries-long struggle between two deities, and between their two groups of constituents.

This compromise leaves other subtle traces in folklore and contemporary ritual. Popular understandings simultaneously maintain and blur the distinctiveness of the two deities. Recall the complaint of the wife of the Pumei temple-keeper that there was no need for the parade to have come so early. In her view, the timing of a visit by one god to another is dictated by the relative status of the two gods. An inferior god must show proper respect to a superior, for example by coming early in the day. As she puts it, the Houshan procession visit to Pumei is actually a visit of equals, one Emperor (Supreme Emperor of the Dark Heavens) visiting another (Emperor Guan). Two equals need not make such an effusive show of respect. So the visit could have been held at a more civilized time. But recall that Zhenwu, the Dark Emperor, did not actually visit the Pumei temple. The Houshan temple was represented by the King alone. For the temple-keeper's wife, Master Zhang is simply Emperor Zhenwu's emissary.

In Shanghu, the fourth stop on the procession, the gods of the village temple are brought out to meet with the visitors. Chief among them is an official with a red face. Ordinarily this iconography would indicate Guandi, but this god is different. He is Master Zhan, the first magistrate of Anxi county when the county was founded late in the tenth century. The local people tell a story that on some New Year's festival long ago, Magistrate Zhan was also touring the county when his cortege encountered that of the gods of Houshan temple. Observing the Venerated King's black face, indicating his lowly status as a charcoal burner, the Magistrate haughtily refused to yield the road. Little did he realize that the Emperor was right behind the King. Things soon started to go wrong for the magistrate as the gods took their revenge for the slight. In order to remedy his bad fortune, the magistrate promised that whenever the gods of the temple went out on procession, he would always present himself to pay his respects. Even after he died and became a god himself, his image would come out to show respect. In this story too we see signs that the two deities of Houshan are effectively fused into one in their relationships with the outside world.

Of course the ritual as I witnessed it in 2014 cannot be taken as a simple reflection of a tradition fixed in time since the Qing. It is rather a new chapter in the ongoing history of ritual transformation. The Houshan temple's ritual network expanded dramatically as recently as 2014, with the creation of the "outer" parade, about which I have so far said very little. This is a new innovation, and it generates much complaining. Even the visitor from outside gets a sense that all is not well. When the procession passes through Shangtian, the home village of the organizers, several groups of men sit by the side of the road playing cards and very deliberately ignore the proceedings to show their disdain. People complain that with the procession divided, the focus of the event has been dispersed. It is not as "hot and noisy" (*renao*) as it should be. The quality of the hired performers is poor; they don't show enough enthusiasm. Many complain that the innovation of two processions was not the genuine desire of the gods. They see it rather as an expression of the greed of the chief organizer—for he owns the local fireworks factory, and more processions means more fireworks. This contemporary social tension reminds us that village rituals are always shaped by local micropolitics. Even though ritual performers typically aspire to the reproduction of tradition, their rituals are always susceptible to change. Even something as fundamental as the scope of participation in a multivillage alliance changes. But the core villages of the "inner" procession are precisely those villages associated with the initial founding of the temple plus those communities that were settled by the military colony farmers in the early Ming. To this day, the festival creates and reinforces a ritual network that simultaneously affirms the unity of the area and the historically produced differences within it.

The Houshan temple is a small, out-of-the-way temple. Before 1949 there were millions like it in China. But it turns out to be possible to recover a history of the temple and its community. Each reconstruction of the temple involved more than simply repairing decayed walls and patching a leaky roof; it could involve a reconfiguration of the deities and deified humans worshipped in the temple. In his analysis of the cult the Three Immortals of Huagai, Robert Hymes identifies two different modes of interaction with the gods in late imperial China, a bureaucratic and a personal mode. People make choices about which mode they prefer to use in their interactions with the gods.[38] In Hutou, the gods themselves are the product of choices by local people. The sequence of reconstructions and renovations, of gods being entered into the temple and gods being removed from it, of ritual networks expanding and contracting, of events being added to and removed from the calendar, is actually an archive of local politics. Each of the changes is a reflection of changing configurations of power in the community, an expression of community micropolitics at that moment. The rituals by which the different gods are worshipped, the processions, offerings, and services by professional Daoists or Buddhist monks may superficially resemble one another. But which gods are worshipped is a product of local history. The tensions in this history, the contradictions between the different narratives, explain why in Hutou today the inscriptions lie broken on the ground, not restored to their full glory and proudly displayed.

Conclusions: Hutou and Dapu

In this chapter, I have told two stories about two places, one to show how military households strategized within the Ming state's registration system, the other to show how their assignment to the region generated new kinds of social relations. While the everyday politics of these stories were little affected by affairs of state, at times the history of the world beyond could have a direct impact. From Hutou, the village with the two inscriptions, to Dapu, home of the mysterious stranger Lin Chunzhai, is only a few miles as the crow flies. But they are worlds apart. The plains around Dapu are smaller than Hutou, the hills steeper, and there is no navigable waterway to the sea. So Dapu has always been poorer and more isolated than its neighbor. Another difference between the two places is more closely related to the themes of this book. In the civilian administrative system in Ming, the counties in which the colonies were located were both under the jurisdiction of Quanzhou prefecture. But in the military system their position was different, since they belonged to different guards. The colonies in Hutou supported Yongning Guard. The colonies in Dapu supported guards further up the coast, Xinghua and Fuzhou. These differences in geography and administrative hierarchy had profound consequences for the colony soldiers assigned to the two places, consequences that echo down through the centuries to the present.

One of the darkest moments in the collective memory of the descendants of the farming soldiers of Dapu is when their ancestors were called up to active duty in the mid-fifteenth century. They were assigned to garrison duty to replace the guard soldiers who were off fighting Deng Maoqi's rebels in northern Fujian—this was the episode of political turmoil, recall, that brought disaster on the Yan family in chapter 5. By this time families had been farming their assigned lands for generations, with little or no connection to the guard to which they were nominally assigned. Now officers from the guard descended on the colony and rounded them up. Colony officers were also ordered to be vigilant about ensuring the supply of grain from the colonies to the guard and thence to the front. This meant they had to find someone to replace the newly conscripted soldiers. The guard officers and their predecessors had been lax in their monitoring and record keeping and had lost track of the supernumeraries—the close relatives of the serving soldiers—who would have been the obvious choice. All sorts of people were pressed into service. They "were called supernumeraries, but how is it possible that they were all the sons and grandsons of dead soldiers?" The gazetteers even had a term for this problem: "false substitution of collateral kin (*fangzu er maoding zhi bi*)."[39] The colonies collapsed into chaos.

When the soldiers returned from active duty they learned the dire consequences. Local civilians had taken advantage of their absence to seize land and property. "Our lands were gone and our houses destroyed; everything had been seized by the local civilians. There remained only the foundations of one building. Facing up, we could not meet our tax obligations; facing down we had nothing to eat each day . . . The conflicts with civilians over land went on for years . . . It even came to the point that the colony soldiers had the burden of paying tax [without the income from the land that was taxed]."[40] Officials tried repeatedly to straighten up the situation but without success. Only a few of the families initially assigned to the colonies could even be located.[41]

Compared to Hutou, religious organizations in Dapu have played a much smaller role in the structuring of local society and in particular the relations between civilian households and soldier-farmers. There is no clearly articulated community of military households' descendants nor a visible structure linking these groups with prior residents. In Dapu, the integration of the soldiers assigned to the colonies in early Ming into local society was a matter of their gradual integration into the civilian structure, in particular the civilian tax and corvée structure. The more challenging local ecology and the disruption of the mid-fifteenth century meant that most soldier-farmer households disappeared through desertion or extinction. There was no critical mass of military households able to constitute themselves as a community and take over local institutions in the same way as those in Hutou took over the Houshan temple. Lineages that evolved from military households had to find ways to come to terms with the communities in which they found themselves, but how they did so was highly contingent on local conditions.

The policies of the central government transplanted colony soldiers into new environments; demographic increase forced them to come up with answers to the challenges of interacting with the people who already lived there. Chapter 5 explored some of their material strategies, ways of taking advantage of regulatory overlap to secure benefits in the local land market. Military households also had to resolve the larger question of how they would integrate into the existing communities around them. This chapter has explored two dimensions of that issue, seemingly quite different but actually both closely tied to the need to transcend the limits of the community's foundation. Some military households, notably but not only the upwardly mobile, used a textbook form of regulatory arbitrage to circulate between two systems of registration that, nominally, should have been mutually exclusive. They registered as civilians to evade the pressure of local military officers, to rule out the risk of conscription, to protect their wealth and facilitate their sons' participation in the examinations. Where their numbers were sufficient, farm soldiers asserted leadership over existing social organizations like temples, taking them over and transforming them in the process.

Colony soldiers thus used a variety of approaches and methods, sometimes infiltrating and taking over existing community organizations and thereby developing and maintaining a separate communal identity within the larger society, sometimes integrating as individuals and families with that society and blending into it. Local conditions and local histories shaped their choice of strategy. In one place, they made a deal with local clerks to alter the register archive; in another, they built a temple with two gods.

PART IV

After the Ming

CHAPTER SEVEN

A God Becomes an Ancestor

POST-MING LEGACIES OF
THE MILITARY SYSTEM

TODAY MOST OF THE RESIDENTS of the former battalion of Tongshan no longer live in traditional courtyard-style homes but in modern brick-and-tile houses. But they still leave the main doors of homes open during the day, and domestic life still spills out over the threshold. In the narrow lanes women prepare food and wash clothes; the old folk sit on stools chatting and minding the grandchildren. Ritual life too still defies any strict boundary between public and private. In most homes the domestic altar, located in the front room facing the street, is in full view to passersby through the open doorway. Within the walls of the old battalion, the place of honor at the center of the altar is given not to tablets to the ancestors, as is the norm elsewhere in this region, but to a large image of Guandi, Emperor Guan. No one finds it strange for Guandi to be in this spot, because as an old temple-keeper told me, the people of the town "worship Emperor Guan as our ancestor." This way of looking at things is actually a legacy of the Ming military household system.

Today Emperor Guan's temple is the liveliest in the town. It is filled at all hours with worshippers making prostrations and burning incense. Emperor Guan's procession festival is the highlight of the local ritual calendar. In contrast, the temple of the God of the Wall next door has few visitors and no one pays him much mind; he never leaves his temple to tour the town. Townsfolk today recognize this is unusual; they know that in towns only a few miles away people proudly carry their God of the Wall in procession, just as villagers do in Pinghai, Fuquan, and other former garrison communities. They explain that because the God of the Wall is associated with dangerous *yin* forces, it is safer to keep him at a distance.[1] But the god's *yin* energies do not seem to bother the people of nearby towns, nor of the countless towns and cities across China where the annual procession of the God of the Wall is an important ritual event. Guandi's striking preeminence in Tongshan does not actually have much to do with the inhabitants' cosmological ideas or, for that matter, their genealogical origins. It has everything to do with history, and the legacies of the Ming military system after its dissolution in the early Qing.

Institutional legacies constrain the choices open to every state. Even a state established through conquest is subject to legacies of the institutions of its defeated predecessor. Even if the conquering state dissolves or replaces the formal institutions of its predecessor, institutional legacies may still shape the choices of people living in new states. Detached from their original institutional context, residual elements from defunct institutions can take on new life as elements of everyday politics under the new situation.

The end of the Ming meant—eventually—the end of the Ming military system. Some parts of the institution were eliminated; others were incorporated into the civilian administrative system. This was a gradual and piecemeal process that took almost a century from the fall of the Ming in 1644. But the institution still left many legacies, both in the interim period and beyond. Some, such as the persistence of distinctive tax levies, were top-down legacies created by officials dealing with the challenges of the transition. Others were produced from the bottom up. People within the system, and their descendants, sought to retain prerogatives granted them in the past by the now-defunct institution. Or they tried to rework elements of the institution in order to deal with new situations. Where they were successful, these legacies became political resources to be redeployed in different contexts. Thus the institution continued to produce new social relations even after it had formally ceased to exist. We can call such efforts to deploy old institutional arrangements in new institutional contexts strategies of precedent.

The Ming was the nearest and the natural model for the conquering Manchus as their nascent Qing state grappled with the challenges of governing a more complex society. Qing legitimacy rested in part on claims to have received the Mandate of Heaven to restore order to the realm, and reviving moribund institutions was one way of demonstrating this. So for both practical and ideological reasons, the Manchus adopted many elements of the Ming state. Indeed the Manchu precursors to the Qing had begun to adopt Ming institutions well before the dynasty was formally established in 1644. The process only accelerated thereafter.

The similarity in organizational structure between the two dynasties used to be a key element in the conventional wisdom that the Qing was a completely "sinicized" regime. More recently, scholars of the so-called New Qing History school have stressed the Qing and the Manchus' enduring distinctiveness. Not even the most ardent New Qing History proponents would suggest that everything about the Qing was new. Institutionally the Ming-Qing transition was as continuous as it was discontinuous. But the military was different. The Manchu army of conquest was organized on principles fundamentally different from the army it defeated. At the core of the Qing army were the Banners, a hereditary force established earlier in the seventeenth century. After the conquest, the Qing created a second military branch, the Green Standard Army, out of surrendered Ming soldiers. Some Green Standard soldiers belonged to military households; others were drawn from the ranks of professional soldiers, that is, mercenaries, who by the late Ming made up much of the army. But the Green Standard was not hereditary. This basic two-branch structure remained in place for most of the Qing dynasty. Early Qing rulers do not appear to have ever seriously considered retaining the Ming system of hereditary military households and guards or integrating it as a third branch.[2] Because they never seriously discussed the topic, we don't know if this was because they saw the Ming system as flawed or because the challenges of integration seemed insurmountable. Whatever their reasons, the Ming system had to be eliminated. Suddenly in some places and gradually in others, the guards and battalions were dissolved. So too was the hereditary status registration system; "military registration" officially disappeared.[3]

This did not mean that former guards simply disappeared or became indistinguishable from other communities, or that former military households simply dissolved into the undifferentiated body of ordinary commoners. This chapter is about the persistence of institutional differences from the Ming military into the Qing and beyond. Here as throughout this work my focus is not on the legacies for military matters narrowly defined—for recruitment, logistics, and fighting—but rather on the legacies for ordinary people. The descendants of the families we met in previous chapters inhabited an institution that formally no longer existed. But it persisted in unexpected ways after its formal dissolution because people continued to find it useful in their everyday lives. Understanding these legacies can help us better understand not only the longer history of the Ming institution, but also the Qing. For Qing rule consisted not only of the institutions it inherited from previous Chinese tradition nor only of distinctive Manchu institutions, but also the legacies of institutions which, while formally eliminated, lived on in the everyday politics of Qing subjects.

A Difficult Interregnum

Before the people of the southeast coast could give any thought to institutional arrangements, they had first to survive the massive disruptions of the late seventeenth century. After decades of peace and prosperity following the "pacification" of the pirates, the southeast coastal region was thrown anew into turmoil by the dynastic transition. It took forty years from the time the first Qing emperor took the throne in Beijing in 1644 before peace was restored.

For much of this period the main threat to Qing control was Zheng Chenggong, also known as Koxinga, the scion of a merchant family whose operations once stretched from Japan to Southeast Asia. In the 1650s, in the name of restoring the Ming, his forces seized control of much of the coast, including former battalions like Jinmen and Tongshan. Tongshan was occupied by Zheng's armies for more than a decade.

Having overreached himself in an ill-conceived 1659 campaign to restore the Ming, Zheng retreated to Taiwan where, until their defeat in 1683, he and his successors maintained what was, despite claims of loyalty to the Ming, effectively an independent regime. Several lineages in Taiwan today claim that their founding ancestor was a resident of a coastal battalion who followed Zheng's forces to Taiwan.[4]

To cut off logistical support for the Zheng regime, the Qing ordered the entire coastal region forcibly evacuated to a distance of several miles from the sea. Most of the communities we have discussed in previous chapters lay in the evacuation zone. In Tongshan, Qing troops "toppled the walls and burned the dwellings. The residents all fled. It was miserable beyond words. The ancestral shrine was burned to the ground; the houses turned to wasteland, and the tombs became cold and desolate."[5] We know little about what became of the evacuees and how they found refuge in the interior. Even if some may have stayed behind, as some historians have argued, they must have led a furtive existence evading Qing patrols.[6]

The evacuation order was only repealed when Zheng's forces were defeated. Former residents of coastal battalions now straggled home to find scenes of devastation. In Fuquan, "the land was emptied and all the structures burned." The residents "gradually returned, but what could be recovered was not one ten-thousandth part of what had been destroyed."[7] The ancestral tombs of the Chen family of Tongshan were "overgrown with weeds, and had been completely dug up by other people."[8] Townsfolk today tell the story that their town had become so infested with deadly snakes that they had to hire a Daoist Master to drive the monsters away.

Two Qing Families Fight over Their Ming Taxes

Forced evacuation and the destruction of homes and property were of course far more immediate and dire threats to the residents of the guard than administrative reorganization. But reforms to local government and the elimination of the guards too would ultimately also have profound effects on their society. In Fujian, the disappearance of the guards was a two-stage process. First the actual guards were disbanded, while the military colonies remained. Then in the early eighteenth century the colonies were also dissolved, rolled into the civilian administrative system. Institutionally the guards and battalions were no more.

Many Qing and Republican gazetteers from Fujian summarize the state of taxation in the early Qing in a few words: "followed the Ming."[9] These deceptively simple accounts do convey a basic truth: the new Qing rulers did not overhaul the tax system nor, despite the turmoil of the transition, conduct a comprehensive census or a land registration. Even after the threat from Koxinga was neutralized, an enumeration of key tax data was not thought crucial. To us this seems strange. Modern states view comprehensive, accurate statistical information about populations as a prerequisite for effective governance. Officials in premodern Chinese states had no such illusions. Early Qing officials for the most part thought that they had inherited sufficient information to do their job. The surviving Ming records assigned tax obligations to the registered households in each jurisdiction. If these obligations were met, then the necessary revenue would be delivered. If revenue proved insufficient to meet expenses, then the existing records provided the framework to levy surtaxes.

So the descendants of military households in the former colonies typically remained liable for the tax obligations of their ancestors, which were now folded into the tax quotas of the civilian county where the colony was located. The Hu of Anxi were still paying a "surplus tax" well into the Qing. (Recall that the term "surplus tax" was a legacy of the early Ming system. Soldiers initially paid a "basic tax" that was returned to them as rations and a "surplus tax" that supplied the guard; the basic tax was later eliminated.) In chapter 5, we traced their story up to 1584, the year that they registered an allotment with the colony authorities. This allotment was in the name of Wang Bingzai, because the Hu belonged to a composite military household, sharing their military registration with the Wang and another family. The allotment was physically located in Nan'an county, but the Hu had long since returned to their ancestral home in Hutou and the land was obviously being rented out to tenants. The farmer-soldiers were no longer farmers but landlords (or at least, they were not farming the colony lands; I don't know how they made a living back in Hutou). They collected rent on the allotment from the tenants and passed on a portion of it to the guard to meet their "surplus tax" obligations. The three families took it in turns to manage the allotment, collect the rent, and submit the tax. In the early Qing, after the military colony system was eliminated, they paid the tax to the county magistrate in Nan'an. Then in the early eighteenth century, the nearby counties of Anxi and Hui'an had a shortfall in revenue, but Nan'an county was flush. To smooth out the imbalance, some revenue from Nan'an was transferred to the other two counties. Like their predecessors, the Qing authorities did not think of tax revenues as being pooled in a central fund, a percentage of which could be transferred. Rather, a tax on a specific plot of land that had formerly gone to one county was now to be sent to another. The tax on Wang Bingzai's allotment was included in the transfer. The allotment was a plot of land that had originally belonged to the military colony of Fuquan Battalion under Yongning Guard. But now neither battalion nor guard even existed as administrative entities. Nor did their military colonies. What survived was a tax obligation. More precisely, a record in the county archives identified certain lands, the tax due from them, and the household that was liable for payment of that tax. With the change in dynasty, the authority to collect that tax had been transferred from the military system to the civilian system. Now it was transferred from one civilian jurisdiction to another. This was a very concrete way that the institution continued to matter to the people who were descended from the military households that had once belonged to it. They now took their tax grain, or more likely its equivalent in silver, to the new jurisdiction. This actually made their lives easier—the new jurisdiction happened to be the very one where they lived.

The three families collected the rent on the land and paid the tax without incident for several decades. Then in the mid-eighteenth century a problem arose. The tax went unpaid. The Wang sued the Hu, claiming they were responsible for the arrears. As is so often the case, we only have one side of the story—the Hu's. As they tell it, the real problem was that the tenants refused to pay their rent, so there was no income with which to meet the taxes. Why did the Wang family sue the Hu family, rather than the tenants who had not paid their rent? The only explanation that makes sense is that the Wang lawsuit referred back to the old agreement between the three families that they would take responsibility for the land in rotation. The Wang must have claimed that since the tax had gone unpaid during the Hu's term in the rotation, the tax shortfall was the Hu's problem, not theirs. The case dragged on for years. Eventually the Hu produced the 1584 register and pointed out that although they might have helped to pay the tax obligation in the past, their name did not actually appear on the register (this of course helps us understand why they had decided to copy the register into their genealogy).

The case hinged on whether the original agreement to rotate tax responsibility was still in force. The Wang argued that it was. As they saw it, the former allotment was still a special sort of property, subject to rules that persisted from the previous tax regime. The tax obligation continued to be shared between the multiple families who comprised the original military registration. The unpaid tax was the Hu's problem because it was their turn in the rotation. The Hu family argued that the 1584 register should now, two hundred years and a change of dynasty later, be considered simply the equivalent of an ordinary land deed. The Wang owned this land; paying the tax was their problem. This was a dispute over which regulatory regime applied to the land. Both families were trying to situate the land under the regulatory regime that was most favorable to them. In the Hu's ideal world, the agreement would be in force when it was their turn to collect the income from the land, but not when it came time to pay taxes. They were working the system by taking advantage of the difference between two overlapping systems.

The judge was persuaded. He found for the Hu and ordered the Wang family to pay the outstanding taxes. But there was more to the story. For the judge saw what was going on. He ordered that once the back taxes were paid, the land was to be sold. He wanted to be sure that the problem would not recur to trouble him or his successor. The complexity of claims to the land created loopholes, and he wanted to close them. A specific tax obligation was associated with this land; because of ambiguity in regulatory regimes there were different possible interpretations of who was liable for it. Both the Wang and Hu hoped to use certain elements of the Ming regulatory system to support their interests. Once the land was sold, the purchasers could no longer play such games. They would have no connection at all with the military registration system of the previous dynasty. Having purchased the land, they would become liable to pay the tax. The obligation on the land was still a distinctive kind of tax called the "surplus tax," and many aspects of it were a legacy of the defunct Ming colony system. By removing the ambiguity over how the tax obligation was to be decided, the judge hoped to resolve the troubling headache of who was responsible for this tax. His judgement was designed to close off the possibility of regulatory arbitrage in the future.[10]

The Tian Family Turn an Old Estate to New Purposes

With hereditary military registration eliminated, the various institutions that had developed around it should in theory have become obsolete. Or so it might seem. But these institutions structured rights and access to material resources, especially property. Just like the Hu's tax obligations, these resources did not disappear just because a Manchu emperor sat on the throne in Beijing. They still needed to be managed. This created another kind of legacy.

The Tian family of Xiaoshan, near Hangzhou to the north of our main focus, resembles many of the military households discussed in chapter 1. After their conscription in the early Ming, they set up a system of rotation through the branches of the lineage to resolve the issue of who should be the serving soldier. To encourage the serving soldier to fulfill his obligation, they endowed a corporate estate to pay him a stipend. In the late sixteenth century, an internal dispute led to a lawsuit that ended with the magistrate confirming the right of the current serving soldier to receive the income from the estate. The collapse of the Ming dynasty, the dissolution of the guards, and the elimination of military registration did not change this. In 1677 the former serving soldier returned to the ancestral home, demanding the income from the estate. Nobody questioned his right to do so. He and the "whole lineage" drew up an agreement confirming this right. Obviously the income from the estate was now entirely separated from its original function; it no longer had anything to do with military service.

The parties to the contract agreed for the sake of convenience that the serving soldier—who was now a soldier in name only—did not have to come personally to receive the funds but could send a delegate. To this end, they made a special tally. The soldier could give the tally to his delegate, and this would confirm that he should receive the funds. This arrangement was obviously supposed to make things more convenient for the soldier. It turned out to have the opposite effect. Somehow he managed to lose the tally. (There was probably foul play, for another member of the lineage miraculously "found" it.) When the soldier next returned in 1681, he could not produce the tally, so his kin turned him away empty-handed. Since they themselves had the missing tally, they knew they did not have to worry about him coming back a second time. This gave them the luxury of deciding what to do with the income stream. If they divided it up and gave each member of the lineage a share, it would dwindle into insignificance. So they decided to maintain it as a kind of corporate estate but to transform its function. It became part of the sacrificial estate of an early ancestor of the lineage. The property set aside in the Ming to support a soldier thus now became part of the material basis of the lineage, ensuring the continuity of its rituals and promoting solidarity among its members.[11]

Such stories of the conversion of military estates, which were common in early Qing, reveal an entirely unexpected consequence of the military registration system, which was to encourage lineage cohesion. I have argued previously, building on the work of Zheng Zhenman, that military households were on balance more likely than commoner households to develop into organized corporate lineages. My argument was that military registration made groups of patrilineally related kin more likely to organize to address their shared obligation, and the lineage provided a suitable organizational vehicle.[12] I still think this argument is correct, but can now offer an additional reason. Military registered households were early adopters of the system of corporate estates as a way of addressing their shared obligations. When these estates were no longer needed to fulfill their original purpose, they could provide a ready-made material foundation for the ideological vision of neo-Confucian elites, a convenient vehicle by which they could implement their ideas about the power of kinship to transform social order. But this did not happen everywhere in China, so we must recognize that surplus property and neo-Confucian elites were not sufficient conditions for the emergence of lineages.

The "Soldiers" of Dacheng Battalion Invoke Precedent and Appeal for Tax Relief

In the temple to the God of the Wall of the town of Dachengsuo in northern Guangdong stands a stone inscription dated 1730. Erected by the "gentry, elders, soldiers and civilians" of the town, it is a permanent and public record of a decision by the local magistrate. The background to the inscription was a petition for tax relief. The residents of the town had long complained to the magistrate that greedy tax collectors were demanding payment of surtaxes to cover "corvée labor obligations." They asked to be exempt from these levies on the grounds of a long-standing precedent. "The territory of the battalion is all registered as belonging to military households." They had repeatedly petitioned the magistrate to "eradicate accumulated injustices and manifest benevolence impartially." Now he had finally agreed to their requests. "Let all the soldiers and civilians in Dachengsuo know: From this day forward, whenever miscellaneous exactions [of corvée labor] are levied to support public needs, in accordance with past [precedent] they are exempt."[13]

Dachengsuo refers here of course to the former Dacheng Battalion. By 1730 the battalion was long dissolved; the residents were using Dachengsuo as the name for the town that stood on the site of the former military base. The transition from Ming to Qing had not eliminated the area's strategic significance; the Qing had set up a Green Standard garrison nearby. But the term "soldiers" (*jun*) in the inscription does not refer to Green Standard soldiers of the Qing. The "soldiers" here are the descendants of the military households that had been stationed in the battalion since the early Ming.

The precedent to which they were appealing was more complicated than they let on. The townsfolk were arguing that prerogatives that their ancestors had enjoyed under the Ming tax code should still apply now, under the new dynasty. As we have seen, military households in the Ming were granted exemptions from corvée for the obvious reason that they provided labor to the state in the form of their military service. It made no sense for them to also provide civilian corvée service. This would mean they were being taxed twice, something the Ming state forbid not out of an abstract commitment to fairness but because such a heavy burden might lead to desertion. In the early Ming, exemption from civilian corvée labor service meant exactly that. But by the early eighteenth century, almost nobody in China was actually providing corvée labor anymore. The so-called Single Whip Reforms of the mid-Ming commuted most taxation in kind and corvée labor to payments of cash. So in the Qing "corvée labor" was a euphemism for surtaxes. When the authors of the inscription asked for an exemption from labor service they were really asking for an exemption from certain surcharges. But by the time this inscription was composed, the residents did not provide military service either. The battalion had been dissolved and the very category of military household no longer existed. The people who went to the magistrate for relief were essentially saying that they were entitled to the same prerogatives as their ancestors, while neglecting to mention that they no longer provided the very services for which their ancestors had been given these prerogatives.

There is yet another wrinkle to the story of this stone. The area around Dacheng was a salt-producing region. Over the course of the Ming, some hereditary saltern families had grown extremely wealthy, converted their wealth into education, and become members of the literati elite. They had moved into the town and become influential in its social life. Their names and the names of their descendants also appear on this stone and other inscriptions around Dachengsuo, commemorating their local leadership before and after the dynastic transition.[14] Thus many of the people calling for tax relief were thus not actually descended from military households at all. They were claiming exemption from taxes on the basis of prerogatives that soldiers in the battalion had once enjoyed, on the grounds that they resided in the physical location where those soldiers had once lived.

On the face it, it would seem like the magistrate should have sent them packing. Why didn't he? There are two likely possibilities. The first is that the magistrate had decided to rely on surviving records from the Ming in assigning taxes to the locality. These records would have specified how much tax was to be collected and under what accounts. If he were to ignore these records, he would need new registers to replace them. Collecting this data surpassed his administrative capacity. All he would accomplish with such an effort would be opposition from local elites and a grand opportunity for corruption and extortion by his clerks. It was easier just to rely on the information he had. But this meant that he had to allow precedents inherited from the prior dynasty to stand, even though the rationale for those precedents was gone. The other possibility is that the labor service obligations had been added as a surcharge to regular land taxes, which the people of Dachengsuo were already paying. So they were already paying their fair share, and what they were objecting to was demands that they pay even more.

Everyone involved in this story was engaging in regulatory arbitrage. The military households were asking to be treated as they had been under the Ming system. The wealthy saltern households who had moved into the town were asking to be treated as if they were military households. Even the magistrate was choosing to apply an outdated regulatory regime (or perhaps simply accepting the logic of that regulatory regime to justify his decisions) because he saw no alternative. Such claims to prerogatives from defunct institutions were another legacy of the Ming system. They are a form of regulatory arbitrage made possible because of the unspoken coexistence of two regulatory systems, the Qing system that was recorded in the compilations of laws and institutions published in the capital, and the Ming system that lingered in everyday political interactions.

Recycling Institutions:
How Guandi Became an Ancestor

Qing subjects, like their rulers, reworked the principles, practices, and records of the defunct Ming system to deal with new concerns in the new
context. The story of Emperor Guan in Tongshan, both god and ancestor,
is the result of one such attempt.

As we saw in chapter 3, there had been a temple to Lord Guan at Tongshan ever since the battalion was first established. By the late Ming, the
spirit had been given the title by which he is now best known: Guandi,
Emperor Guan. Over the course of the Ming the population of the settlement, initially made up largely of soldiers and their families, had become
much more diverse. Soldiers deserted or disappeared. Outsiders moved in
to take advantage of opportunities, including opportunities for overseas
trade. Tongshan grew into a prosperous coastal community. The surviving preface to a Ming edition of the town gazeteer, now lost, records that
"within the walls, soldiers and civilians live interspersed."[15] These broader
changes were reflected in the religious life of the community. As happened
in countless towns around China, the temple to Lord Guan, first built
around 1388 by battalion officers, became a cult site for a broader community. Ordinary residents of the town and the surrounding area offered
devotion and financial contribution to what had initially been a cult in the
official register of state sacrifices.

Then came the disasters of the Ming-Qing transition. After several
difficult decades, residents were allowed to return in 1675. Soon thereafter the battalion was formally abolished and the town became part of
the surrounding Zhangpu county. Reconstruction was surprisingly swift—
perhaps the destruction was not so severe as the sources claim. The Nanyu
Chen, a lineage that had grown out of a military household stationed in
Tongshan for more than two hundred years, was able to rebuild their ancestral hall within a decade of the evacuation order being rescinded.

While the returnees set about reconstructing local social order in the
early Qing, local officials set about rebuilding the local fiscal order. This
complex story has recently been explained by Liu Yonghua and Zheng
Rong.[16] To make full sense of it requires delving a little deeper into the operation of the tax system in the Ming. The Dacheng inscription asserts the exemption of military households from corvée labor duties, which by the Qing
really meant exemption from surtaxes allocated on the basis of these duties. As we saw in chapter 2, labor service in Ming was coordinated through
the *lijia* system. The wealthiest and largest households in the locality were

called "hundred" and "tithing" heads and given responsibility for assessing and collecting tax and labor from the households under their charge. In principle, the assignment of households to headships was supposed to be revised every ten years. In practice, households assigned to each status in the beginning of the Ming retained that status for the whole dynasty. Moreover, we have also seen that what the term "household" (*hu*) referred to also changed over time. In the early Ming, the household was both social and fiscal unit. As the number of people descended from the original household rose through natural increase, an ever-larger group of people, living in multiple social households, would belong to the same fiscal household. Indeed, a single registration might cover an entire lineage descended from the man who had originally been registered. A "household" in the registration system would eventually become primarily a unit of account for the assessment of corvée. But over time the fiscal distinctions blended with the social in a new way; headman households were often the elite of the community.[17]

Despite the many changes in the fiscal system, the basic function of the *lijia* system, to coordinate payment of tax for the locality, remained in place to the end of the dynasty. And beyond. Early Qing officials kept the system in place. The fiscal-cum-social distinctions remained as well. According to an early Qing report from Zhangzhou:

> The hundred-head households all have many members and much property, so they always bully the weaker households. Even the elderly and the children refer to themselves as hundred-head. They treat the tithing households like children, as if they were people under their control. When they encounter the children of a hundred-head household, even the elderly and white-haired members of the tithing households must use [respectful] terms of address [appropriate] to a man of a more senior generation (*shuhang*) When members of the tithing households die leaving behind sons and daughters, the hundred-head household can decide who they should marry, or even sell them off.[18]

It was chafing against these social distinctions that led officials in Fujian to overhaul the tax system, prompted by complaints by a local gentryman. Though Zheng Zhihui (*juren* 1657) was a learned scholar, successful in the examinations, and holder of a minor official post, he belonged to a household that at some forgotten time in the Ming past had been registered as a low-level household within the *lijia* system. In 1687, he wrote to the magistrate to complain about bullying by the hundred-head household to which his own household had been assigned. He asked that the county recompile its registers so that his family could receive the fiscal status—and therefore the social status—that was their due. His proposal made its way slowly up the administrative hierarchy, eventually reaching the governor, who approved it. The governor's approval meant that registers across the province had to be recompiled, provoking all sorts of opposition, and perhaps explaining why the governor was soon transferred to another post. But his former subordinates continued the work he had started.

One of these subordinates was Chen Ruxian (1656–1714) who became magistrate of Zhangpu county, in which Tongshan was located, in 1696.[19] To deal with the problem of abuse by headmen households, he hoped to go beyond the initial suggestion and simply abolish the position. His objective was to do away with the whole intermediary structure of the *lijia* system, allocating tax responsibilities directly to individual registered households. This would require a clear understanding of the actual situation of these households, and Chen ordered a new census and land survey. But this turned out to be beyond the administrative capacity of his staff, and no doubt provoked the opposition of local vested interests. So he retreated from his initial position and stuck with the existing list of registered households. Now each registered household, rather than negotiating its obligations with the headmen who had once stood between them and the county yamen, would be assigned a levy proportional to the overall tax obligation of their district and would pay this levy directly to the tax collector. Chen recognized that the "households" were both units of tax accounting and social organizations. He realized that many of the households on his register had grown since the early Ming into much larger groups of descendants sharing kinship ties with one another. In other words, they had developed into what we could call a lineage. This mattered a lot to the household's existence as a social organization, but not so much to its role as a taxpaying unit. So long as the household-cum-lineage organized its internal affairs sensibly, their tax obligation would be paid and all would be well.

This solution appealed to Chen because it appeared to settle the question of how to deal with future changes as well. Periodic adjustments of the registration had been tried and failed; Chen did not want to repeat the mistake. So long as all the descendants of a registered household continued to pay their collective obligation, it did not actually matter what happened to them as a social organization. Of course Chen did not manage to avoid antagonizing all vested interests. The old hundred-head households were the most adversely affected by the reforms, and a group of them rioted in protest. But Chen prevailed, and the reforms held.[20]

Because the reform made descent from a registered household the criteria for assigning tax responsibility, the fiscal reform was known as "allocating [responsibilities of registered] tax-paying households to the patriline" (*lianghu guizong*)—the term is much less ungainly in Chinese. As Liu Yonghua and Zheng Rong have shown, the reform linked genealogical connection and lineage organization to lawful tax-paying status and had the unintended effect of strengthening the role of lineage in local society.

But the reform created a new kind of problem. Not everyone belonged to a registered household. Those who did not had no place in the system. They could not participate in the civil service examinations because they would be unable to register. They were vulnerable to being taken advantage of by their neighbors who were registered. People in this situation sought out solutions. Some "looked for a household of the same surname with which they could combine," working out arrangements for sharing in the tax burden in exchange for the benefits of being registered.[21]

Among the people excluded from the new system were the former military households of Tongshan. Like their fellows in Dacheng, soldiers in the battalion and in the colonies who had not previously acquired civilian registrations had never been registered in the civilian system, but only in the military registers. In the Ming this distinction had made sense. Now their status had become problematic. In Jinjiang county to the north, an innovative magistrate allowed previously excluded categories to register for new households, which he categorized according to the circumstances that led to their being registered. One such special category was the "military tithings" (*junjia*), former military households who now registered as civilian taxpayers.[22]

Some went to the magistrate and purchased a registration, just as people had sometimes done in the Ming. In Yongchun, the Tang family decided they had to regularize their status in response to the additional taxes levied on the old military colonies. In 1691, members of the family purchased a civilian registration and established a household in the name of Tang Gui. The author of the genealogy, writing a few decades later, was quite explicit about the shifts in their regulatory position over time. "The ancestors had been civilians and became soldiers. Then from soldiers they became civilians. To be both soldiers and civilians simultaneously is respectable and no cause for shame."[23]

In Zhangpu, the former military households of Tongshan who remained excluded from the formal registration system looked for solutions as well. The Chen genealogy suggests that attaching themselves to registered households had a long tradition: "Ever since troops were transferred here in 1394, our lineage together with all the other surnames of Tong[shan] have always been registered as soldiers. Our lands were registered under the names of other households for tax purposes, and we have never been liable for corvée." When the magistrate reorganized the tax obligations in 1701, he expanded on this tradition, by assigning the households of Tongshan to previously registered households within existing tithing units.

> The various surnames in Tongshan were divided up amongst tithing 1 and tithing 2 of sector 6, plat 1 . . . The surnames in tithing 2 were attached to the household registered under the name Gong Moulie. Our lineage was attached to tithing 2, and [within this tithing] the Chen surname was assigned eight fiscal males (*guanding*). These eight fiscal males were recorded under the name Chen Deguang [the second-generation ancestor] of our lineage.[24]

This is a difficult passage to interpret. (The author did not intend to be cryptic, he just assumed that anyone who was liable to read the document would be familiar enough with the system being described to make sense of it.) The key point that the author wanted to convey is that his lineage accepted and fulfilled its due tax obligations. Under the reform, a certain household registered in the Ming tax-rolls—the household of Gong Moulie—was confirmed as a tax-paying unit. Then the tax officials had identified lineages that did not have registration—that were not listed as households—and assigned them to lineages that did. The total tax obligation due from the registered household was divided up amongst the lineages that had been assigned to that registration. This was expressed in terms of fiscal males, which must here have been a counter for a corvée surtax obligation. In a sense, the officials and their clerks who did this were engaged in their own form of regulatory arbitrage, manipulating multiple household registration regimes to ensure that the tax revenues kept flowing.

So even as Chen's reform eliminated the intermediary role of the old headmen for some households, it introduced a new intermediary role for others. The relationship of the former military households with the tax-collecting state was now mediated by people who predated them in the civilian registration system and to whose registration they had been assigned.

The residents of Tongshan decided they did not like this new arrangement. Perhaps old patterns of social distinction reemerged; perhaps the new intermediaries levied taxes excessively or unfairly; probably both. Ten years later, in 1711, when the tax rolls were next updated, the former soldiers of Tongshan took action.

To understand what they did, we must go back to the Guandi temple. In the main hall, off to one side, is an inscription dated 1713 (figure 7.1). It is titled, "Stone record of the public establishment of Guan Yongmao":

7.1. Inscription in the Tongshan Guandi temple

Investigation of the past [reveals that] our Tongshan used to be an island on the outer seas, where fishermen sometimes stepped [ashore] temporarily but where no [registered] civilians had ever lived. In the early Ming, Zhou Dexing . . . created a battalion here, and named it after Tongshan hill. He transferred people from Puxi in Xinghua [Putian] to guard the fort. Officers and soldiers held their posts through hereditary inheritance, and thus were registered under military registration. The *lijia* corvée and land tax were never heard of here.

When [the Qing] dynasty was established, the guards and battalions around the empire were maintained without change.[25] Only in Fujian were they abandoned because of the maritime turmoil [caused by Koxinga]. Those who had been registered were scattered and lost their registration. Can there be people under Heaven who are without registration? So in 1701 Magistrate Chen registered the households in Tongshan in the Yellow Registers, and it was from this point that there came to be head and land tax [obligations] in Tongshan. But [those people who were] scattered and had no descent line were forced to affiliate to other people's households. This was truly not a good method.

We heard that in Zhao'an county there were military households who were not [registered under any] descent line. They reverently took Imperial Lord Sage Guan to be their collective ancestor and applied to register a household under the name Guan Shixian [Guan Virtuous through Generations] for the payment of land and head tax. The [resulting] convenience was greatly praised.

In 1711 when the tax registers were re-compiled, we discussed this case together. We also expressed [our wish] to register a household under the name of Guan Yongmao [Guan Ever Flourishing]. Everyone agreed it could be done. So we applied to County Magistrate Wang requesting that we be allowed to establish a household. Permission was obtained for Guan Yongmao to take on the payment of land and head tax for sector 17, tithing 9, plat 6. Not only did this bring the benefit of uniformity in the payment of land tax and corvée, but it also meant that there were no longer people of other households interspersed among us [for payment of tax]. Those who were scattered were now gathered; from nothing there was again something; we could look forward to flourishing in the future even more than we had in the past.[26]

This part of the inscription in the Guandi temple is actually the story of how the people of Tongshan cut out the middleman and established a new relationship with the Qing state. Because of the problems of paying tax under the umbrella of another household, and informed by the analogous experience of former military households in a neighboring county, the military households of Tongshan banded together to register directly with the magistrate. In Qing times, this meant registering a "household." Inspired by their military background, they took Guan as their nominal surname, creating a fictional ancestor named Guan Yongmao to serve in the role that in other households was played by the first ancestor to register in the early Ming.

After their initial meeting in the temple, representatives went to the county offices. According to the genealogy of one of the participants, "They agreed to purchase [the registration associated with] the household of Chen Zixin of tithing 9, plat 6, sector 17 to serve as the flourishing household (*shenghu*) of Tongshan."[27] The text does not explain why Chen Zixin's registration was for sale; perhaps the household had died out or fled, perhaps the descendants agreed to sell their registration to the families of Tongshan. It took almost two years, and one hundred taels, for the deal to be done.

The Tongshan taxpayers now had a more satisfactory method to pay their taxes. But they soon learned of a potential problem with their arrangement. It seemed that other people were trying to infiltrate the new organization for their own nefarious purposes. The inscription continues:

> Recently [we] consulted the household registration record in the county yamen, and learned that the registration for the household under the name Guan Yongmao includes such names as Huang Qitai and others [that is, people who were not signatories to the original agreement]. We became very concerned about this matter of stealthy substitution and malicious concealment. A mere three years have passed [since the household was set up] and there is already this sort of complication. How can we ensure that in the future crafty tricksters like this will not encroach on our descendants?
>
> Therefore, it was publicly announced that we would gather before the deity to draw lots, and divide ourselves into seven branches.
>
> Any trivial matters shall be managed by each branch; important affairs shall be negotiated by assembling everyone [from the different branches]. Uncles and cousins [should treat one another like] brothers. There is to be no differentiation between hundred and tithing, and no discrimination between larger and smaller. The rich should not bully the poor; the strong should not oppress the weak. If someone has different ideas and does evil, it is permitted to call him out and attack him. In this way, there will be no partiality or factionalism. This is the height

of fairness and prudence. We therefore inscribe this [agreement] on stone so that it will last forever.[28]

The inscription ends with the names of more than forty signatories, drawn from twenty-seven surnames, each corresponding to a different lineage or lineage subdivision of a former military household. They are organized into seven branches of a lineage descended from the founding "ancestor," Guan Yongmao, who is named for their collective ancestor, the martial spirit Emperor Guan, with each branch responsible for a specified share of the overall tax obligation.

This temple inscription is thus, in fact, a contract. It is an agreement between the descendants of the soldiers of the garrison to formalize their relationship with the tax-collecting state. It is a contract that creates a new organizational form, the multisurname tax-paying fictive lineage, sanctified in the presence of a god who also takes on some of the attributes of an ancestor.[29] The contract uses the idiom of kinship and the lineage to specify group membership and the principles of the lineage to shape its internal management. This information could be produced if ever again someone tried to sneak in and create new social relations beyond the ones they had produced themselves.

In the years since 1711, whenever Guandi is carried out of his temple and paraded through the lanes of the town, what occurs is thus not only a ritual of purification and protection but also a commemoration of the creation of an organization. One might even say that this festival is a ritual that celebrates a contract.

Tongshan is not unique. In Fuquan, the battalion up the coast where Jiang Jishi once celebrated his dalliance with a pirate's sister, one finds today the ruins of an ancestral hall, the shrine of the Quan surname. But there is no one living in the town who actually has the surname Quan. Nor has there ever been. This strange lineage that seems to have no people not only has an ancestral hall, it even has a genealogy. The origins of the Quan lineage are explained in a 1714 contract that has been copied into the 1895 genealogy. The contract's fourteen signatories explain:

> The makers of this contract are [formerly] scattered military households. We have never had a household registration, and we [live] in the midst of powerful lineages and frequently suffer bullying and humiliation. So we all discussed and agreed that we should take over one household registration. Reflecting on the fact that our surnames are numerous, we decided to take the [second character from the] name of this place, Fu*quan*, as our surname, Quan.[30]

Just like the lineages of Tongshan, the various lineages of military house-holds in the former Fuquan battalion dealt with the legacies of their Ming status by uniting together into a common, fictive lineage, with an invented surname taken from the name of their community. They established an invented common ancestor, Venerable Quan, and installed his tablet with those of their individual ancestors into a "Quan" ancestral hall, the ruins of which can still be seen in the village. They too registered this "lineage" with the local authorities for payment of tax. The Guan lineage of Tong-shan and the Quan lineage of Fuquan are products of efforts by the Qing descendants of Ming military households to use their former shared status as an organizational resource to produce new kinds of social relations in a new context.

Later the history that gave rise to such arrangements would be entirely forgotten. In his early nineteenth-century account of the peculiarities of Fujian province, Chen Shengshao (*jinshi* 1805) wrote:

> For the state to levy its taxes justly, it must rely entirely on the fish-scale registers and an accurate taxation register. But Zhao'an is different. The Liao of Guanpi and the Shen near the county seat [are registered] as Xu, as Chen, or as Lin. It is not known how many thousands of mu of land they possess or how many tens of thousands of households they number. They register only the name of one or two general households (*zonghu*) with the authorities. [The households registered under the names] Liao Wenxing, Liao Rixin, Xu Lifa, and Xu Shipu are examples of this. There are furthermore cases of several households combining into one household in order to evade corvée duties. For example, the Li, Lin and other households combined into [a single household registra-tion under the name] Guan Shixian; the Ye, Zhao and other households have combined into Zhao Jianxing. . . . Can this be called an accurate tax register? No.[31]

For officials like Chen, the Tongshan arrangement was simply a form of resistance to state power, an organized attempt to evade taxes rather than an organized attempt to meet them. This forgetting is more than a historical curiosity. Chen could not understand the motivations of the Guan household members, nor did he realize that local officials and their clerks, for their part, faced with a society of sometimes unfathomable complexity, implicitly recognized that there were at least some useful functions for the local social order to ensure tax payments and maintain local order. Twentieth-century intellectuals might have called the Tong-shan contract an expression of local autonomy (*zizhihua*). Such informal institutions are not intrinsically challenging to the larger political order but may indeed be supportive of it. The failure of twentieth-century political elites to grasp this point is surely one of the great tragedies of China's recent past.

Conclusions

Even after the Ming military institution and the state that created it were both long gone, the institution continued to matter to the people who had lived under it. It continued to matter even to their descendants, people who had no direct personal experience at all of the institution itself. In this chapter, I have explored several types of institutional legacies: obligations that persisted after the institution was gone, prerogatives that people tried to maintain after the institution was gone, and reinventions of the institution for new purposes. In this third type, exemplified by the cases of Tongshan and Fuquan, members of former military households used their existing social relations as an organizational resource to meet the challenges of a dramatically different situation.

The chief reason states create archives is as a tool to aid in seeing their population. As James Scott has shown, the modern state seeks to create a detailed "map" of its population and its territory, and such maps both depict and enable state interventions.[32] But efforts to make such maps did not begin with modernity. Earlier states had also made maps in order to render their population more legible. It is too simplistic to dismiss these efforts on the grounds that premodern states lacked the technology to produce the same maps as modern states. Premodern states had different technical capacities from modern states, to be sure, but they also had different ambitions. Just like modern states, premodern states engaged in a calculus that evaluated the returns from greater legibility against the administrative burdens it imposed.

Early Qing officials were generally content to use the surviving Ming archive because the alternatives seemed too costly. This decision created the conditions for a systematic misfit between the archive and reality. In the Ming, the military households in the garrisons had been recorded in a separate archive, one that no longer existed. The surviving civilian archive did not include them. In the late seventeenth century, Qing magistrates in Fujian implemented compromises to address this misfit. Structurally these compromises were nothing new. In Ming, households not liable for direct taxation because they were too small or poor had been attached as "subordinate" households to registered households. The expectation was that the registered households and the subordinate households would work out equitable arrangements themselves. Qing officials tried something very similar for the legacy military households, attaching them to the households that were recorded in the surviving registers and expecting that those involved would work out the details.

To use Scott's term, the early Qing state did not "see" the military households; it saw right through them. The social organizations that the people of Tongshan and Fuquan created, and that found physical expression in the Guandi temple and the Quan ancestral hall, were their responses to this situation. They were unseen by the state, and they decided to find a way to make it possible for the state to see them. The families in these organizations were not made legible by the state. They made themselves legible.[33]

In chapter 1, I argued that the techniques devised to handle military obligations resembled techniques devised to address risk in commercial transactions. It may be too much to suggest that the one preceded the other, that people in south China learned to deal with the market by dealing with the state. But I think it is reasonable to assume that the two domains were mutually constitutive or mutually reinforcing, that these strategies derived from a shared cultural repertoire for dealing with problems, and their effectiveness at dealing with one kind of situation encouraged people to use them in other situations. Something quite similar explains the early Qing forms of organization that were created to deal with the new tax system. People used familiar types of informal institutions to negotiate their relationship with the state.

The Guandi temple's function as the organizational structure by which the people of Tongshan paid their taxes in early Qing, or to put it another way, as the site where social actors organized their relations with the state, was only possible because local officials recognized that informal local organizations could be effective guarantees of local order. In other words they turned a blind eye to the manipulations of the tax system. Our sources are silent on the subject, but turning a blind eye must have come with an implicit agreement that there were limits to these manipulations, that social actors could calibrate their relations with the state with some but not infinite flexibility, that there were rules that had to be followed. By the same token, the men of Tongshan who decided to declare themselves descendants of Emperor Guan as part of an effort to manage their tax obligations were not operating in a vacuum and were not simply exploiting a loophole, but believed with some confidence that their manipulations of the tax code would be acceptable to the yamen clerks with whom they had to deal.

Calibrating one's relations with the state was a key part of everyday politics in late imperial China. Individuals and groups considered the demands of the state and reflected on the best ways to meet those obligations. This meant optimizing the structure of the relationship and determining the most appropriate language to use to explain that structure. They carefully calibrated both how they would relate to the state and how to talk about their relationship. Households and groups of households used the language of the state and a set of familiar organizational idioms both in dealing with the state and as a political resource in their dealings with other groups in local society. This was not an assertion of independence but rather an implicit recognition of state authority coupled with an assertion of the legitimacy of meeting state claims in ways that did not necessarily conform to the letter of state law. This partial adoption of state forms framed not only their grievances but also ordinary social organization. It proved useful not just in relations with state agents but also in their relations with their neighbors. It was a critical element of their everyday politics.

Conclusion

THE FAMILIES WE HAVE MET in this book faced some distinctive challenges because they were registered as military households. But the fact of their having to deal with state institutions did not make them distinctive. It did not even make them unusual. For these families, as for most of the people who in the past several centuries have lived in what is today China, the critical political decision was not whether to engage with the state but how best to do so. For most people, most of the time, politics was largely about everyday and mundane questions: how to manage, negotiate, and manipulate encounters with formal state agents and their informal delegates to best advantage, and how to use their relationship with the state as a resource in other interactions. Except in very unusual circumstances, engaging with the state did not mean escaping the state or changing the state or openly resisting the state; it meant dealing with the state and the demands of its agents as best one could. The genealogies, contracts, and stone inscriptions in this book are an archive of the everyday politics of Ming subjects, a record of their efforts to secure advantage within and as defined by the political and cultural systems they inhabited. To interpret their highly sophisticated art of being governed merely as variations on the themes of subjection or resistance would needlessly impoverish our understanding of Chinese history.

The chapters of this book make up a partial typology of the strategies used by Ming households to manage their obligations to provide labor service to the state. The typology is a partial one because it deals only with the strategies used by a single type of household, registered military households (though these comprised a significant proportion of the total population). Moreover not all types of military households are equally represented in the discussion. Because hereditary officers had some enviable privileges that ordinary soldiers did not, they were more likely to remain in service and so our sources are disproportionately drawn from their numbers. Because the obligations on colony soldiers were typically lighter than on garrison soldiers, fewer of them deserted, and so genealogies of military colonists survive and can be located in greater numbers. The typology is also incomplete with respect to the types of strategies that people used. It is heavily weighted to strategies that shared two characteristics. The strategies discussed here were recorded by the people who used them, and they could be recorded in ways that made them appear to be compliant (chapter 3 on smuggling is perhaps the exception, though even there we saw officers insisting they were on legitimate missions even as they engaged in smuggling).

But even an incomplete typology can tell us something. The chapters illustrate four broad types of strategies: strategies of optimization, strategies of proximity, strategies of regulatory arbitrage, and strategies of precedent. Chapters 1 and 2 explored the optimization strategies by which households managed their obligations to provide labor to the army. These solutions were mostly internal to the early Ming household—and the larger kinship group into which it evolved—methods by which military households and lineages organized themselves to manage their obligations to the state. The regulatory position of these groups was straightforward— they had to provide one soldier for military duties—but their reality was more complex. Families had multiple sons or no sons; households developed into lineages with multiple branches whose members were not all equally willing or able to serve. Family strategies sought to optimize the difference between the regulatory position and their actual situation.

From the perspective of the household, state policies intended to maintain constant troop strength could be arbitrary and unpredictable. The death of a distant relative on the other side of the empire or a bookkeeping failure by a local clerk could suddenly make a person liable for conscription. So in the early decades of the dynasty, in the late fourteenth and early fifteenth centuries, military households devised ways to manage their obligations under these conditions, to ensure service responsibilities were fulfilled at minimal possible cost, to make obligations more predictable and reduce uncertainty. They used three basic approaches to accomplish this: rotation, concentration, and compensation. They set up mechanisms to rotate the obligation systematically through their own internal divisions or to concentrate the obligation on a single individual or division. Substitution, arranging for a third party to fulfill the obligation on one's behalf, was the natural extension of concentration. Substitution strategies almost always involved payments, but compensation was often part of other strategies too. My interpretation—that these strategies aimed to optimize the difference between rules and social reality—is supported by subsequent efforts by state authorities to specify rules for a broader range of social possibilities and to specify with greater precision how such differences should be managed.

Once stationed in the guard, soldiers and their families faced different challenges. In chapters 3–6, we saw how military households of the mid-Ming, in the fifteenth and sixteenth centuries, developed strategies that were outward-looking, that went beyond the internal management of the family itself. They made use of overlaps and discrepancies between multiple government systems to their advantage. Some soldiers and officers in the garrisons even took advantage of their special position in the military system to gain advantage in illicit commerce. We can label strategies like these strategies of proximity, because they took advantage of proximity to certain parts of the state apparatus in order to gain advantage with respect to others. Soldiers assigned to the military colonies became adept at arbitrage strategies that took advantage of the differences between military colony land and ordinary land, turning these differences to their benefit. These strategies involved more than simply identifying and using loopholes. Their practitioners recognized and took advantage of the multiple regulatory regimes that shaped everyday life and sought to position themselves within the regime that was most advantageous to them. This can be called regulatory arbitrage because it involved taking advantage of the differences between multiple regulatory systems.

Finally the last chapter showed how military households sought to maintain prerogatives from the Ming system or recycle its institutions to serve their interests in the Qing. These were strategies based on appeals to precedent.

The history that I have told here is thus not a cumulative history but an episodic one, illustrating four cycles of human interaction with a changing institution. Within each cycle, people deployed their ingenuity and elements from their repertoire of cultural resources to better manage individual, family, and communal interaction with the institution. The institutional chronology reveals how the evolution of the institution generated different sorts of challenges for different groups of people, and how they responded strategically.

Regulatory arbitrage, a term I have borrowed from economics, can serve as an umbrella term for the various types of strategies that emerged in the different cycles. For all of the four types are in fact variations on a single theme: the arbitraging of differences between multiple regulatory systems, or between regulatory position and reality, to one's advantage. The term highlights the ways household strategies exploited opportunities and minimized costs; took advantage of overlapping jurisdictions and precedents to reduce uncertainty, increase predictability, and gain financial advantage; converted obligations of one type to another type; used compliance with state requirements as a resource in other contexts, and developed informal institutions to manage their relationship with the state. The specific forms of arbitrage that people developed and deployed were not timeless—they had to adapt to changing institutional configurations—but the impulse to arbitrage endured.

Attention to arbitrage strategies challenges still-influential paradigms that explain Chinese history either with regard to purely formal structures—such as the imperial institution—or to cultural preconceptions—such as familism or Confucianism—that are thought to underlie and animate the whole of society. This approach has implications for Ming history, for the history of the state in China, and for the history of early modern empires. It can also suggest an agenda for the study of everyday politics in general.

Informal Institutions and the Ming State

Ming extractive institutions were designed to supply the needs of a small state with minimal overhead costs. To accomplish this goal, the Ming state deputized semiformal and informal agents to collect taxes and perform other local functions, in effect passing much of the cost of running the system onto families and communities. Philip Huang had the Qing dynasty in mind when he coined the term "centralized minimalism," but the term can be usefully applied to its Ming predecessor.[1] Centralized minimalism in operation required that the state and its agents accept the informal institutions and procedures that families and communities created to meet the demands the state made on them.

The hereditary aspect of military households' obligations meant that the informal arrangements to which they gave rise inevitably became linked to patrilineal kinship. The spatial distribution of other obligations such as *lijia* duties meant that informal institutions in the villages, especially temples, also frequently served to mediate engagement with state agents. The effective state sanction of such informal management institutions encouraged their spread—lineage, temple, and market growth in Ming all owed something to the state system. This is not of course to suggest that kinship groups or temple festivals were Ming inventions; patrilineal kinship and temple affiliation had been powerful structuring or orienting principles of Chinese society since long before the Ming. But the spread of particular institutional expressions of these principles was driven at least in part by the exigencies of everyday politics in this particular period.

The informal institutions of late imperial China are a good example of the way social and cultural history can reveal how phenomena that might appear to be rooted in eternal cultural elements are better understood as historical. Lineages with highly complex internal organization and temple festivals that simultaneously affirm unity and mark difference may seem like quintessential expressions of Chinese culture. But we have seen that the origins of particular expressions of these phenomena can sometimes be specified with some precision. Indeed these origins are not simply historical but more narrowly institutional, that is, they were produced by the interaction of individuals and groups with the institutions of the Chinese state.

It is no coincidence that later observers noticed a resemblance between the Chinese lineage and the modern corporation. A corporation is, on the most simple definition, a group of people legally authorized to act as a single entity.[2] With their shared obligation, explicitly recognized in law, to provide labor service to the state, military households meet this definition precisely. I have argued here and in previous work that the pressure of meeting hereditary military responsibilities encouraged military households in Ming to organize themselves, thereby creating corporate lineages.[3] Lineage organization was not simply an already-existing static social form that happened to suit these purposes. It was itself a product of everyday political strategizing. The constraints and opportunities of everyday politics encouraged certain patterns of organization. These may subsequently have been represented as ideologically orthodox but orthodoxy alone cannot explain their emergence or spread. Kinship structures are not simply cultural givens nor passive outcomes of historical processes. They are, as James Scott has argued, political choices.[4] In Ming China, the art of being governed included using informal institutions to mediate with the state and its agents.

The Ming reliance on informal institutions was self-reinforcing; to secure the resources it needed the state had to sanction local arrangements. The passing of the dynasty did not fundamentally change this dynamic. But in the nineteenth century, a combination of internal pressures and outside stimuli created new tensions that launched China into a process of state-making. When that happened, the same informal institutions that had made politics function now came to be seen as part of the problem of China's premodernity. Reformers of all political stripes now concluded that these institutions had to be eliminated if China was to build a modern state. This was the cause of much trauma in twentieth-century China.

Legibility and State Vocabulary

One common feature of the family strategies explored in this book is that they are accessible to us because they were recorded. But notation was not just a convenient (to us) side effect of the strategy; it was actually part of the strategy itself. For at the core of many family strategies was managing how the state and its agents perceived the family. Unlike the modern state, the Ming state had no aspirations to a perfect understanding of society. It did not seek to make society completely legible. The Ming state's perception of its realm was a product of its own methods of making, keeping, and accessing records. It was not just a rule-bound state but a document-bound one. Its smooth operation relied on the creation, circulation, retention, and referencing of documents. These were written in a distinctive, specialized vocabulary. When functionaries (in any system, not just China) fill out the forms recording details about a population, they must use a common vocabulary in order for the exercise to be useful. If they describe every household in different terms—the archival equivalent of Borges's famous map as big as the world—then to their superiors the population would remain completely illegible.[5] A shared language is a form of administrative simplification and standardization that is intended to minimize ambiguity and therefore maximize efficiency. State documents must use state language.

Because the way one was inscribed in state records affected how one was governed, Ming subjects learned to use that language, and the principles and practices it served, to their advantage. They sought to manage how they were represented in the state archive. The ways documents were produced, circulated, and archived mattered in the lives of ordinary people in Ming. In a sense this book is a study of the social consequences of Ming bureaucratic practices.

Families sometimes even took the initiative in state record keeping by seeking to have the state create information about them. One way they could do this was by initiating a lawsuit. Huang has shown that bringing a lawsuit could be a complex strategic act, intended not only to obtain a favorable judgment but also to gain advantage in informal mediation. We have seen that in Ming, and probably later as well, it could also be a strategy to enter the state archive, to "establish a documentary record" (*li'an*), in ways that might be useful in the future. "Establishing a documentary record" meant something like creating a precedent, not in the narrow sense of a judicial decision that is binding on other courts, but rather in the sense of a demonstration that something—some behavior or some situation—had been acknowledged and authorized or legitimated by a magistrate.[6]

Avner Greif argues that use of state vocabulary can reduce transaction costs because all parties to a transaction understand it.[7] This is not the only reason. Using state language to demonstrate or even to claim adherence to state rules could also be productive in one's subsequent encounters—not only with state actors but also with other non-state actors. The use of state language increases the likelihood that a transaction can be represented as being authorized. So a state-provided precedent was a resource that could be used in claims against other actors in the future. This was part of the reason why families carved court judgments into stone inscriptions that they erected in their ancestral hall or copied official documents into their genealogy. To use the language of the state is to borrow the state's legitimacy and prestige and turn it into a political resource for one's own purposes. This is one way the state can thus be an instrument of productive as well as repressive power. The Ming state was an authorizing machine even as it was an extracting machine.

The value of this kind of resource lay, at least in part, in the degree to which it could be used in ways other than what the author of the precedent actually intended. To optimize regulatory position, effective strategies took advantage of the appearance of compliance to do things that were subtly different. Families adhered to the forms of regulation in order to manipulate the substance. The principle of bureaucratic government by precedent is always undermined by the reality that precedents are open to interpretation. From the perspective of the judge, the more precise and less ambiguous the precedent the better. But from the perspective of social actors, the more ambiguous the precedent the better (at least in general—in some cases certain actors might well prefer precision). The functional power of a precedent in Ming society was thus in a sense directly related to its ambiguity. Part of the everyday politics of social actors involved estimating the degree to which the ambiguity latent in a precedent could be exploited.

This capacity to use interaction with the state as a resource in other types of politics illustrates that, by the Ming, state forms and state language did more than simply govern subjects' interaction with the state. They had become embedded in local culture. Cultural parallels between state and society facilitated arbitrage strategies. The Ming state's mode of seeing, intended to simplify social reality so it could be governed, created the possibility, indeed the inevitability, of differences between aspects of society as they were lived and as they were perceived by the state apparatus, between reality and regulatory position. The state that cannot see everything misses things. Or, more precisely, it mis-sees. This creates the possibilities of regulatory arbitrage, of seeking advantage within and through the state's institutions without explicitly violating its rules. If the interface between state and society was as Duara suggests a sort of translucent canopy, actors in society could seek to distort the transluscency to their advantage, or even deliberately vary the degree of transluscency and transparency.[8] Knowing the ways of the state created political resources for social actors.[9]

James Scott has shown that modern states have distinctly modern ways of seeing. But seeing like a state is not unique to the modern era. Premodern states had their own way of seeing, their own methods of making administration, accounting, and control possible. This inspired responses from those the state tried to see. In Ming China, social actors were not only seen by the state, they also sought to *be seen* by the state in particular ways. And this required the ability to *talk* like a state. In Ming China, the art of being governed meant acquiring idiomatic competence in the language of the state.

Commodification and Contract in Ming

Many of the strategies we have encountered in this book involved the use of what are recognizably contracts. This tells us something important about the society in which these strategies were deployed. To borrow a distinction made by Myron Cohen, since the Song dynasty if not earlier China's southeast coastal region had become both commercialized—in the sense that its economy was characterized by specialized production and market exchange—and also commodified—in the sense that the market was central to economic culture. Buying and selling things was part of everyday life; so too was the idea that things could be bought and sold. These processes only accelerated in Ming. Military households in Ming Fujian treated not just material goods but also rights to land use, political obligations, and even social relations as things that could be bought and sold.[10]

In many parts of the world commercialization and commodification—of property rights, obligations, and social relations—thoroughly disrupted the existing social order. With a few exceptions this was generally not the case for Ming China. One obvious reason is that these processes did not occur simultaneous with or as a result of colonialism.[11] But perhaps there is also something to the different chronologies of the two processes. In southeast China, commodification was not simply a response to commercialization; the transformation of social relations was not simply a direct result of the penetration of the market into the economy. Commodification did not just follow commercialization in Ming; in some respects it was simultaneous and in others it may even have preceded and stimulated it. Ordinary people in Fujian were already turning labor obligations into financial obligations in the late fourteenth century, centuries before the influx of foreign silver that drove late Ming commercialization. Was this the revival of a process that had been interrupted by the Mongol conquest? Was the disruption of the commercialization process not so serious as previous historians have thought? Or did the process by which Ming subjects learned to be governed follow a distinctive chronology from the process of their learning about markets? Whatever the answer to these questions, it is clear that the everyday political strategies of military households were both rooted in their experience with the market and also shaped their further experience with it.

A key piece of evidence for commodification is the prevalence of contracts. We now know that contracts were widely used in late imperial China and contractual agreements relating to land rights and marriages were routinely presented as evidence in lawsuits.[12] Such agreements formalized relationships in which parties made promises in exchange for a consideration. There continues to be lively debate over whether these agreements fit the modern definitions of a contract, and the degree to which they were enforceable.[13] The genealogies and court records of the Ming show that magistrates did enforce the terms specified in internal agreements by military households. Magistrates *did* choose one member of the family to be conscripted over another on the basis of their reading of a written agreement. The Ming state was clearly willing to enforce contracts where state interests were directly concerned.

But magistrates intervened in such cases not out of an abstract commitment to contracts or a sense that certain rights were guaranteed, but because the realities of centralized minimalism gave them little choice. They intervened because to fail to do so would leave army ranks empty, which would generate a paper trail that led back to the magistrate himself. What made these agreements enforceable was precisely that they governed the fulfillment of state obligations. The evidence from lawsuits over colony lands supports this argument. There is no evidence that the notion of rights to colony allotments existed prior to or outside of the obligation to pay the surplus tax; they were created at the very moment of fiscal perception.

One of the core issues in debates over Chinese contracts is the link between enforceable contracts and stable and secure property rights. Some have argued that secure property rights and contracts are a necessary condition for economic modernization. China's economic performance over the last four decades has shown to the surprise of many that the absence of secure property rights is not incompatible with rapid economic growth.[14] Nor, clearly, are contracts a sufficient one. But this does not make China's history of contracts irrelevant. We should not allow economic modernization narratives to blind us to other historical possibilities. Contracts in premodern China played a different role in economic and political life than they did in the West. One of those roles was to facilitate everyday politics. In Ming China, the art of being governed included the capacity to use contracts effectively to optimize one's interaction with the state.

State and Society in the Ming

In this book, I have explored everyday political strategies and the social relations arising from them in relation to a specific microecology, the southeast coast. Some of the distinctive features of the region were geographic; others were historical. The proximity of the sea shaped the strategies that were available to military households—taking up piracy would not be a winning strategy in a landlocked region. The sea and the people who sailed on it also shaped the military functions to which they were assigned. Except during the upsurge of violence in the sixteenth century, and especially after the opening of licenced trade, soldiers in coastal garrisons did not face relentless military attacks or even military threats like their colleagues in the north. The main responsibility of coastal soldiers was a predictable, seasonal obligation to put out to sea; this resembled in some ways the tasks of soldiers in garrisons along the Grand Canal, to accompany the boats carrying tax grain to the capital. On other frontiers guards were sometimes the only form of government; on the coastal frontier and in the interior the guard coexisted with the civilian county administration, and this created its own possibilities for strategizing. Finally, locally specific cultural traditions shaped the available repertoire of strategies. Highly elaborated traditions of village religion in the southeast coastal region help explain why temples were such important sites for the practice of everyday politics.

The specifics of early Ming recruitment and assignment in the region, whereby serving soldiers were mostly assigned first to garrisons close to their native village and later reassigned to garrisons elsewhere along the coast, had an impact on the ties between serving soldiers and their kin—such ties were probably maintained longer than in other places.

Moreover even within the microecology, there were distinctions. The strategies that made sense in the upland colonies were different from those in the garrisons along the coast. The distinction between colonies whose serving soldiers were mobilized to deal with the Deng Maoqi rebellion and those that were not—a product largely of the location of the garrisons to which those colonies were attached—was hugely consequential for local society and politics thereafter.

Given local distinctiveness, were the strategies and social relations discussed here more broadly distributed in Ming society? Even to consider this question here poses a basic methodological challenge, since I have argued that strategies must be situated in relation to local ecologies, meaning not only distinctive physical environments but also local social structure and culture. But to demonstrate that these strategies are of more than parochial interest, I cannot avoid the subject.

Yu Zhijia's research—more extensive that my own—shows that the basic strategies of rotation, concentration, substitution, and compensation were widely used across the empire, though with distinctive local features in different places.[15] On every one of China's frontiers, not just the maritime, military households took advantage of their competitive advantage to engage in smuggling and raiding, though of course when they were discovered they were labeled in terms other than "dwarf bandits."[16]

This is not to say there was no significant variation in strategy. The sources from the southeast coast almost uniformly treat military service as a burden to be avoided; probably in less prosperous parts of Ming China, providing military service in exchange for a ration—even if it was not always paid on time—could be an attractive career. Strategies for dealing with the service obligation must have been very different in such places and would have generated different strategies. Xu Bin has shown how many of the greatest landowners of Hubei in Ming and Qing were people with military registration who used corvée exemptions to accumulate land from others less fortunate.[17] In those parts of the hinterland where unlike on the southeast coast corvée duties were crushingly heavy, military households could probably have parlayed their corvée exemptions to greater effect.

Different local microecologies provided different institutional tools that could be used to pursue strategic ends. This was a product of the evolution of local society. So whereas the rich temple traditions of southern Fujian provided the people of Tongshan with the mechanism to regularize their status in the early Qing, this approach does not seem to have been considered by their counterparts in Nanling in Hunan, studied by Xie Shi. Lacking the vocabulary of the communal temple to solemnify the social networks they developed to deal with the Qing state, they had to find other bases for communal identity. They also do not appear to have compiled a joint genealogy like the people of Fuquan. But their descendants are surely hinting at a sense that the community is an alliance of lineages when today they describe the old battalion gazetteer as a "joint genealogy."[18]

The most striking variation across space is one that this book cannot explain. If the nature of the hereditary military system meant that institutions of patrilineal kinship would always be part of people's strategies to deal with their obligations, and kinship institutions are not a cultural given but political choice, how can we explain the variation in the development of corporate lineages? Why if military households were found everywhere did corporate lineages develop in some parts of China in this period but not others?

The core strategies discussed above were widespread in part because they worked. Perhaps the best indication that strategies by military households could be effective is the large number of successful members of the Ming elite who belonged to such households. Besides Ye Xianggao and Lin Xiyuan—two men we have encountered in this book—other well-known examples of men with military registration include Xia Yan (1482–1548), chief grand secretary to the Jiajing emperor; Wen Zhengming (1470–1559), the celebrated painter and calligrapher; the great travel writer, Huang Xingzeng (1490–1540), and many others. None of these men owed their position in society to military exploits, their own or those of their ancestors. Just like the strategies that generated them, these successes could persist even after the fall of the Ming. Qing historians have noticed that in many places the social hierarchy even as late as the nineteenth century showed the legacies of changes in the early Ming, and that descendants of military households were often among the wealthy and powerful local elite. Working within the Ming system could obviously lay the foundations for long-term prosperity and status.[19]

What about beyond the ranks of military households? The basic strategies that military households used to manage their obligation to provide military service and to deal with the various consequences of this obligation were also found widely distributed in society at large. Civilian lineages in Huizhou, Anhui, used the same basic repertoire of rotation, concentration, and compensation to deal with their corvée labor responsibilities. Liu Zhiwei has shown that civilian-registered households in the Pearl River Delta of Guangdong made use of similar sorts of everyday political strategies to those that I have characterized as regulatory arbitrage—by registering and therefore engaging with the *lijia* system, the Ming state's key tool to regulate local society, families secured a variety of legal benefits.[20] Even something as specific as the combination of multiple lineages into a single registration was a strategy used by civilian as well as military households. Two of the most prominent lineages in late-Qing Anxi, where Hutou is located, were actually comprised of previously unrelated groups who fabricated a genealogical connection in the early Qing in order to associate themselves with a household registration in the face of changing registration policies. In Chaozhou too, groups of people with several different surnames changed their names in order to attach themselves to a registration.[21]

These parallels should not surprise us. Both military and civilian registered households were called upon to provide both labor and material goods to the state, and those obligations were managed through state agents and their informal and semiformal delegates. Both types of households shared similar cultural and organizational repertoires to bring to the task of managing their relationship with the state.

Ming military registered households were subject to an additional level of state record keeping compared to civilian households. To put this another way, state legibility schemes for civilian households were less well developed than for military households. This must have affected the types of regulatory arbitrage that were possible for the two groups. But regulatory arbitrage operated at the nexus of limited state capacity and state sanction of informal institutions, and this was broadly true of late imperial China in general. The state commitment to informal procedures meant that state officials could expect to be called upon to intervene in disputes or to enforce agreements between non-state actors, military or not. This created the expectation that one could ultimately call upon state agents to enforce agreements, both agreements that were registered with the state and agreements that were not. It encouraged the use of the appropriate state language in agreements of all sorts, because doing so increased the likelihood that they would be enforceable.

The Ming state may not have had the same degree of penetration as modern states, but it was sufficiently present in everyday life that it could create opportunities to be exploited. Being able to interact with the state could be a benefit and not just a cost, providing not just reasons for resistance but also opportunities for manipulation. The same is true of being close to the state. One's freedom of action and movement did not vary directly with one's distance from state agents and institutions. On the contrary, in Ming times it could be productive to get close to the state, to cultivate one's art of being governed.

On Ming History

The analysis here complicates the prevailing narrative arc of Ming history, a story in which market displaces autocratic state so that by the early seventeenth century the vision of the Ming founder "had attenuated to nothing more than a textual memory."[22] In this conventional version of the story, as the heavy weight of the state is lifted, Chinese society becomes more free—mobile and fluid rather than fixed and static, flexible and creative rather than rigid and hidebound. I have argued in this work that the study of the Ming is better served by a more archaeological approach that uncovers the sedimentation that lies beneath each phase of Ming history. State institutions and state agents continued to structure people's everyday political strategies over the whole of the dynasty, and even beyond. Zhu Yuanzhang's vision may never have become a reality. But it also never ceased to matter, not to people's interactions with the state nor to the social relations that were produced as an unintended consequence of the state institutions established in the early Ming. The history of state-society relations in the Ming is not simply a story of subtraction, of the disappearance or withdrawal of the state. The changing relationship of state to society in the Ming must also be told as a story of addition, of new responses and new relationships.

These changes were not just the result of developments in people's art of being governed. The state changed too. On the one hand, state policies were often "mediated by capillary effects that worked to reshape [institutions like the] *lijia* to local preferences"; on the other, state officials adjusted policies to contain and sometimes to counter the everyday political strategies they encountered.[23] These efforts, and for that matter the very localization policy that gave rise to so many of these strategies, show that the conventional image of the Ming state as static and unresponsive is overstated. It may still be true that the institutions of the Ming state were unable to respond structurally to the changing world. But the reality is that institutional inertia is a characteristic of all states to some degree; no state system of any complexity can turn on a single cash coin.[24]

Informal management coupled with strong institutions produced relatively high state capacity at relatively low cost. But even as this capacity declined, the system became even harder to change. As local institutions responded to the incentive structures created by the system, they became vested interests that both opposed and increased the costs of change. This, coupled with constitutional elements and intellectual imperatives towards small government, meant that Ming inertia was overdetermined; there were forces from below as much as above that shaped its path.

While the current view that the Ming population became increasingly involved in market-oriented production over the course of the Ming is no doubt correct, the commodification of culture did not simply follow from commercialization of the economy. On the contrary, it may have preceded and in some ways shaped it. From the very first years of the Ming, the notion that things—including social and political relationships—could be bought and sold was already becoming part of everyday political culture. Economic growth and social change in the late Ming caused considerable elite anxiety, "the confusions of pleasure" in Tim Brook's evocative book title. The new social mobility of the late Ming led them to try to defend the boundaries of their community and to bemoan the decay of morality. But it is too simplistic to see this as just the Ming version of a common tension in early modern and modern societies between the formalistic operation of the state and market and the moral codes of communities. The Ming constitution was itself a moral code, resting on and legislating a set of assumptions about the relationship between social categories and appropriate behavior.[25] Social actors were conscious of that code, and while they were generally uninterested in living according to its precepts, they claimed fealty to it when it served their purposes, sometimes evading the code and sometimes manipulating it. The evolution of their strategies reflects a politics far more complex than simply the substitution of a post-market for a premarket ethos.

Physical mobility is another element of the "from state to market" narrative for which our findings have implications. In early Ming, according to the standard narrative, society was largely static; people mostly stayed put. Then in the late Ming, people responding to market forces moved this way and that. In fact the early Ming was actually a time when large numbers of people were on the move.[26] Serving soldiers assigned to new guards were only one of several groups of such people. There was indeed a fundamental shift in mobility during the Ming, but it was not an absolute shift from immobility to mobility. Rather, the shift was in the character of mobility, from regulated to unregulated mobility, from mobility by state fiat to mobility on personal initiative. The limits of the data make a quantitative estimation of this shift impossible. But we can say that mobility was constituted as a different kind of problem in late Ming than it had been in early Ming.

The State in Chinese History and Beyond

Having moved from a series of anecdotes about several families living in southeast China in the Ming to some broader claims about the Ming, I now wish to make some more ambitious claims about the state in Chinese history, about the early modern state, and about studying states in general—with a digression into contemporary China along the way. This book has sought to explain what "working the system"—which is just another way of saying "everyday politics"—meant in a particular context. Can its findings also shed light on how people work the system in other contexts?

The institutions of the early Ming can be seen as one solution to a long-term tension in the history of Chinese politics—between *dirigiste* and *laissez-faire* approaches to the economy, between central authority and local initiative, or between the centralizing state-building initiatives of the early Song and the neo-Confucian reaction. Ultimately the latter pole proved stronger for much of the last centuries of imperial rule, but there was no linear shift from direct control towards informal management and local initiative. The tension between state intervention and informal management was not a zero-sum contest.[27] Indeed Zhu Yuanzhang deliberately tried to create a system that had both. The Ming, though claiming to be a return to nativist tradition, actually incorporated many techniques of control adapted from the steppe in the Mongol period, while also turning back towards local initiative and informal governance. The early Ming was thus simultaneously an interventionist state that sought new channels to penetrate into the lives of its subjects and a *laissez-faire* state that permitted considerable scope for people to negotiate and strategize over how best to handle obligations. Some scholars have argued that the Ming state was "precociously modern" in the sense that it had modern visions of state capacity but lacked the technical capacity to realize them.[28] But Ming statesmen did not design their political institutions in anticipation of the fax machine being invented. The Ming Chinese state, like all states, balanced objectives against available technologies.

The balance may have shifted over time, but the dualism in approach persisted through Ming and Qing. There were periodic efforts, sometimes at the local level, to shift to direct rather than indirect control, to formal rather than informal management of local society. But such efforts never fully took root, in part because of ideological concerns, in part because there was no way to implement direct control without raising the costs. In some ways, the shift from informal to formal mechanisms of state control is still ongoing in China even today. The widespread notion that the transition to modernity is a linear process of state penetration and the building of uniform control should not blind us to the possibility of other historical trajectories.

The strategies that ordinary people used to respond to this situation of course had their antecedents. But their elaboration and widespread applicability and application was time-bound. They were phenomena of the Ming, and therefore invite discussion of whether similar patterns occurred elsewhere in the centuries preceding the transition to modernity. Did the Ming configuration of state power and patterns of negotiation with social actors have parallels in other empires? To put this another way, is it helpful to think of the Ming as an early modern empire, the everyday politics of which can productively be compared to that in other early modern empires?[29]

Notwithstanding Jack Goldstone's caution that the very term "early modern" runs the risk of being meaningless, much recent scholarship on Chinese history in the period from Song to Qing has benefited from careful comparison with contemporary societies elsewhere.[30] Such comparisons are otiose so long as early modern is defined in relation to a presumed universal pattern of development culminating in universal modernity, or such that the key features of modernity must be the logical outcomes of indigenous processes. Rather, we want to inquire into similarities and differences across societies in the period that was the "crucible in which the armature of the modern world was forged," that is, when the preconditions that would shape modern transformations were established.[31] By the twentieth century, a condition labeled "modernity" had come to be the universal aspiration of states. The proper way to attain that condition—the modernist agenda—was defined differently in different places, and implemented in different ways and to different tempos. In the process, many elements in society came to be constituted either as impediments to or resources for that agenda. These elements are part of what we ought to be investigating when we pursue early modern comparisons.

The study of everyday politics is not at the stage where the sorts of broad comparisons that have been made for economic performance or political structure are possible.[32] Here I wish simply to sketch out an agenda for future comparative study. In the centuries when the Ming and its successor state the Qing ruled China, the pursuit of centralization of control over large polities and extensive territory was a feature common to many states and empires. This was not just a matter of increasing control but also making it more uniform. In theory, in a modern state the degree of state control does not vary across state territory. One might assume that in premodern states central state capacity varied inversely with distance from the center. But in reality, places that are distant from the center are often precisely those places where military defense is most important, necessitating a high state presence. So perhaps the relationship between distance and state impact is direct on the frontier and inverse in the hinterland. But even this adjustment does not fully capture the complexity of the premodern state. Premodern state penetration was also not uniform across different issues; for matters that the ruler or bureaucracy saw as particularly significant, higher levels of engagement and penetration (or, to use Michael Mann's formulation, greater infrastructural power) were possible.[33] This variation in state penetration might be seen as a common characteristic of early modern states—or rather, it is in early modern states that this variation came to be constituted as a problem.

Reliance on informal and semiformal mechanisms as a tool of governenace was a common way for early modern states to deal with the challenge of centralization under conditions of partial legibility and limited resources. In seventeenth-century France, the main direct tax, the *taille*, was assigned to parishes, within each of which the parishioners themselves allocated and collected the tax. James Collins calls the system "a very rational adaptation to the practical realities of the early modern state." Karen Barkey describes the Ottoman Empire as a kind of "negotiated enterprise," because the state willingly ceded a degree of autonomy to local actors in order to secure a more stable polity. A common by-product of negotiations between central and local actors was that ties to the central power could become a political resource for local actors in their own struggles. Farhat Hasan writes of the western Mughal Empire in the seventeenth century that "imperial sovereignty was appropriated by social actors to suit their purposes, increasingly embroiling it in local conflicts for access to symbolic and material resources."[34]

Peter Perdue has noticed successive Chinese states engaging in similar patterns of negotiation on the frontiers, and David Robinson has observed that the Ming state negotiated with men of violence not only on the periphery but also at the center. In this book I have showed that such negotiations occurred not just on the margins of Ming society but were very widespread among ordinary people.[35] Accommodation and other forms of negotiation between the central state and local elites or other local power systems was of course nothing new in the Ming. But the combination of reliance on informal institutions and negotiation, new impulses to centralization, and the limits of state legibility projects probably created new opportunities for what I have called regulatory arbitrage in many polities of the time. Because people were able to arbitrage the presence of the state and leverage their relationship with it, engagement with state agents became potentially useful, and not simply something to avoid as much as possible. One shared characteristic of early modern states might therefore be the creation of new possibilities for regulatory arbitrage, and therefore new patterns and processes of interaction with the state and its agents. Did early modern governance mark the moment when getting closer to the state, being seen by the state, talking like a state, could be used to serve one's interests, generating new patterns of everyday politics?

In premodern and modern societies alike, the everyday politics of ordinary people can have consequences that go well beyond their communities. In Kerkvliet's classic study of everyday politics, Vietnamese peasants through their everyday politics ultimately forced the national government to reverse its policies on collective farming.[36] In the Ming, shortfalls in the number and quality of soldiers from military households, coupled with the emergence of new threats in the northeast, forced the state to come up with a new solution to the universal challenge of mobilizing labor for military service. The main response was to recruit paid soldiers, that is mercenaries, to supplement the depleted ranks. This created a fiscal crisis that contributed significantly to the fall of the dynasty. So the everyday household strategies discussed here could easily be linked to large-scale political events. But this has not been my main concern here.

Rather, I have sought to shed light on everyday politics themselves, on how ordinary people respond to the challenges of dealing with the state. Everyday politics being universal in human societies, the specific patterns of regulatory arbitrage that obtain in any given polity past or present ought to be part of the comprehensive analysis of that polity. A generalized approach to the study of regulatory arbitrage would include four necessary elements: the institutional system itself—the traditional subject of institutional history; the space for regulatory arbitrage, that is, the gaps between regulatory regime and social reality and the overlapping jurisdiction of different parts of the regulatory regime that make arbitrage possible; the cultural and organizational resources that people have available to them to make sense of and respond to their situation; and the strategies they devise on the basis of those resources to optimize their politics. The interaction of these four elements over time is what produces everyday politics in different societies.

With its focus on individual and group strategies, concrete encounters with state agents, and the development of informal institutions to mediate between the two, regulatory arbitrage makes it possible analytically to transcend oversimplified analyses of monolithic state and monolithic society. Since securing manpower for the military is an all but universal challenge for states, regulatory arbitrage in relation to military service is a particularly promising arena for comparative study.

Much of the literature on the history of the Chinese state focuses on the issue of state capacity. But a comprehensive analysis of any state requires that we consider not just its effectiveness but also its effects. The term "state effect" has been coined by Timothy Mitchell to describe how the processes of the modern state create "the appearance of a world fundamentally divided into state and society."[37] In the absence of those processes, Mitchell argues, this fundamental division between state and society can hardly be meaningful. But this is not to say that the processes of mobilization and extraction that enable the premodern state to perform its core functions do not have consequences that go beyond these functions themselves. These processes produced a sort of premodern "state effect." That is, they generated behaviors that would not have made sense in the absence of the state. Presumably people develop strategies to optimize their situations whether or not they live with a state. We might call the generation of certain expressions of everyday politics and certain patterns of legitimacy that depend on the existence of the state for their operation the "premodern state effect."

Contemporary Echoes/Contemporary Consequences: Another Visit to Pinghai

An old folk saying that one still hears in China today, "to comply overtly but violate covertly" (*yangfeng yinwei*), captures well the spirit of the strategies discussed in this book. As it happens, one of the early appearances of the phrase is in a late Ming memorial on corvée obligations— though people who use the phrase today are generally not aware of this.[38] Examples of "complying overtly but violating covertly" abound in contemporary China. Many of China's greatest fortunes were made in the early reform era through regulatory arbitrage, by people purchasing things in the command economy system and selling them at a higher price in the market economy (in this case I do use the term in the narrow sense, with its contemporary negative connotation). Jiang Jishi and his fellow naval officers from Fuquan in the Ming would have been right at home in the PLA Navy of the 1980s and 1990s, in which smuggling and collusion with smugglers was rife.[39]

Among the three observations I made above—concerning contracts, informal institutions, and the use of state language—the third at least seems to retain a certain validity today—and is certainly the one most noticed when I talk about the subject in front of Chinese audiences. In the Maoist period, people continued to use state vocabulary deliberately to frame their political claims, and they still do so today.[40] For example, in some parts of China one finds newly rebuilt local temples that also house "recreation centers for the elderly" and "folklore research centers." Gao Bingzhong explains that when organizers rebuild a temple whose legal status is ambiguous, they deliberately create an unambiguously legitimate social organization at the same time. He calls this phenomenon "double-naming." The temple organizers take advantage of one regulatory regime—that governing activities for the elderly or folklore studies—to secure authorization in another—popular religion. Robert Weller develops this argument further with the notion of blind-eyed governance, a "don't ask, don't tell" attitude on the part of the government to social forms and actions that are outside the strict letter of the law but are nonetheless tolerated. He suggests that officials turning a blind eye is actually a fundamental principle of politics in contemporary China.[41] But it is also a modern analogue of the reliance on informal management in the Ming.

Another parallel in linguistic practice lies in the contemporary repertoire of protest. Elizabeth Perry, criticizing the notion that contemporary protest reflects a developing rights consciousness in public discourse, agues that what seems to be a consciousness of rights is actually a consciousness of rules. Protestors know the importance of "playing by the rules . . . adopting official language to signal that one's protest does not question the legitimacy of the central state."[42] The contentious issues that drove the theoretical insights of Gao, Weller, and Perry—house churches, environmental protection, and so forth—do not have obvious analogues in late imperial society. But looking at how local communities inhabited, manipulated, and deformed state institutions in service of their own interests suggests intriguing parallels in the everyday politics of state-society relations. Perry writes that protestors in China are simply "parroting" the language of the state, as do their counterparts in many other places. But we can also see this creative use of language as part of a longer history of indigenous structures of living with the Chinese state. It would be unproductive to devote much time to these similarities; "working the system" is not a uniquely Chinese phenomenon. But to the extent that the ways in which ordinary people in late imperial times secured and pursued their interests and the ways their claims-making proceeded without reference to legal rights have some bearing on their political struggles in the present day, these modes of politics are not a primitive relic produced by an unchanging culture, but rather the product of their long history of interaction with states old and new.

Whether or not there are continuities between Ming everyday strategies and contemporary ones is not a question I can answer decisively. But there can be no doubt that the former had enduring legacies for social institutions and social relations. The consequences of the strategies used by military households did not end with the fall of the Ming, and the evidence for them is found not only in libraries and archives. We can still see traces of them in the Chinese countryside today.

Ming military policy moved individuals and families from one place to another. It lifted people out of the social settings they knew and placed them in new ones. This in turn generated efforts to create new social relationships and new communities; deterritorialization spawned reterritorialization. Members of military households who were not serving soldiers sought to maintain ties—sometimes over long distances and many generations—with their kin who were. Once they had settled in a guard, battalion, or affiliated colony, soldiers joined or formed communities of interest and ultimately of identity with their fellow soldiers and the previous inhabitants, through marriage practices, temple networks, participation in the examination system, and a host of other practices. The movement of people in Ming China thus led to the disruption of communities and the linking of spaces that had not previously been linked, the transformation of existing communities and the creation of new ones. State interventions and the responses of people affected by those interventions generated transformations in the architecture of social space. These transformations persisted after the instititutions that gave rise to them were long gone, in some cases lasting to the present day. By relating these legacies to the phenomena that drove them, we can actually see the processes that went into the making of local society in late imperial times. Following a temple procession route or assembling evidence of the history of a lineage alliance proves to be not only a way to better understand everyday politics long ago, but also a way to link past and present in Chinese society.

The challenge for historians to give voice to those people in history who stood outside hegemonic structures of domination is sometimes framed as a question of whether the subaltern can speak.[43] Since the original meaning of the term "subaltern" was a low-ranking officer, is there anyone better than the subjects of this book about whom we can ask this question? Can the Ming subaltern speak? The genealogies, stone inscriptions, and other family documents of this book are part of a vast-dispersed archive that provides an extraordinary and insufficiently utilized resource for the social history of rural China. They make it possible for us to trace the history of ordinary people back many centuries. Of course the voice of the Ming subaltern in the genealogies and other sources reaches us through texts; it is not unmediated. But there is also another way for us to listen. The procession festivals I have described here are today gaudy affairs, with *qipao*-clad women, "artillery trucks," and neon lights. But underneath this cacophony are murmurs—so quiet they are easily missed—when the parade route turns this way and not that, when the women from this village bring offerings but those from that village do not. These are indeed messages transmitted from the soldiers of the Ming. The only way to access these materials and create the archive that makes it possible to tell this story is through the work of local history—to visit the communities where these rituals are being performed even in times of extraordinary change, to read the materials that community members have preserved in the face of danger and difficult odds, and to listen to the descendants of the Ming subjects of this book tell their own stories about their ancestors.

In Pinghai, the God of the Wall is once again taking his annual tour of the community, as he has done for centuries. The villagers' ears are ringing from the cannons and their eyes are watery from the firecrackers. The path of the procession has been swept clean to ensure the purity of the ritual; now it is dotted red with the blood of the spirit mediums, who demonstrate their imperviousness to pain by piercing and cutting their bodies. The children of the village scurry around to get the best view of the spectacle; their grandmothers pull them away to shelter them from the baleful influence of the spirits. As the young men of the village carry the god and the various symbols of his authority, they recall the founding of their town by the god in his human form, more than six centuries ago. They commemorate and enact their identity as townsfolk and their distinctiveness from the villages around them. The organizers know that they should call the procession festival "intangible cultural heritage" or "popular culture," lest the authorities label it instead as "feudal superstition." Organizers and participants alike subtly commemorate and enact a distinctive mode of everyday politics, an art of being governed that they share with people in China past, present, and perhaps future.

ACKNOWLEDGMENTS

IF I HAD A PERSONAL MAXIM as a historian, it would be what the great Chinese historian Fu Yiling used to tell his students: "you can't study history only in a library." The historian who adopts such an approach incurs a lot of debts. My greatest are to the Chinese people who have helped me learn more about their history. They include farmers and factory workers, village party secretaries and county cadres, lineage elders and temple mediums. I often wonder what I would do if a stranger knocked on my door and asked to talk about my ancestors or see my private family papers. Hundreds of people in rural China have responded to just such a request with warmth, courtesy, and endless tea and oranges. They have guided me on walks through their neighborhood, dug out their genealogies, and turned the pages as I photographed their family records. I am very grateful to all of them.

I am also very grateful to the colleagues who have accompanied me on trips to the countryside and patiently shared with me their knowledge of local history. Many are scholars at Xiamen University: Gao Zhifeng, Huang Xiangchun, Lin Changzhang, Liu Yonghua, Rao Weixin, Zhang Kan, Zheng Li, and Zheng Zhenman; others include Chen Chunsheng, Cheng May-bo, Ding Yuling, Liu Zhiwei, Wang Lianmao, Yang Peina, Yu Zhijia, and Zhao Shiyu.

Many friends and colleagues have read some or all of the manuscript and offered their comments. They include Peter Bol, Sam Clark, Nara Dillon, Mark Elliott, Fred Grant, Francine McKenzie, and Eric Schluessel (and I apologize in advance if I have left someone out). Chen Song, Maura Dykstra, Siyen Fei, Devin Fitzgerald, Joanna Handlin-Smith, David Howell, Elisabeth Koll, Robert Weller, and Zhao Shiyu participated in a book workshop, kindly funded by the Fairbank Center for Chinese Studies (of which I was not at the time director!) and provided detailed and helpful advice. I wish to single out for special thanks two fellow historians of the Ming, David Robinson and Sarah Schneewind, who generously read the entire text with great care.

The wonderful staff of the Fairbank Center for Chinese Studies helped make a congenial environment in which to finish the book. Jeff Blossom prepared most of the beautiful maps. My old friend Jiang Bowei was kind enough to share some of his detailed architectural drawings, which were reworked to illustrate the layout of the garrisons. Wang Weichu and John Wong collaborated with me on some critical parts of the research. Lu Cheng-heng (Rex) found and copied a genealogy that was crucial to part of my argument. Jiang Nan and Li Ren-yuan generously shared valuable sources.

I may not work *only* in a library, but I am fortunate to work some of the time in one of the greatest libraries for Chinese studies anywhere, the Harvard-Yenching Library. Its remarkable resources include people as well as books. Ma Xiaohe and Kuniko McVey in particular helped me to obtain some rare works for this project.

I thank the Chiang Ching-kuo Foundation for support for the early phases of research for the book, and the James P. Geiss Foundation and the Harvard University Department of History for subventions to support publication. It has been a pleasure working with Princeton University Press. I thank Brigitta van Rheinberg and her excellent team, including Amanda Peery, Brittany Micka-Foos, and Debbie Tegarden. Bruce Tindall prepared the index.

I have presented portions of this work at the following institutions: Xiamen University, National Taiwan University, Academia Sinica, Georgetown University, University of Pennsylvania, National University of Singapore, Columbia University, Guangdong University of Finance and Economics, Chinese University of Hong Kong, Harvard University, University of Toronto, Ohio State University and the Education University of Hong Kong. I thank my hosts at these institutions for inviting me and the audiences for stimulating discussions.

I dedicate this book to three teachers: Tim Brook, who first introduced me to the study of Chinese history; David Faure, who taught me that to study Chinese history one ought to go to China; and Zheng Zhenman, who taught me that to study Chinese society one ought to go to its villages. Their guidance has made me into a historian, and I am deeply grateful to each of them for their support over years and decades.

I am grateful in a different but even more profound way to Francine, Robert, and Kathleen.

baihu company commander 百戶
Balang Eighth gentleman 八郎
bazong squad leader 把總
bendihua localization 本地化
chengding succeed to substitution/to take over a military allotment 承頂
Chenghuang God of the Wall 城隍
congzheng fellow campaigners, early adherents of Zhu Yuanzhang 從征
Danmin Dan boat dwellers 蜑民
Dawang Great King 大王
deye jun soldier by virtue of having acquired property 得業軍
diao transfer 調
difanghua localization 地方化
ding adult male 丁
dingzhong to substitute as cultivator of a military allotment 頂種
fangzu er maoding zhi bi "the problem of false substitution of collateral kin"
　房族而冒頂之弊
fen share [of colony allotment] 分
fenjia household division 分家
fenxiang division of incense 分香
Folangji Franks/Portugese 佛郎機
fu guye "recover the old property" 復古業
fuji attaching registration 附籍
gong public 公
guanding fiscal male 官丁
Guan Shixian Guan Virtuous through the Generations 關世賢
Guan Yongmao Guan Ever-Flourishing 關永茂
guifu submitters [to Zhu Yuanzhang]/the former troops of his defeated rivals 歸附
haose fondness for women/sex 好色
hu household 戶
Huangce Yellow Register 黃冊
huomai conditional/live sale 活賣
jia unit of ten households in *lijia* system 甲
jiangji to descend to communicate [through planchette writing] 降乩
jiji temporary registration 寄籍
Jinhua gong Master Jinhua 金華公
Jiulihu xiangong Sages of Nine Carp Lake 九鯉湖仙公
jun soldier 軍
junhu military household 軍戶
junhua soldier dialect 軍話
junji military registration/military-registered 軍籍

junjia military tithings 軍甲

junmin soldiers and civilians 軍民

junshu soldier-uncles 軍叔

junyao military service record 軍徭

junyu supernumerary 軍餘

junzhuang military subsidy 軍裝

Kaishan Miao Temple of Opening Up the Mountain 開山廟

kaizhong grain-salt exchange system 開中

lao basket 栳

li unit of 110 households in the *lijia* system 里

li'an create a record 立案

lianghu guizong allocate [responsibilities of] tax-paying households to the patriline 糧戶歸宗

lijia system of household registration 里甲

Linshui furen Lady of Linshui 臨水夫人

lizhang headman in the *lijia* system 里長

Longxian Dragon Immortal 龍仙

Lufu furen Lady Lufu 魯府夫人

maigang selling the harbor 賣港

ming name [term for a single unit of colony allotment] 名

nüxu jun soldier by virtue of being a son-in-law 女婿軍

paoche mobile artillery 炮車

pidian hire as tenant 批佃

qianhu battalion commander 千戶

qidao cult of the Banner 旗纛

qijia banner-head, a minor functionary in the military colony system 旗甲

qingli zhi dangran "in accord with both particularities and principle" 情理之當然

renao hot and noisy 熱鬧

renzu recognize common ancestry 認祖

Sanshan guowang Cult of the Kings of the Three Mountains 三山國王

shenghu flourishing household 盛戶

sheren houseman (supernumerary of a hereditary officer household) 舍人

shouyu qianhu suo independent battalion 守禦千戶所

shuhang more senior generation 叔行

shuizhai maritime fort 水寨

Shuntian shengmu Sage Mother who Follows Heaven 順天聖母

si private 私

suo battalion 所

tiaoli substatute 條例

tie auxiliary 貼

tie form 帖

tongxing jun soldier by virtue of having the same surname 同姓軍

tun military colony 屯

tuntian military colony lands 屯田

tunzhi military colony record 屯誌

wei guard 衛

weiji guard registration 衛籍
weiren man of the guard 衛人
weisuo guards and battalions/the military system 衛所
weixuanbu military register 衛選簿
weixue guard school 衛學
wokou [Japanese] pirates 倭寇
wuyao zaiwu shengu "it is his duty to die in the ranks" 務要在伍身故
xianghua flower and incense [Buddhism] 香花
xiaojia headman in the military colony system 小甲
xiehuo collecting [incense] fire 擷火
Xuantian shangdi Supreme Emperor of the Dark Heavens 玄天上帝
xunfu grand coordinator (effective provincial governor) 巡撫
xunjiansi police office 巡檢司
yangfeng yinwei overt compliance; covert disobedience 陽奉陰違
yi'nan adopted son 義男
Yingtian zunwang Venerated King who Responds to Heaven 應天尊王
Yingwu Heroic Martiality 英武
Yingwu zunwang Venerated King of Heroic Martiality 英武尊王
yuanji junhu military households [residing in] the original place of registration
    原籍軍戶
yuliang surplus tax in the military colony system 餘糧
Zhang gong Master Zhang 章公
zhaofu pacification 招撫
zheng primary 正
zhengjun serving soldier 正軍
zhengliang basic tax in the military colony system 正糧
Zhenwu Perfected Martiality 真武
zhihui shi guard commander 指揮史
zizhihua local autonomy 自治化
zongfa descent-line system 宗法
zonghu general household 總戶
zongzi descent-line heir 宗子

Introduction. A Father Loses Three Sons to the Army

1. Weber is the usual locus classicus for this position: "A state is a human community that (successfully) claims the monopoly of the legitimate use of physical force within a given territory." "Politics as a Vocation," 78.

2. Indeed, some scholars see it shaping the very nature of modern state formation. As Tilly puts it, "war made the state and the state made war," *The Formation of National States in Western Europe*, 42; see also Roberts, *The Military Revolution 1560–1660*. For a typology of state approaches to conscription, albeit with an emphasis on modern states, see Levi, "Conscription: The Price of Citizenship."

3. Composite households are discussed in more detail in chapter 1.

4. *Ming Xuanzong shilu* 3/2/2 (1428), in *Ming shilu*, 36:892. Citations to the Ming shilu (*Veritable Records of the Ming*) are in the form: imperial reign, date (year of the Western calendar), *juan* number: page number according to the *Hanji quanwen ziliaoku (Scripta Sinica)* database.

5. "Ji Wuji," in *Yanshi zupu*, 119*ff*. Where possible, citations to genealogies include the title of the essay or subsection being cited.

6. He passed the provincial examination in 1604 and held a series of posts, the highest of which was prefect of Chuxiong in Yunnan. Ironically, this unsettled region was the very place to which many soldiers from his home region of Quanzhou were transferred.

7. Foucault seeks to resolve a similar dilemma with the term "counter-conduct," but I find this term unsatisfactory because it still overemphasizes opposition. *Security, Territory, Population*, 260. Elsewhere he writes of "the art of not being governed like that and at that cost" and "the art of not being governed quite so much," which is unsatisfactory for the same reason. "What Is Critique?", 45.

8. Kerkvliet, "Everyday Politics in Peasant Societies (and Ours)," 232.

9. Foucault, "Governmentality"; Scott, *The Art of Not Being Governed*.

10. Rosenthal and Wong propose, following Hirschman, that if people in late imperial China were ever truly dissatisfied, they would have tried to reformulate their relationship with the state through some combination of strategies of "exit" and "voice." I will argue below that this way of thinking about possible strategies is too narrow. The reformulation of the relationship went on all the time, as people pursued strategies that they believed would serve their own interests. *Before and Beyond Divergence*, 211.

11. Hobsbawm, "Peasants and Politics," 7.

12. For some estimates of the scale of desertion, Xu Xianyao, "Mingdai de goujun," 139–40.

13. Scott, *Weapons of the Weak*; Sivaramakrishnan, "Some Intellectual Genealogies for the Concept of Everyday Resistance."

14. Deleuze and Guattari, *Anti-Oedipus*, 34–35; *Nomadology*, 65–68.

15. Chinese scholars often use the term "localization" (*difanghua* or *bendihua*) to describe the process I call reterritorialization. See for example Lin Changzhang, "Ming-Qing dongnan yanhai." The other main sense of the term deterritorialization—to signify that, under conditions of contemporary globalization, various types of interactions such as financial transactions do not occur in any particular place—is different from the usage here. Scholte, *Globalization: A Critical Introduction*, 17, 75–78.

16. Taylor, "Yüan Origins of the Wei-So System."

17. Farmer, *Zhu Yuanzhang*, 10.

18. Ibid., 16–17; Tackett, "A Tang-Song Turning Point," 3; Deng Xiaonan, *Zuzong zhi fa*, ch. 4, and for the consequences, ch. 6.

19. For example, "the second and related significance of the Ming founding was the enhanced concentration of power in the imperial institution: Ming autocracy." Farmer, *Zhu Yuanzhang*, 100. In the Chinese literature, see Fan Wenlan and Cai Meibiao, *Zhongguo tongshi*, vol. 8, especially ch. 1.

20. For a discussion of the intellectual background to this position, see Struve, "Modern China's Liberal Muse: The Late Ming."

21. This has sparked new interest in state-society relations, including a largely fruitless attempt to identify an indigenous "public sphere" and "civil society" in the late Ming, as well as more productive accounts of negotiation between social actors and state agents, such as the ways in which the state was subject to "capillary" flows of influence from social networks or in which the social realm "colonized" state institutions. Brook, *The Chinese State in Ming Society*; Schneewind, *Community Schools and the State in Ming China*; Wang Fansen, *Quanli de maoxiguan zuoyong*.

22. Dreyer, "Military Origins of Ming China"; Li Huayan, "Jin sanshinian lai Ming-Qing ding'ge zhe ji junshishi yanjiu huigu." For a survey of the literature in Chinese, Zhang Jinkui, "Ershinian lai Mingdai junshi yanjiu huigu"; in Japanese, Kawagoe Yasuhiro, "Mingdai junshishi de yanjiu zhuangkuang."

23. Much of the Chinese language literature is strongly nationalistic; it criticizes the Ming, especially the late Ming, for subordinating martial valor and neglecting strategic concerns. Swope's recent revisionist approach challenges this narrative of decline and weakness, arguing that late sixteenth-century successes against the Japanese show that even towards the end of the dynasty there was nothing fundamentally wrong with its military. Swope, *A Dragon's Head and a Serpent's Tail*.

24. Johnston, *Cultural Realism*; Robinson, *Bandits, Eunuchs and the Son of Heaven*; Waldron, *The Great Wall of China*.

25. Yu Zhijia, *Weisuo, junhu yu junyi*, as well as many other works; Zhang Jinkui, *Mingdai weisuo junhu yanjiu*. Yu's 2010 book is a study of the military institution in Jiangxi but in my opinion is less interested in situating the study in relation to the local ecology of the province. In the substantial historiography on the Ming military, there is also a large body of work focusing on a single part of the larger system. One example is the grain-salt exchange (*kaizhong*) system, by which licenses to trade in salt were issued in exchange for supplying provisions to troops on the frontier. For example, Raymond Huang, "The Salt Monopoly," in his *Taxation and Governmental Finance*; this literature is reviewed in Puk, *The Rise and Fall of a Public Debt Market*, 13–18.

26. Geertz, *The Interpretation of Cultures*, 22.

27. In terms of Skinner's influential schema of macroregions of China, the bounds of this study correspond almost exactly to the core areas of the Southeast Coast macroregion.

28. For example, Clark, *Community, Trade and Networks*; Billy Kee-Long So, *Prosperity, Region and Institutions in Maritime China*; Zheng Zhenman, *Family Lineage Organization.*

29. An excellent study of urban guards is Luo, "Soldiers and the City."

30. Only a small fraction of the extant texts is to be found in public repositories such as libraries, of which the Shanghai Municipal Library is the largest. To give just one example, the most comprehensive catalog of Chinese genealogies, Wang Heming ed., *Zhongguo jiapu zongmu*, lists forty-seven known Anxi genealogies, of which the Shanghai library holds a single one. On a brief collection trip in 2012, I was able to photograph more than twenty genealogies from the single town of Hutou, one of twenty-four townships in the county. Only four of these even appear in the Wang Heming catalog. The Center for Research in Local Historical Documents at nearby Xiamen University has collected over a hundred genealogies from Hutou. Since even their collection is not exhaustive, this suggests that the total number of genealogies is some two orders of magnitude larger than the number in the catalog.

31. Joyner, *Shared Traditions: Southern History and Folk Culture*, 1.

Chapter 1. A Younger Brother Inherits a Windfall

1. Such special arrangements might include, for example, setting aside a dowry for an unmarried sister, an allowance to support an elderly mother, or a fund to pay for sacrifices to the parents after their death. See Wakefield, *Fenjia*. The legal requirement is discussed in Farmer, *Zhu Yuanzhang*, 159.

2. On the ways that lineages in late imperial times diverged from ancient principles, see Makino, *Kinsei Chūgoku*, 5–9

3. The genealogy does not say so explicitly, but these elaborate strategies suggest a possible explanation for the widow's decision to send her two younger sons back to Quanzhou beyond her devotion to her husband's memory. Perhaps they were sent away not just to care for the patriarch's grave, but also to insulate them from the family's military service obligations. "Jiapu xiaoyin," in *Zhangpu Liu'ao Yingli Rongyang Zhengshi zupu*, 8ff. A transcription of this text, as well as other unpublished texts used in this book, can be consulted at https://scholar.harvard.edu/szonyi/ABGreferences.

4. *Ming Taizong shilu* 27/8/21 (1404), in *Ming shilu*, 33:589; Wang Yuquan, *Mingdai de juntun*, 232; Zhang Songmei, "Mingchu jun'e kao," 47–52.

5. As it happens both of these are older genealogies, but these types of materials are often copied and recopied with every periodic recompilation of a genealogy. So even newly published genealogies sometimes contain much older texts within them, though of course these must be treated with care.

6. Freedman, *Chinese Lineage Society*, 31.

7. More recent analyses include Oakes, "The Alchemy of the Ancestors"; Pieke, "The Genealogical Mentality in Modern China"; Rao Weixin, "Daoyan: Zupu yu shehui wenhuashi yanjiu"; Zheng Zhenman, *Family Lineage Organization.*

8. Zemon Davis, *Fiction in the Archives*, 3. See also Stoler, *Along the Archival Grain*, 20.

9. The connection between population registration systems and military conscription in China goes back to the earliest references to registration in the sixth century BCE. von Glahn, "Household Registration, Property Rights, and Social Obligations."

10. On the study of these registers, see Wilkison, "Newly Discovered Ming Dynasty Guard Registers"; Yu Zhijia, *Mingdai junhu shixi zhidu*.

11. See Wenxian Zhang, "The Yellow Register Archives of Imperial Ming China"; Wei Qingyuan, *Mingdai huangce zhidu*; Luan Chengxian, *Mingdai huangce yanjiu*; Zhang Jinhong and Xu Bin, "Wang Jinghong jiqi houyi xintan."

12. The surname suggests they may have been descended from a prominent Arab family in the region in the Song dynasty. But this would not have had any significance with regard to recruitment.

13. *Zhongguo Mingchao dang'an zonghui*, vol. 64, 346–47.

14. Genealogies were updated and republished periodically—this process of continuous transmission is one reason for confidence in the reliability of information in them. Subsequent editions usually reprinted the prefaces to earlier ones, allowing us to trace the publication history of the work. The earliest preface in the extant edition dates from 1641, which tells us that Ni Wulang's descendants first compiled a genealogy no later than this date. "Shizu Wulang gong," in *Jinmencheng Nishi zupu*, 24.

15. This was not the only type of government soldier in Ming, but it is the only one that need concern us for the moment.

16. Langlois, "The Code and *Ad Hoc* Legislation in Ming Law," 102–12; Wu Yanhong, *Mingdai chongjun yanjiu*, 132–38.

17. Yang Peina argues that these drafts were also a way to bring people—such as non-Chinese groups—who had not previously been incorporated under state control. "Binhai shengji yu wangchao zhixu," 24–26.

18. *Ming Taizu shilu* 20/4/8 (1387), in *Ming shilu*, 181:2735; *Ming Taizu shilu* 20/11/13 (1387), 187:2799; *Minshu* 39:957. The number of sons a household happened to have in the 1380s could thus be consequential for the descendants for centuries to come. Yu Zhijia, "Zailun duoji yu chouji."

19. The different categories and ranks of officers in the Ming army are discussed in Liang Zhisheng, "Shixi Mingdai weisuo wuguan de leixing," 83.

20. *Ming Taizu shilu* 27/6/26 (1394), 233:3404–5.

21. *Xinghua fuzhi*, 48:1237; *Chongwu suochengzhi*, 20.

22. *Minshu* 39:957. The general rule is described in *DaMing Huidian*, 20:359.

23. There is an enormous literature on the definition of lineage in Chinese history. For a brief discussion, see Szonyi, "Lineages and the Making of Modern China," 436–41.

24. For the former position, Wang Yuquan, *Mingdai de juntun*, 236; for the latter, Yu Zhijia, "Mindai gunko no shakaiteki chii ni tsuite: gunko no kon'in o megutte;" Yu Zhijia, "Mindai gunko no shakaiteki chii ni tsuite: kakyo to ninkan ni oite."

25. Raymond Huang, *Taxation and Governmental Finance*, 36.

26. Yang Shiqi, "Lun goupu nanbei bianjun shu," in Chen Zilong, ed., *HuangMing jingshi wenbian*, 15:7a.

27. Ibid.; *DaMing Huidian*, 124:10a.

28. To put this another way, camp followers can have a reterritorializing effect on deterritorialized soldiers.

29. *Ming Taizu shilu* 7/10/27 (1374), 93:1628; *Ming Taizu shilu* 20/run6/7 (1387), 182:2752.

30. *Ming Taizong shilu* 15/5/27 (1417), 188:2005.

31. "Qijie junren shenkan qixiao" (1436), in Tan Lun, *Junzheng tiaoli*, 6:2b; Zhang Jinkui, "Junhu yu shehui biandong"; also see Yu Zhijia, "Shilun." The early Qing writer Pu Songling (1640-1715) offered a satirical take on this rule in a story set in the early fifteenth century, a dramatization of the life of Xue Lu. Xue was the unimpressive son of a military household, thought to be so dull-witted that he could not find a wife. But when it came time for the household to provide a conscript, he volunteered to go in his elder brother's place so long as the brother allowed him to marry a housemaid. The brother agreed, Xue and his wife went off to the garrison, and his subsequent bravery earned him a hereditary noble title. "Yangwu hou," in *Liaozhai zhiyi*, 5:188.

32. Shen Jing, *Shuangzhu ji*, 37-46.

33. See for example Robinson, *Bandits, Eunuchs and the Son of Heaven*, ch. 3, 163-64.

34. "Zhike gong lishu junyou," in *Fuzhou Guoshi zupu*, 10:6a-7a; *Fuzhou Guoshi zupu* 2:12b. See Szonyi, *Practicing Kinship*, 61-64.

35. *Yingqiao Wangshi zupu*, 6:140.

36. Faure describes several examples of what I label substitution strategies in the Pearl River Delta. The Zhao surname of Sanjiang village claimed descent from the Song imperial house, but this did not stop one of their number from being registered as a military household in the early Ming. When conscripted in 1391, he sent a "purchased son" to serve in his stead in a Nanjing garrison. Though the genealogy of the Guan family of Nanhai records that they were registered as a civilian household, they were also called upon to provide military labor. The obligation was fulfilled by two adopted sons. *Emperor and Ancestor*, 72-74.

37. "Guofang zinü tingbu fuwu," (1429), in Tan Lun, *Junzheng tiaoli*, 2:3a-3b.

38. On the translation of the term, see Jones, *The Great Qing Code*, 3.

39. *Yingqiao Wangshi zupu*, 6:140.

40. "Taichang gong zixu junyuanyou"; "Zheshu, gaishu, ji junzhuang ji," in *Qingxi Lishi jiapu*, 3:42a, 3:33a.

41. McKnight, *Village and Bureaucracy in Southern Sung China*, 158-68.

42. "Jinjiang Dalun Caishi zupu fulu quanshou," in *Shiyou Dalun Caishi zupu*, 1:20-22.

43. The text says this happened in the twentieth year of the Zhizheng reign, corresponding to 1294—a century before the establishment of the Ming dynasty—so this is obviously wrong. The actual date must have been miscopied at some point in the intervening seven centuries. A likely candidate for the actual date would be the second year of the Zhengtong reign, 1437, for two years later the assignment was transferred again to a guard in Guangzhou. The current edition, a printed one, is marred by multiple obvious errors of punctuation, including one in the very phrase where the date appears. Traditional genealogies, like other premodern texts written in classical Chinese, are generally unpunctuated, so it may be that the text was copied and typeset by someone who did not have mastery of classical Chinese.

44. "Wenshui Huangshi puxu," in *Huangshi zupu*, A14, B29–30.

45. "Xu," in *Jinghai Rongshi zupu*, 6.

46. "Junshi huding buxu lunti," (1436), in Tan Lun, *Junzheng tiaoli*, 2:8a–b.

47. Ibid., 2:22a–23a.

48. Ming regulations required military households to provide a soldier's allowance or subsidy (*junzhuang*) to their serving members. But the size of the subsidy and precisely whose responsibility it was to provide it are not specified, and the rule seems to have been little enforced. (For the text of the rule, "Wunian yisong junzhuang," in Huo Yi, *Junzheng tiaoli leikao*, 3:23a–24a.) Most crucially for our purposes, the sources from military households even when they use the term *junzhuang* for such payment invariably describe it not as an obligation but as a way to compensate family members for their efforts and discourage desertion. Wang Yuquan argues that the supernumerary who accompanied the serving soldier to the garrison was responsible for providing the allowance. This would mean that after the localization policy, household members living in the place of registration were free of any obligation to provide support after the serving soldier was sent on his way. *Mingdai de juntun*, 52.

49. These estimates are in line with William Guanglin Liu, *The Chinese Market Economy*, 180. See also Li Bozhong, *Agricultural Development in Jiangnan*, 125–32.

50. "Churong gongyi," in *Changle Zhuti Linshi zupu*. The alert reader will have noticed that this is a story about a man named Huang in a genealogy bearing the Lin surname. The explanation is that the wealthy member of the lineage who paid for the estate learned that the family had changed its surname to Huang in the early Ming and he requested of the emperor that he be allowed to "restore the surname." This boon was granted. The details are in Szonyi, *Practicing Kinship*, 64–68. It may well be that the attempt to change the surname was also linked to a desire to insulate the family from the consequences of the military registration. If so, this might be an elite version of what Guo Wei had done when he tried to alter the name on his own military registration.

51. On the Yuan origins of the composite household, Hsiao, *Military Establishment*, 19–27. Composite military households in Ming were formed when general drafts were imposed on households with few adult males; two or sometimes three households were conscripted together, with joint responsibility to provide a single serving soldier. See *Ming Taizong shilu* 35/12/13 (1402), 15:7713. On saltern-military households, see Rao Weixin, "Mingdai junzaoji kaolun." Rao thinks this was a deliberate strategy to optimize tax obligations. On saltern households in the region in general, see Ye Jinhua, "Ming-Qing zaohu."

52. Acharya and Richardson, "Causes of the Financial Crisis," 195–210.

Chapter 2. A Family Reunion Silences a Bully

1. For travel times in Ming, see Brook, "Communications and Commerce," 619–30.

2. Ye Xianggao, "Jiapu zongwu zhuan," in *Cangxia cao*, 15:29a–30b. Though this text comes to us from Ye's collected works, the title shows that it was written for inclusion in the genealogy.

3. "Kezhong gong," in *Shejiang yanpai Fuquan Chenshi zupu*.

4. Ibid.

5. Zheng Zhenman, *Ming Qing Fujian jiazu zuzhi yu shehui bianqian*, 243, translated in Zheng Zhenman, *Family Lineage Organization*, 288.

6. Feng Menglong, *Stories to Awaken the World*, translated by Shuhui Yang and Yunqin Yang, vol. 3, 205–25. Several examples from literature of Ming soldiers traveling to collect a payment from their kin are noted in Li Pengfei, "'Sanyan erpai' zhong."

7. Qi Biaojia, *Puyang yandu*, 193.

8. Zheng Ji, "Yu Pang Dacan shu," in *Fujian tongzhi*, 49:21a–b.

9. *Ming Xuanzong shilu* 1/6/12 (1426), 1:28; *Ming Xuanzong shilu* 2/1/18 (1427), 24:638; "Jinzhi weili wanggou wangjie," (1572), in Tan Lun, *Junzheng tiaoli* 5:34b–36a.

10. "Fujian dengchu cheng xuan Buzhengshisi Fuzhou fu Gutian xian niansan du di'er tu min" (1462), in *Wugongtang Boyuancun Sushi jiapu*, 15–16; Li Renyuan, "Making Texts in Villages," 126–30.

11. *Ming Xuanzong shilu* 3/2/16 (1428), 36:889–93.

12. "Zhike gong lishu junyou," in *Fuzhou Guoshi zupu*, 10:6a–7a.

13. "Tianfang Zhike gong di-er ci chongxiu zhipu xu," in *Fuzhou Guoshi zupu*, 1:14a–b.

14. "Ruiyun shiji ji," in *Ruiyun Yaoshi zupu*. Elsewhere in the genealogy, we learn that the Yao were first registered not under their own name but under a household of the Zheng surname. Perhaps they inadvertently inherited the military obligation through marriage or adoption, in other words that they became "soldiers by virtue of being a son-in-law (*nüxu jun*)" (on which see chapter 4).

15. "Ruiyun shiwu ji," in *Ruiyun Yaoshi zupu*; Li Ren-yuan, "Making Texts," ch. 3.

16. Chen Wenshi, "Mingdai weisuo de jun," 198.

17. Brook, "The Spatial Structure of Ming Local Administration," 30.

18. Kuhn, *Chinese among Others*, 14–16.

Chapter 3. An Officer in Cahoots with Pirates

1. *Ming Shizong shilu* 8/7/9 (1529), in *Ming shilu*, 103:2424 for the initial reporting; 8/12/16 (1529) 108:2551 for the subsequent investigation.

2. Ibid., 26/11/16 (1547), 330:6064. The episode also appears in Zhu Wan, *Piyu zaji*, 6:8a.

3. As I noted in chapter 1, on the southeast coast guards were physically located within counties and prefectures but were administered under a different system from the civilian one. Yongning lay in Jinjiang county, but it was under the jurisdiction of the military administrative hierarchy that reached all the way up to Chief Military Commissions in the capital. The civilian magistrate of Jinjiang had no formal authority over matters in the guard. The guard was in Jinjiang not of it. Commanders and magistrates had to develop many procedures to deal with issues that spanned the two administrative systems, including complex fiscal and judicial issues. For a specific example, see chapter 5.

4. "Jianzhi yange xiuli zhi," in *Nanyu Chenshi zupu*, 8b.

5. Many people outside of China know about Zheng He too, through Gavin Menzies's book *1421: The Year China Discovered the World*. Unfortunately not so many

know that most of the claims of the book have been thoroughly debunked. Zheng He's ships did not sail to America. See www.1421exposed.com.

6. On the tribute system in early Ming, see Wills, *Embassies and Illusions*, 14–23.

7. Li Kangying, *Ming Maritime Trade Policy*, 97–135.

8. On the abuse of power by officers in general, see Hucker, *The Censorial System*, 126–29. For some specific examples of the hard lot of garrison soldiers, *Ming Yingzong shilu* 8/7/20 (1443) in *Ming shilu*, 106: 2157; *Ming Yingzong shilu* 10/2/7 (1445), 126:2515.

9. "Fengling dingjian Lijiang Chenghuang miao beiji," inscription in Chenghuang temple, Puxi; Putian xian difangzhi biancuan weiyuanhui and Putian xian minsu xuehui, *Puxi suocheng zaji*, 45.

10. Zhu Wan, "Yueshi haifang shi," in Chen Zilong, ed., *HuangMing jingshi wenbian*, 205:2158.

11. Li Kangying, *Ming Maritime Trade Policy*, 177; So Kwan-wai, *Japanese Piracy*, 145–56.

12. Much of the scholarly literature agrees that the underlying issue was the tension between imperial rhetoric and the realities of the southeastern coastal region. But this tension had been present since the start of the dynasty. A satisfactory explanation for the emergence of the sixteenth-century crisis remains elusive. So Kwanwai, *Japanese Piracy*; Geiss, "The Chia-Ching Reign"; Higgins, "Piracy and Coastal Defense in the Ming Period." Chin speculates that the Portugese fought against the Ming military in support of their trading partners. "Merchants, Smugglers, and Pirates." Also see Calanca, *Piraterie et contrabande au Fujian*. For earlier studies, Lin Renchuan, *Mingmo Qingchu de siren haishang maoyi*; Zhang Bincun, "Shiliu shiji Zhoushan qundao zousi maoyi"; Chen Chunsheng, "Cong woluan dao qianhai."

13. Tu Zhonglü, "Yuwo wushishu," in Chen Zilong, ed., *HuangMing jingshi wenbian*, 282:2979; *Ming Shizong shilu* 34/5/9 (1555), 422:7310.

14. Zheng Ruozeng, *Chouhai tubian*, 11:4a, p. 819.

15. Dahpon Ho accurately characterizes the region in this period as a "frontierlike zone of dubious legality, a region both militarized and lacking in institutional means to resolve local conflicts or the increasing complexity of exchange and bribery without resort to violence." Ho, "Sealords Live in Vain," 81.

16. Reid, "Violence at Sea," 15. Dardess points out that they thus used the sea just as terrestrial bandits used mountains and peripheral areas—as sanctuary and place to launch their raids on coastal settlements. Chen Chunsheng takes Dardess's analogy further, arguing that the pirates and mountain bandits of Chaozhou were often the very same people, the differences in terms reflecting not distinctive groups of people but the particular choices the same people made at particular times. Dardess, *A Political Life in Ming China*, 95; Chen Chunsheng, "Mingdai qianqi Chaozhou haifang ji qi yingxiang," pt. 2, 46–52. For an intriguing argument that pirates could form "escape societies" similar to the upland societies of Scott's Zomia, see Joseph McKay, "Maritime Pirates as Escape Societies." McKay's analysis is weakened by the assumption of a strict divide between pirates and ordinary coastal residents.

17. Li Jinming, *Mingdai haiwai maoyi shi*, 80–108, 173–83; Lin Renchuan, *Mingmo Qingchu*, 40–84.

18. Zhu Wan, *Piyu zaji*, 3:38b; the phrase is repeated at 8:64a.

19. *Ming Shizong shilu* 4/8/17 (1525), 54:1332-33. The same phrase appears in the repeated prohibitions against private maritime trade. Thus, from the early years of the dynasty: "Soldiers and civilians are forbidden from private intercourse with foreign lands, or from going to sea themselves to trade in foreign goods." *Ming Taizong shilu* 5/6/1 (1407), 68:946.

20. *Ming Taizu shilu* 4/12/16 (1371), 70:1304; *Ming Taizong shilu* 5/5/29 (1407), 67:942; *Ming Xuanzong shilu* 9/3/14 (1434), 109:2448.

21. Zhu Wan, *Piyu zaji* 4:24b-25a. See also Yamazaki Takeshi, "Junbu Shu Gan no mita umi—Mindai Kasei nenkan no enkai eijo to 'Daiwakō' zenya no hitobito," 13-14.

22. *Zhongguo Mingchao dang'an zonghui*, vol. 4, 41.

23. Cai Jiude, *Wobian shilue* 2:9b; Wang Yu, "Tiaochu haifang shiyi yangqi suci shuxing shu," in Chen Zilong, ed., *HuangMing jingshi wenbian*, 283:2996. The Hongwu emperor's decision to rotate troop assignments away from their native place was reportedly provoked by a memorial that reported "the troops of the locality are strongly attached to their native place, leading to laxity in defense" (*Xinghua fuzhi*, 48:1237). Could this be a subtle reference to their turning a blind eye to smuggling by their fellow villagers?

24. *Ming Xuanzong shilu* 6/7/19 (1431), 81:1880-81.

25. Tu Zhiyao (*juren* 1654), reprinted in Yu Dazhu ed., *Yurong guqu*, 225.

26. There were some exceptions, for example when multiple members of a single military household were simultaneously conscripted. Later in the dynasty, surplus men were also often given the opportunity to serve in the military to fill depleted ranks.

27. *Ming Xuanzong shilu* 9/2/24 (1434), 108:2431; 9/3/1 (1434), 109:2439 for specific cases.

28. *Ming Taizong shilu* 2/2/22 (1404), 28:511, *Ming Xuanzong shilu* 7/9/7 (1434), 95:2148.

29. Biography of eighth-generation ancestor, name illegible, in *Fuquan Jiangshi Sifang Beisha Xupu*.

30. Hong Shou (fl. 1565-68), *Canghai jiyi*, 91.

31. Tan Lun (1520-77), cited in Zheng Ruozeng, *Chouhai tubian*, 11:22b-23a

32. Girard ed. and trans., *Le voyage en Chine d'Adriano de las Cortes (1625)*. Girard proposes a different identification for one of the places in which de las Cortes was held, but Nicolas Standaert, in a private communication, gives a more persuasive explanation that the places he mentions are the garrisons at Jinghai and Pengzhou.

33. *Ming Yingzong shilu* 10/2/7 (1445), 126:2515.

34. Fang was a one-time salt smuggler along the Zhejiang coast who became a successful pirate and smuggler. Repeatedly submitting to and then turning against the Yuan had allowed him to build up a personal empire of hundreds, perhaps thousands of vessels. In 1367, his nascent empire ran up against Zhu Yuanzhang's, and he negotiated a surrender. A few years later, in 1372, Zhu Yuanzhang ordered Fang's surviving followers conscripted and registered as military households. Goodrich and Fang, eds, *Dictionary of Ming Biography*, vol. 1, 433-35.

35. *Ming Taizu shilu* 25/12/18 (1392), 223:3262. Much the same happened a few years later, when Zhu Yuanzhang decided there was no dealing with the people of Jianguo county in Ningbo. Far too many of them, seemingly the entire population,

were involved in piracy. Zhu ordered the county abolished and the entire civilian population conscripted, registered, and placed under the authority of the local guard, where their seafaring experience would, in theory, be put to more legitimate use. *Ming Taizu shilu* 25/6/9 (1387), 182:2745.

36. On naval technology in Ming, see Needham, ed., *Science and Civilization in China*, vol. 4, pt. 3, 477ff.

37. "Fujian shiyi," in Zheng Ruozeng, *Chouhai tubian*, 4:20b.

38. *Ming Yingzong shilu* 5/12/5 (1440), 74:1433–34.

39. Zheng Lichun, *Zheng Duanjian gong nianpu*, 1:24b–26a.

40. Qiu Junqing (ca. 1520–91), cited in "Fujian shiyi," in Zheng Ruozeng, *Chouhai tubian*, 4:32a–b.

41. *Ming Xuanzong shilu* 8/7/8 (1433), 103:2308.

42. *Ming Xianzong shilu* 5/9/25 (1469) in *Ming shilu*, 71:1398.

43. "Yi shuizhai buyi ru Xiamen," in Hong Shou, *Canghai jiyi*, 40–42.

44. *Minshu*, 40:34a.

45. *Ming Xianzong shilu* 1/7/3 (1465), 19:379.

46. Wang Zaijin (*jinshi* 1592), *Haifang zuanyao*, 8:28b.

47. Dennis, *Writing, Publishing and Reading Local Gazetteers*, 121–26.

48. Biography of Jiang Jishi, in *Fuquan Jiangshi Sifang Beisha Xupu*. It is possible the entire file is a forgery. However, numerous other sources both internal and external to the genealogy make clear that the Jiang were indeed who they claim to be, hereditary military officers in Fuquan. So even if the file itself is fake, the outcome, the assignment of the lineage founder to Fuquan, is real. The genealogy in its present form may reflect the explosion of genealogical compilation in the Qing, which meant that all sorts of people who did not fully understand the conventions of the genre were busy compiling their genealogies. Printed genealogies record what must be recorded for the purposes of the family, so genealogies of military households rarely include stories of military exploits. Ordinarily we must look elsewhere for tales of enemies routed and heads captured. But the compilers of the Jiang genealogy do not seem to have understood this convention either.

49. Ibid.

50. Robinson, *Bandits, Eunuchs, and the Son of Heaven*, 164–68; Tagliacozzo, *Secret Trades, Porous Borders*, 5–6. Robinson is responding in part to Tong's earlier study of illegality in Ming, *Disaster under Heaven*.

51. Wan Biao (1498–1556), *Haikou yi*, 3a. See also Yamazaki Takeshi, "Junbu Shu Gan no mita umi."

52. Li Kangying, *Ming Maritime Trade Policy*, 177.

53. In a style typical of Ming cases, Yan's account ends by trailing off into questions of accounting. The cargo was a huge haul; the total value of trade goods amounted to almost ten thousand taels. What standard should be used in calculating the value of the goods? Since the goods were to be confiscated, this created a difficult situation. Unless the value of the goods was specified precisely, how could the investigators be sure the amounts for goods confiscated and goods received matched? The text ends with a request for instruction from higher-level officials about how to handle the matter. Yan Junyan (*jinshi* 1621 or 1628), *Mengshui zhai cundu*, 699–702. A similar case in the same work involves merchants claiming to be company commanders, 77.

54. *Chongzhen changbian* 5/1/1 (1632) in *Ming shilu*, 55:3183ff.

55. Girard, *Le voyage en Chine d'Adriano de las Cortes (1625)*, 242.

56. Cai Jiude, *Wobian shilue*, 2:1b.

57. "Zhejiang wobian ji," in Zheng Ruozeng, *Chouhai tubian*, 5:26b.

58. Gu Yanwu, *Tianxia junguo libing shu*, 26:2332. Local lore in Dongshan has it that a famous defeat of the Portugese was made possible when soldiers disguised their ship as a merchant vessel to lure in the enemy. Sun Wenlong, ed., *Dongshan wenwu mingzheng zhi*, 8.

59. *Fuquan Jiangshi jiamiao*, 5; *Yongning Nanmenjing Lishi zupu*. We might also consider the story of the Minh-huong, several thousand loyalist Ming soldiers and their families who left China and settled in Vietnam as the Ming was collapsing. Li Tana, "An Alternative Vietnam?"

Chapter 4. An Officer Founds a School

1. *Jinjiang xianzhi*, 7:14b.

2. Peng's mother was the great-granddaughter of a famous scholar from nearby Nan'ge village, Zhang Lun (1413–83).

3. "Bashizu Laiyi Donghuan gong lüli," in *Puqi Heshi zupu*.

4. Zheng Ji, "Yu Pang Dacan shu," in *Fujian tongzhi*, 49:21b–22a.

5. *Mingshi*, 158:4309.

6. *Puqi Heshi zupu*.

7. Qi Wenying has used epigraphy to good effect to recover marriage patterns of soldiers in the north, but there is little relevant epigraphy from the southeast coastal region. "Beiming suojian Mingdai daguan hunyin guanxi."

8. Hong Shou, *Canghai jiyi*, 94. Genealogies of officer families like the Puqi He include many biographies of "exemplary" women like Qiu Yinniang who killed themselves to demonstrate their chaste devotion to their husbands. Qiu was from a poor family, but women who were willing to make this sacrifice were probably more likely to come from literati families. To the degree that this generalization is true, it confirms that officer families were increasingly marrying not just families in the locality, but elite families. In terms of the marriage market, officer status had become just one of the ways by which families indicated their status and therefore shaped the pool of possible spouses.

9. *Anxi xianzhi* (1757), 9:6a. The story of the family's evacuation from their home and conscription is related in *Minshu*, 6:18a.

10. "Houshan miao Longxian gong ji," in *Anxi Hushi zupu*, 1460–61; *Anxi xianzhi* (1552), 2:6b.

11. "Xinjian Xia Chen xiaozongci xu," (1806), inscription at Yongning.

12. *Yingyang Panshi zupu*, 108. The Pan ancestor certainly settled in Jinxiang; the claim that he was an officer is more dubious.

13. ter Haar, "The Religious Core of Local Social Organization."

14. A fourth type also appears in the sources, but has disappeared and is no longer part of communal life today. The cult of the Banner (*qidao*), a military cult of great antiquity, was mandated for all Ming guards. But of the more than a dozen Banner temples, including one in Tongshan, reported in a fifteenth-century gazetteer, not a

single one survives. (On the mandating of the cult of the Banner, *Mingshi*, 50:1301–2; on the distribution of its temples in the fifteenth century, *BaMin tongzhi*, j58–59; on the installation of the cult in the temple of the God of the Wall of Chongwu, "Fuxiu Chenghuang miao xu," (1717), in *Chongwu suochengzhi*, 123; on the cult in Tongshan, *Tongshan zhi*, 336. For discussion, see Guo Hong, "Mingdai de qidao zhi ji.") Of course the gods discussed here do not even begin to exhaust the range of religious forms in Fujian past and present; I do not consider sectarian traditions, monastic traditions, Islam and Christianity, or private devotional altars, any and all of which are to be found in some former guards and battalions. Here I discuss only communal temples in which all the members of the community participate or are expected to participate.

15. *Tongshan zhi*, 315.

16. Another example of a cult brought by soldiers is the cult of Lady Linshui (*Linshui furen*) in Fuquan, almost certainly brought there by soldiers from Fuzhou when they were transferred there. The Lady Linshui is the apotheosis of a Tang-era woman from the Fuzhou region who became an important figure in the Lüshan Daoist tradition and is particularly associated with easing the troubles of childbirth. Her cult is among the most important in the Fuzhou region. She is worshipped in a few temples elsewhere in the Putian region, but generally under different names—either *Lufu furen* or *Shuntian Shengmu*. The use of the Fuzhou name by Fuquan residents suggests that she is also a deity who was brought by the soldiers, and local folklore is clear on this point.

17. They are today a prominent cult in Taiwan, taken there by Hakka migrants.

18. Today they are worshipped in a temple called the Temple of the Great Envoy. The chief deity of the temple is Chen Zheng, the apotheosis of a historical figure who lived in the seventh century. Together with his better-known son, Yuanguang, Chen Zheng is celebrated for leading an army from central China to southern Fujian to establish Tang rule over the region. Chen Yuanguang is widely venerated as the "Great Sage Who Pacified Zhangzhou," the region in which Tongshan Guard was situated. It would be tempting to speculate that Chen Zheng was also a preexisting cult in the region even before the soldiers arrived there, but he is also worshipped in Putian so there is a chance the soldiers from Putian were already familiar with his cult even before they were assigned to Tongshan. But the Kings of the Three Mountains must have been new to them.

19. The 1516 inscription commemorating the reconstruction shows this transformation from official to communal temple: "In 1388, a wall was built around Tongshan in order to defend against pirates. An image [of the god] was carved and sacrificed to, that he might protect the officers and soldiers. The officers and soldiers relied on [the god]. Later officials came in constant succession. Those making prayers, holding festivals and asking fortunes might number as many as several dozen at one time. People all regretted that [the shrine was too small] to contain them all. There were good-hearted people who wished to address this, but the project was large and the funding was difficult. In 1508, Wu Ziyue of Yunxiao together with the good man Hong Zongji and eight others gathered funds from the people to reconstruct the temple." *Tongshan zhi*, 336; "Dingjian Tongcheng Guanwang miao" (1516), inscription in Dongshan Guandi temple (the former Tongshan battalion is today located

in Dongshan county, created in 1916). Lord Guan is today more commonly known as Emperor Guan, Guandi. But Guan Yu's spirit was only given the title "Emperor" by command of the terrestrial emperor in 1615. This inscription, carved a century before the god's elevation to the imperial title, refers to him as King Guan. On the history of Guan Yu's titles, culminating in Guandi, see Duara, "Superscribing Symbols"; ter Haar, *Guan Yu.*

20. We have already met the God of the Wall of Pinghai, in the Introduction.

21. *BaMin tongzhi*, j79. On the early history of these cults see Johnson, "The City God Cults of T'ang and Sung China"; on Ming, see Taylor, "Official Altars, Temples and Shrines."

22. Hou Fang, "Jinshan wei chenghuang miaoji," cited in Xu Shuang, "Fujian chenghuang xinyang yanjiu," 29. People today, conscious that their temples might appear to usurp the privileges of places higher up in the administrative hierarchy, use the same justifications as their Ming ancestors. Guards and Battalions, I am often told, are walled. Therefore, they must have their own God of the Wall.

23. Hamashima Atsutoshi, "Communal Religion in Jiangnan," 154–56.

24. Curiously this is not the county in which Fuquan is located, but rather where many of Fuquan's military colonies were located. On military colonies, see chapters 5 and 6.

25. Wang Mingming, "Place, Administration and Territorial Cults," 64–65.

26. In Ningcheng and Hai'an in Wenzhou, the God of the Wall is Zhou Dexing's Zhejiang equivalent: Tang He, the early Ming official who built the guards there (see chapter 1). Residents of the town today say that Tang He initially had a terrible reputation in the surrounding area because of his merciless conscription of local labor to build the walls of the guard. But people changed their minds about him when the pirates came. They realized they owed their lives to his farsightedness. Entry for 1940/2/28 in Zhang Gang, *Zhang Gang riji.* I thank Lo Shih-chieh for bringing this reference to my attention.

27. In Meihua, the main deity is known as "Great King" (*dawang*), the term used by the villages in the area for their tutelary deity, rather than God of the Wall. He too was a member of a local military household, an officer who distinguished himself in the defense of the community against the pirates.

28. Elman, *A Cultural History of Civil Examinations*, 127.

29. Cai Jialin, *Mingdai de weixue jiaoyu*, 102–6.

30. *BaMin tongzhi*, 55:276.

31. Tang Shuyi et al., *Qian shi jilue*, 9:160–61.

32. *Putian xianzhi*, 9:13a–b; *Xinghua fuzhi*, 15:14a–b.

33. *Shishi shizhi* (1998), 733.

34. Zhang Yi (*jinshi* 1415), "Xinjian Zhenhai, Taicang weixue ji," in Qian Gu, *Wudu wencui xu ji*, 7:16a.

35. On the related term "guard registration" (*weiji*), see Gu Cheng, "Tan Mingdai de weiji."

36. A well-known case is the former guard located at Zhongshan town in Wuping county in southwestern Fujian, where the local dialect still has traces of Gan dialect from Jiangxi. See Zhuang Chusheng, "Shilun Hanyu fangyan dao"; Huang Xiaodong, "Hanyu junhua gaishu."

37. "So up to the present the soldiers of coastal garrisons do not speak the dialect of their prefecture, but still maintain the tongue of their ancestors." *Minshu*, 40:25a; "The ancestors of [the people of Zhenhai] Guard are all from Putian, so they still esteem the Putian dialect," *Zhangzhou fuzhi* (1572), 33:697. Wen Duanzheng, *Cangnan fangyanzhi*, 28–29, 202–4.

38. Individual village reports in an anthropological survey of the area show that the differences are striking. In the town itself, there is no evidence of delayed transfer marriage or the wearing of the distinctive Hui'an costume, but both are reported in a village only one kilometer away (where delayed transfer marriage "has a long history") as well as in a nearby fishing village (where women wear the traditional costume "like in the other villages outside the walls of Chongwu"). The editors ascribe the differences to "urbanization," but this explanation is unconvincing. Chen Guoqiang and Shi Yilong eds, *Chongwu renleixue diaocha*, 81, 123, 167.

Chapter 5. A Soldier Curses a Clerk

1. The genealogy records that this happened at a place called Yanjin; this must be an error for Yanping.

2. Fazhen is said to have have been transferred to Yongtai in 1404 and the clerks took their revenge almost fifty years later. It may be that the problems between the men developed in the intervening decades and that Fazhen was already an old man when he was attacked. A more likely explanation is that the date of the transfer is incorrect. Perhaps by the time the genealogy was compiled, the exact date had been forgotten, but since it was widely known that the military colony policies had been reformed in 1404, the compilers hit upon this as the most likely date for their ancestors' arrival. *Linyang Yanshi jiapu*, 3:1a–2b.

3. Affinal kin were critical to the survival of other family members: "Jin survived because of his mother Li"; "Yu survived because of his maternal uncle Lin." Even the boy who was sold was later rescued by his aunt's husband, who tracked him down and redeemed him. Ibid., 1:3b; 3:2a.

4. Ibid., 4:2b.

5. Master Jinhua's name does not appear in the records of his native place or either of the places he is reputed to have served—though it is possible his name was expunged after his disgrace. His name does appear in county gazetteers from the Yanping area, but this does not really tell us much; the story could have made its way into the gazetteers through his descendants.

6. Ibid., 3:10a, 4:2b–3a.

7. For a theoretical account, see Margaret Levi, "Conscription: The Price of Citizenship."

8. *Ming Shenzong shilu* 17/10/1 (1589) in *Ming shilu*, 587:11239.

9. The conventional translation for the term *tuntian*, "military colony," is more apt for guards on the frontier. There the colonies were generally geographically concentrated; their residents lived together in their own settlements, and their officers were often the chief or even the sole political authority. The situation was very different in Fujian and other provinces of the interior. There the institution had little to do with our usual understanding of the word "colony." Soldiers of the colony lived dispersed

among the existing population, and the lands they worked were not concentrated together but scattered among civilian fields. But I will stick with the conventional translation in the absence of an obvious alternative. See Wang Yuquan, *Mingdai de juntun*; Liew, *Tuntian Farming*, 2-5.

10. "Zutun," in *Anxi Hushi zupu*, 1417.

11. This was probably the terms of recruitment, but it is also possible that this was an arrangement they worked out amongst themselves. See *Ming Taizong shilu* 3/2/11 (1405), 39:652.

12. Liew, *Tuntian Farming*, ch. 4; Ma Wensheng (1462–1510), "Qing tuntian yi fu jiuzhi shu," in Chen Zilong, ed., *HuangMing jingshi wenbian*, 63:3a–5b.

13. *DaMing Huidian*, 18:334–35.

14. "Zutun," in *Anxi Hushi zupu*, 1417–18.

15. *Ming Xuanzong shilu* 4/2/19 (1429), 51:1224–25; *Ming Yingzong shilu* 1/6/11 (1436), 18:356. Recall that unpaid rations were to blame for the riots in Panshi mentioned at the start of chapter 3.

16. Zhu Jian, "Qing jian tunjun zimi, jinge jianbi shu," in Chen Zilong, ed., *HuangMing jingshi wenbian*, 35:261–62. Similar complaints are made in "Yingzhao chenyan tuntian shu," by Lin Xiyuan, a native of Tong'an, a man who has come up already several times in this work. Ibid., 163:20b–6b.

17. On which see Puk, *The Rise and Fall of a Public Debt Market*. Puk's analysis is focused on the implications of the system for public credit markets in early modern China. But I think his interpretation of the emergence of speculation in salt certificates and the subsequent state response could easily be fit into a regulatory arbitrage framework.

18. On the early phases of this process, *Ming Taizong shilu* 1/4/26 (1403), 19:349. The process for Zhendong Guard is described in some detail in *Ming Xuanzong shilu* 3/2/11 (1428), 39:753; on the commutation process, see *Ming Xianzong shilu* 16/6/28 (1480), 200:3724. See Yang Peina, "Binhai shengji yu wangchao zhixu," 43*ff.*; Peng Yong, "Mingdai qijun jingji shenghuo tanyan," 171–74.

19. *Gutian xianzhi*, 73–75; *Fuzhou fuzhi*, 7:23a–b.

20. Zhu Jian, "Qing jian tunjun zimi, jinge jianbi shu," in Chen Zilong, ed., *Huang-Ming jingshi wenbian*, 35:261–62.

21. There are several more cases in the casebook that involve military households but in which the type of land is unclear. I have excluded these from the analysis.

22. Qi Biaojia, *Puyang yandu*, 144.

23. Strictly speaking, there were two distinct types of military household members settling in rural areas: military colonists (and their families) and the supernumeraries of garrison soldiers. Because both groups had to find ways to integrate with existing rural residents, I do not distinguish them here.

24. *Ming Yingzong shilu* 14/2/18 (1449), 175:3375; *Ming Xianzong shilu* 18/5/26 (1482), 227:3897.

25. Yan Junyan, *Mengshui zhai cundu*, 537. Qi makes a further distinction between drill and colony soldiers. Probably because the former still, in theory, earned a ration in the guard, Qi holds that the latter should have greater rights to allotments than the former. So in a dispute over an allotment between members of the two groups, he decides that individual members of drill households should be allowed

to register for a single allotment, but that members of colony households should be under no such restriction. Qi Biaojia, *Puyang yandu*, 143.

26. Ibid., 24.

27. Ibid., 141.

28. Yan Junyan, *Mengshui zhai cundu*, 537.

29. On live sale, see Yang Guozhen, *Ming Qing tudi qiyue wenshu yanjiu*, 30–33; Buoye, *Manslaughter, Markets and Moral Economy*, 227. Pomeranz suggests that live sales were a form of insurance by which sellers agreed to accept a lower price in exchange for insurance that they could recover their land. "Land Markets," 128.

30. Qi Biaojia, *Puyang yandu*, 107.

31. Yan Junyan, *Mengshui zhai cundu*, 375, 537; Qi Biaojia, *Puyang yandu* 24, 42, 60, 141.

32. The terms of the transfer are not stated; the text uses the term "hire to tenant" (*pidian*). We do not have enough examples of transfers of military colony allotments from the Guangzhou area to be sure what this term signifies, but it is probably the local equivalent of the term "succeeds to cultivation" that appears in some of the Fujian documents. Because transfer documents involving military colony land did not and indeed probably could not use terms like "sale," since the land after all did not simply belong to the vendor, the transaction is presented instead as a long-term lease.

33. Yan Junyan, *Mengshui zhai cundu*, 375. This interpretation requires making a slight change in the punctuation of the published version.

34. Qi Biaojia, *Puyang yandu*, 433.

35. Ibid., 12.

36. See chapter 3.

37. "Tong'an Dushi fuyeji" (1546), inscription in the Overseas Chinese University library, Jimei.

38. Qi Biaojia, *Puyang yandu*, 24, 185; Philip Huang, *Civil Justice in China*, 10–18.

39. The deeds were found by Li Ren-yuan in the *Longtancun Chenshi zupu*; presumably the lands were later acquired by a member of the Chen family.

40. Qi Biaojia, *Puyang yandu*, 141; Reed, *Talons and Teeth*, chs. 2 and 4.

41. Gu Yanwu, *Tianxia junguo libing shu*, 26:105b in the *Siku quanshu congmu edition*; 5:2226–27 in the modern (2002) punctuated edition.

42. This story has been reconstructed from a genealogy written on the walls of the Li ancestral hall in Taiping.

43. Brandt, Ma, and Rawski, "From Divergence to Convergence: Reevaluating the History behind China's Economic Boom," 54–55, 71–72.

Chapter 6. A Temple with Two Gods

1. The Laisu Li are a different lineage from Li Guangdi's lineage, who live across the river in Ganhua.

2. Incense and flower (*xianghua*) monk is the term used today to describe a kind of Buddhist ritual specialist in southeastern China. The specialists themselves do not use the term but simply call themselves "monks." They wear Buddhist robes and shave their heads but typically have little or no formal training in Buddhist doctrine

and do not observe monastic discipline. They make their living performing a variety of Buddhist rituals for their community. See Tam, "Xianghua Foshi (Incense and Flower Buddhist Rites)."

3. The nature of the offerings is at once highly symbolic and highly variable. Every family offers a chicken, and every chicken must be prepared in the same way, with the heart placed in the beak and a blood pudding under the neck. People know they must do it this way even if they cannot say why. But at the same time, the food offerings are also specific to 2014. There is beer, red wine, dragon fruit (introduced to the region from Southeast Asia only in the past few years), and tins of Danish butter cookies. At one point the gods are offered jewelery, gold watches, and stacks of cash, highlighting that not only do the gods look like officials and behave like officials, they are also corrupt like officials.

4. Lin Liangjun, "Hongbu Linshi shixi cankao," (1806), in *Taoyuan Hongbu Linshi baxiu zupu*, 27–28.

5. *Yongchun xianzhi*, 160–61.

6. Chen Tai, "Conggong xiaozhuan," in *Taoyuan Hongbu Linshi baxiu zupu*, 33.

7. Lin Liangjun, "Hongbu Linshi shixi cankao," (1806) in *Taoyuan Hongbu Linshi baxiu zupu*, 27–28.

8. *Linyang Yanshi jiapu*, 3:6a–7b.

9. The solution he came up with was to allow only supernumeraries, that is, nonserving soldiers, to register as civilian households. Moreover, when supernumeraries registered as households, they were required to state clearly their military origins. This was to ensure that they were available for conscription should that ever be necessary. *Huizhou fuzhi*, 5:36a–b.

10. "Cunliu junyu chongshi junwu," in Dai Jin, *HuangMing tiaofa shilei zhuan*, 24:1057–60.

11. Yuanying's line subsequently produced a number of officials, which suggests that their bid to register as a civilian household may have had something to do with participation in the civil service examinations.

12. Lin Xiyuan, "Tong'an Linshi Xushi lü," in *Taoyuan Hongbu sifang Linshi sanxiu zupu*, 17–18. The text is not signed, but it must have been written by Lin Xiyuan because it contains the phrase "When [I] was compiling the Yongchun county gazetteer."

13. The multiple versions of the story in different genealogies give us a rare view into the "Rashomon effect" in the making of family history. I have assumed that it is just carelessness that has led to the inclusion of a version of the story that undermines the version the compiler is trying to tell. But it could also reflect some other strategy of which I know nothing.

14. *Kuishan Wang zupu*, 3:6–7.

15. Qi Biaojia, *Puyang yandu*, 590.

16. For detailed descriptions of annual procession rituals, see Dean, *Taoist Ritual and Popular Cults*, 64–69, 99–117; on the ways that such rituals reaffirm relationships both symbolically and sociologically, see Allio, "Spatial Organization in a Ritual Context," and Sangren, *History and Magical Power in a Chinese Community*. Also see Dean and Lamarre, "Ritual Matters," 57.

17. Wang Mingming, *Xicun jiazu*, 58.

18. *Anxi Hushi zupu*, 1417.

19. The Lin may actually have been the second of the three families that made up the compound military household with the Hu, but the surviving evidence is inadequate to know for sure. Regardless, that both lineages were registered as military households speaks to just how widespread the institution was in Fujian society at the time.

20. The chronology is further confused because the carvers of a stone inscription raised by the county Historical Relics Management Office in 1998 to mark the tomb of the founding ancestor obviously knew the more recent dating but mistakenly placed him in the wrong millenium, giving his dates as 1785–1819.

21. "Linshi pushuo," in *Qingxi Rulin Linshi zupu*. This story is found in Lin genealogy as well as other Ming sources. I was first told a version in 2011 by the caretaker of a nearby temple.

22. Hutou's Master Zhang (*Zhang gong*) is a different deity from the better-known Master Zhang who is one of the Three Masters of the Way associated with Stone Ox Mountain in Dehua. The two share a surname, but their iconography and folklore are different, and there is no apparent connection between the Houshan temple and the widespread ritual networks of the Three Masters of the Way found throughout southern Fujian and Taiwan. On the Three Masters of the Way, see Ye Mingsheng, ed., *Min-Tai Zhang shengjun xinyang wenhua*; on the distribution of their cult, Dean and Zheng, *Ritual Alliances of the Putian Plains*.

23. The Lin genealogy asserts a further leadership role when the temple was rebuilt and expanded in 1491. At that time, Lin Balang's descendant Tingbin (1441–1501) arranged to have the Three Official Sages, the Daoist gods of Heaven, Earth, and Water, installed in the temple. Biography of Tingbin, in *Qingxi Zhushan Linshi zupu*, 3:4–5.

24. The situation in Ganhua on the other side of the river is clearer. There the Li family, into which Li Guangdi would later be born, had been settled since the late Song, and by early mid-Ming was the dominant lineage. They were among the earliest to build an ancestral hall, under the leadership of one of their first office-holders. Li is today by far the most common surname in Hutou, and the vast majority claim membership in this single lineage. The Su surname, who are also concentrated on the Ganhua side of the river, is a distant second. The Su genealogy claims settlement in the area in the late Yuan. Thus both of the largest surname groups today were already present in Hutou by the start of the Ming. *Hengchan Sushi zupu*, 3.

25. Anxi county had about 140,000 mu or about ninety-three square kilometers of registered arable land in the Ming. Several units of Yongning Guard had colonies in the county, with a total allotment in the early Ming of 16,400 mu, equivalent to just over 10% of the arable land. Yongning Right Battalion had colony land totaling 1,500 mu in Laisu and one other district. If we assume that half of the land was in Laisu, then 750 mu in the district was allotted to the soldiers. At thirty mu allotment per soldier, there should have been twenty-five soldiers assigned to the district. *Anxi xianzhi*, 1:26a, 27b–28a.

26. Biography of fourth-generation ancestor Eryong, in *Yangtou Yanshi zupu*, 25; genealogical charts, generation 1–5, *Anxi Hutou Hongshi shizu*. On conscription of colony soldiers, see Yu Zhijia, "Bangding tingji: Mingdai junhu zhong yuding

jiaose de fenhua." Yangtou is now part of Qiaotou; Shangshi has now become part of Shangtian.

27. The Dong have a pre-1949 genealogy but would not allow me to see it. Like some lineages from northern Fujian, but unusually for this region, the Dong have the custom of "sealing" their genealogy. It can only be opened when the new edition is being compiled or if a dispute arises that can only be resolved by consulting it. Villagers did allow me to see their recently compiled new genealogy and it tells the same story as in the oral tradition. *Chanxian Dongshi zupu*, 16.

28. *Qingxi Zhushan Linshi zupu*, 3316.

29. A surviving preface from an earlier edition, dated 1704, explains that their genealogy was lost "in military turmoil," which is why they do not know the origins of their family. (The biography of an early ancestor records that their ancestral tablets were lost "while fleeing the dwarf [pirates.]" Since Hutou is located many miles inland, this is also as sure an indication as any that the sixteenth-century "Japanese pirate problem" was not just about Japanese and not just about pirates.) Biography of Fobao, in *Qingxi Houshan Zhengshi zupu*, 93.

30. I follow the most authoritative recent study of the cult in translating *zhen* as "perfected." See Chao, *Daoist Ritual*.

31. Crediting Zhenwu for helping him to victory in a battle, Zhu Yuanzhang named the god as one of ten cults mandated to receive sacrifice from officials in the capital. In order to thank Zhenwu for his aid in the coup that brought him to the throne, Zhu Yuanzhang's third son, the Yongle emperor, ordered the construction of a massive temple complex for the god on Wudang Mountain. Liu Zhiwei has traced how worship of Zhenwu became a symbolic expression of loyalty to and incorporation into the Ming polity for civilian communities in Guangdong's Pearl River Delta, even as communities refined the legends of the god to define and assert their own identities. The local cults to Beidi, Liu writes "confirm regional loyalty to, and identification with, the state." Liu Zhiwei, "Beyond the Imperial Metaphor," 15.

32. Zhuang Jichang, "Qingxi Laisuli Houshan Zhenwu miao ji," (1621) inscription in Houshan.

33. A version of this story appears in *Hexie chengxiang you*, 365.

34. "Shenshi zou dengdeng potai shouyun ke." I am grateful to Gao Zhifeng for sharing this text with me and for much assistance in fieldwork in Hutou over many years. The Daoist version is not entirely consistent with my interpretation, as it suggests Zhenwu was not brought by military colonists but came from the Guandi temple on the other side of the river in Hutou. But there is no tradition of Zhenwu ever having been housed in that temple.

35. During the renovations, they found "a record in the belly" in one of the statues in the temple. This is a reference to the practice of inserting a talisman in a cavity in the back of a deity statue when it is commissioned (on which see Robson, "Hidden in Plain View: Concealed Contents, Secluded Statues, and Revealed Religion," 183–85). Lin Tingbin's great-great-grandson now took the lead in setting up a special ritual for the Lin family to venerate these images. Biography of Lin Tingbin, in *Qingxi Zhushan Linshi zupu*, 3:4–5.

36. Perhaps out of respect, the sons elected to carve both their father's error-ridden text and the subsequent correction onto an inscription rather than simply

correcting the mistake. "Houshan miaobei" (1748), inscription in Houshan. The text is also found in the Houshan Hu genealogy.

37. Leadership of the ritual also rotates among the different villages from these two groups. A tattered, handwritten poster pasted on the wall of the temple by its organizing committee in 2004 outlines the leadership responsibilities for the next eight years: 2004 Shangtian (including Shangshi and Qiaotou); 2005 Meiban; 2006 Dengxian (i.e., Dingxian); 2007 Zhushan; 2008 Xuqian and Waipu; 2009 Guoban and Yunlin; 2010 Chanxian; 2011 Dongbu (i.e., Guobu). Another poster illustrating the festival accounts for 2009 confirms the role of these villages as the major contributors to the costs.

38. Hymes, *Way and Byway*, 4.

39. *Quanzhou fuzhi*, 7:17b.

40. "Zupu yin," in *Yongchun Tangshi zupu*. The issue is also recorded in *Yongchun xianzhi*, 125; *Quanzhou fuzhi* 7:17b–18a.

41. *Yongchun xianzhi*, 143–54. In the case of the colony assigned to Luo Guoyi, there were only two, the Ma and Lin families.

Chapter 7. A God Becomes an Ancestor

1. There are echoes of this viewpoint in the procession festival of Zhou Dexing at Pinghai. One member of his retinue, the Master of Yin and Yang, is believed to be a dangerous spirit with control over people's fates. Elderly women still today shield their grandchildren when the Master of Yin and Yang passes by.

2. Gu Cheng, "Weisuo zhidu zai Qingdai de biange."

3. There were some exceptions. The use of hereditary soldiers seemed a good solution to the problem of managing the transport of tax grain along the Grand Canal, so the guards that had been responsible for this task were maintained. Yu Zhijia, *Weisuo, junhu yu junyi*; Zhao Shiyu, "'Bu Qing bu Ming' yu 'Wu Ming bu Qing.'"

4. For example, *Wujiang Zhengshi zupu*. I am grateful to Cheng-heng Lu for locating and copying this genealogy in Taiwan.

5. Entry for Kangxi 3 (1664), in "Jianzhi yange xiuli zhi," in *Nanyu Chenshi zupu*, 9a.

6. The Lin of Meihua tell a legend that their fishermen took refuge from a storm on the nearby island of Mazu in 1665. This reads suspiciously like an attempt to avoid the evacuation by moving offshore. "Meihua Diaogeng jing—Lin Wei gong," in *Meijiang Linshi zupu*, 80.

7. "Guangxu san nian suici dingchou xinxuan Quanzhongpu xu" (1877), in *Fuquan Quan zongpu*.

8. "Chongxiu zufen ji," in *Nanyu Chenshi zupu*, 11a.

9. For example, *Longxi xianzhi*, 5:4a; *Shaowu xianzhi*, 10:3a.

10. "Zutun," in *Anxi Hushi zupu*, 1418–19.

11. "Tianshi shizu," in *Xiaoshan Daoyuan Tianshi zongpu*, 1a–5a. It did not take a change of dynasty for this sort of conversion to happen. As we saw in chapter 1, most of the households of the famous Li lineage of Ganhua in Hutou, the family of Li Guangdi, held civilian registration. One branch of the lineage was conscripted by criminal conviction in the early Ming. This branch later established a corporate

estate, the income from which went to the serving soldier in the distant southwest. By the early seventeenth century, the fortunes of the rest of the Li lineage were on the rise. Feeling sorry for his poor kin who were registered as soldiers, Li Maohui (d. 1621) arranged through his connections for their assignment to be transferred to nearby Quanzhou. Since there was no longer any need for such a large estate, Maohui arranged for it to be put to new purposes. The serving soldier continued to receive 15% of the income from the estate. The remainder was converted into a sacrificial estate, and the income later used to support the construction of an ancestral hall. "Taichang gong zixu junyuanyou," *Qingxi Lishi jiapu*, 3:42a–45a.

12. Szonyi, *Practicing Kinship*, ch. 3.

13. "Raoping xian Zhengtang Zhou wei chengju limian liyi" (1730), inscription in Chenghuang temple, Dachengsuo.

14. This section relies heavily on Yang Peina, "Binhai shengji yu wangchao zhixu," 234*ff.*

15. Chen Jin, "Tongshan renwu zhi xu" (1675), reprinted in *Tongshan zhi* (1751), 309.

16. Liu Yonghua and Zheng Rong, "Qingchu Zhongguo dongnan diqu de lianghu guizong gaige," 81–87.

17. Zheng Zhenman, *Ming-Qing jiazu zuzhi*, 242–57; Zheng Zhenman, *Family Lineage Organization*, 286–308.

18. "Hehu shimo," in *Zhangzhou fuzhi* (1877), 14:20a.

19. The brief, sometimes cryptic, accounts in the gazetteers of the counties where reform was tried make it difficult to work out the precise sequence of events. It may be that some of the steps credited to Chen were actually introduced under his predecessors.

20. "Hehu shimo," in *Zhangzhou fuzhi* (1877), 14:19b*ff.*

21. *Zhangpu xianzhi* (1885), 214.

22. *Jinjiang xianzhi*, 21:1b

23. "Zupu yin," in *Yongchun Tangshi zupu*.

24. "Dingliang yange zaji," in *Nanyu Chenshi zupu*, 13b.

25. This too would change with the dissolution of the guards in the early eighteenth century.

26. "Gongli Guan Yongmao beiji" (1713), inscription in the Dongshan Guandi temple.

27. "Dingliang yange zaji," in *Nanyu Chenshi zupu*, 13b–14a.

28. "Gongli Guan Yongmao beiji" (1713), inscription in the Dongshan Guandi temple.

29. According to Zheng Zhenman's typology of lineage organization, this would be a contractual lineage, a type that became increasingly widespread throughout Fujian in this period. *Ming Qing jiazu zuzhi*, 103*ff.*; *Family Lineage Organization*, 122*ff.*

30. "Kangxi wushisan nian qi yue ri yuezi zhi chongxin" (1714), in *Fuquan Quan zhongpu*.

31. "Huahu ce," in Chen Shengshao, *Wensulu*, 93. Note that one of the general households is registered under the name Guan Shixian, the very household created by former military households in Zhao'an county that had inspired the residents of Tongshan to establish the Guan Yongmao household.

32. Scott, *Seeing like a State*, 2.

33. No new dynasty in Chinese history has ever survived without securing the allegiance of old elites by guaranteeing their interests. The most obvious expression of this principle was the maintenance of the examination system as a recruitment mechanism (Lawrence Zhang proposes an interesting extension of this principle, treating the office purchase system whereby families made payments many years in advance of receiving an official post as a kind of sunk cost that further tied elites to the state. "Power for a price," 269–70). But as our understanding of what constitutes the elite expands, so too must our definition of their interests. Fiscal privileges were among the prerogatives that new dynasties could maintain in order to gain support. The most celebrated demonstration of this was the famous tax-clearing case in Jiangnan in the 1660s. The story of tax reform in Zhangpu carries this theme down to the very local level. Even ordinary registered households protested tax reform as an attack on local interests. Old ways of managing taxes persisted in part because the state could not afford to alienate those who benefited from them.

Conclusion

1. Philip Huang, "Centralized Minimalism," 24–25.

2. Ruskola, "Conceptualizing Corporations and Kinship," 1619–76. For an earlier discussion, Steven Sangren, "Traditional Chinese Corporations."

3. Szonyi, *Practicing Kinship*, ch. 3.

4. Scott, *The Art of Not Being Governed*, xi. Oxfeld offers an intriguing discussion of how political factors can shape the kinship dynamics of Chinese families abroad. *Blood, Sweat and Mahjong*, 9.

5. Borges, "On Exactitude in Science," 325.

6. Philip Huang, "Between Informal Mediation and Formal Adjudication," 265–67. Ocko writes, "by allowing a set of rules or contract to be placed 'on the record,' the magistrate was not issuing a charter or formally recognizing the group, but was acknowledging that the rules and provisions of the contracts would be the matrix for deciding subsequent disputes about the parties," "The Missing Metaphor," 193.

7. Greif, *Institutions and the Path to the Modern Economy*, ch 4.

8. Duara, *The Crisis of Global Modernity*, 171.

9. I thus find Watson's argument that traditional society's main symbolic goal with respect to the imperial state was to keep it at a distance to be only a partial account ("Waking the Dragon," 163). For a challenge from another perspective, see Faure, "The Emperor in the Village."

10. Cohen, "Commodity Creation in Late Imperial China." 323. For other examples of the extraordinary degree of commodification in late imperial China, see Goossaert, "A Question of Control," and Sommer, *Polyandry and Wife Selling in Qing Dynasty China*.

11. Parsons, *The Peasant Rebellions of the Late Ming Dynasty*; Perdue, *China Marches West*, 559.

12. Hansen, *Negotiating Daily Life in Traditional China*.

13. Much of the discussion has focused on state enforcement. Katz has also drawn attention to the question of supernatural enforcement. *Divine Justice*.

14. See the discussion in Oi and Walder, "Property Rights in the Chinese Economy," 3-4.

15. For example, Yu Zhijia, "Mingdai junhu zhong de jiaren, yinan" contains many examples of what are recognizably substitution strategies from different parts of China.

16. Agnew, "Migrants and Mutineers"; Robinson, *Bandits, Eunuchs and the Son of Heaven*, 58, 94-95.

17. Xu Bin, *Ming Qing E-dong zongzu yu difang shehui*.

18. Xie Shi, "Yi tun yi min."

19. Rowe, *Hankow*, 80; Perdue, *Exhausting the Earth*, 170, 173; Dennerline, *The Chia-Ting Loyalists*, 177, 181-82; Beattie, *Land and Lineage in China*, 26-27.

20. Liu Daosheng, *Ming-Qing Huizhou zongzu wenshu yanjiu*, 243-70; Liu Zhiwei, *Zai guojia yu shehui zhijian*, 9.

21. Zheng Zhenman, *Ming-Qing Fujian jiazu zuzhi*, 191; Zheng Zhenman, *Family Lineage Organization*, 231-32; Chen Chunsheng and Xiao Wenping, "Juluo xingtai yu shehui zhuanxing," 55-68.

22. Brook, *The Confusions of Pleasure*, 9.

23. Brook, *The Chinese State in Ming Society*, 176.

24. It is only with the recent publication of the various Ming statutes and precedents that scholars have realized that endorsement of precedents by the reigning emperor was effectively a form of constitutional change; imperial declarations and interventions were rules that had the force of constitutional amendments. These materials will almost certainly lead to a revision of our understanding of Ming law and governance.

25. Farmer, *Zhu Yuanzhang*, 106.

26. Cao Shuji, *Zhongguo yiminshi*, vol. 5, *Ming shiqi*.

27. Lee, *Negotiated Power*, 264.

28. The notion of precocious modernity can be traced back to the work of Naitō Konan, but one can find its echoes, if not always the term itself, in many recent works.

29. For the reasons why a firm distinction between "state" and "empire" does not hold well for the Chinese case, see Ebrey, "China as a Contrasting Case," 31-37.

30. Goldstone, "The Problem of the 'Early Modern' World," 249, 261.

31. von Glahn, "Imagining Pre-Modern China," 49.

32. For example, Pomeranz, *The Great Divergence*; Rosenthal and Wong, *Before and Beyond Divergence*.

33. Mann, "The Autonomous Power of the State," 189.

34. Collins, *The State in Early Modern France*, 20; Barkey, *Empire of Difference*, x; Hasan, *State and Locality*, 127.

35. Perdue, *China Marches West*, 558; Robinson, *Bandits, Eunuchs and the Son of Heaven*, 167. Susan Mann, elaborating on Weber's notion of liturgical governance, has described the delegation of state authority to local merchant and literati elites in Qing. *Local Merchants and the Chinese Bureaucracy, 1750-1900*, 12-18.

36. Kerkvliet, "Everyday Politics in Peasant Societies."

37. Mitchell, "The Limits of the State," 95.

38. Fan Jingwen (1587-1644), "Ge dahu xing zhaomu shu," in *Wenzhong ji*, 2:15b.

39. Goodman, "Corruption in the PLA"; Muscolino, "Underground at Sea."

40. To give just one example, Link notes that in the Maoist period canny people "borrowed the devices of official language . . . to lay claim to a status that might support a claim to access or privilege." *An Anatomy of Chinese,* 260.

41. Gao Bingzhong, "Yizuo bowuguan/miaoyu jianzhu de minzu zhi"; Weller, "The Politics of Ritual Disguise"; "Responsive Authoritarianism and Blind-Eyed Governance in China."

42. Perry, "Popular Protest: Playing by the Rules," 23.

43. Spivak, "Can the Subaltern Speak?"; Hershatter, "The Subaltern Talks Back."

References are listed in the following order:

a. premodern gazetteers
b. genealogies
c. inscriptions
d. other premodern Chinese sources
e. works in other languages and secondary sources.

Entries for gazetteers follow the principles in Dennis, *Local Gazetteers*, 343, with the exception that titles with a prefix (such as "recompiled" or a reign period) are only listed once, without the prefix. For rare works the location is indicated.

Entries for genealogies include as much information as is available: title, date of publication or most recent preface, and any publication details. Genealogies are almost never the work of a single compiler, so listing the name of an editor or compiler is generally not useful. For unpublished or privately published genealogies, which are most genealogies, I indicate where I copied or took notes on the genealogy.

Entries for inscriptions include title, date, and current location of the inscription.

For all categories, I omit authors' names if the work is best known by its title.

Transcriptions of many of the original texts cited from unpublished works may be consulted at https://scholar.harvard.edu/szonyi/ABGreferences.

A. Premodern Gazetteers

Anxi xianzhi [Gazetteer of Anxi County]. Lin Younian, ed. 1552. Reprint *Tianyige cang Mingdai fangzhi xuankan*. Shanghai: Shanghai guji, 1981.

Anxi xianzhi [Gazetteer of Anxi County]. Shen Zhong, ed. 1757.

BaMin tongzhi [General Gazetteer of the Eight Prefectures of Min [Fujian]]. Huang Zhongzhao, ed. 1491. Reprint Fuzhou: Fujian renmin, 2006.

Chongwu suochengzhi [Gazetteer of Chongwu Battalion]. Zhu Tong, ed. 1542. Reprinted in *Hui'an zhengshu; fu Chongwu suochengzhi*. Fuzhou: Fujian renmin, 1987.

Dongli zhi [Gazetteer of Dongli]. Chen Tianzi, ed. 1574. Reprint: Shantou: 1990.

Fujian tongzhi [General Gazetteer of Fujian]. Chen Shouqi, ed. 1829. [*Chongzuan Fujian tongzhi*].

Fuzhou fuzhi [Gazetteer of Fuzhou Prefecture]. Lin Lian, ed. 1579. Reprint *Nanjing tushuguan guben shanben congkan, Mingdai guben fangzhi zhuanji*. Beijing: Xianzhuang shuju, 2003.

Guangdong tongzhi [General Gazetteer of Guangdong]. Huang Zuo, ed. 1561. Reprint Hong Kong: Daming, 1977.

Guangzhou fuzhi [Gazetteer of Guangzhou Prefecture]. Wang Yongrui, ed. Qing Kangxi period. Reprint *Beijing tushuguan guji zhenben congkan*. Beijing: Shumu wenxian, 1988.

Gutian xianzhi [Gazetteer of Gutian County]. Liu Riyi, ed. 1606. Reprint *Fujian wenshi congshu, Wanli Fuzhou fushu xianzhi*. Beijing: Fangzhi, 2007.

Huizhou fuzhi [Gazetteer of Huizhou Prefecture]. Liu Wu, ed. 1542. Reprint *Riben cang Zhongguo hanjian difangzhi congkan*. Beijing: Shumu, 1991.

Jinjiang xianzhi [Gazetteer of Jinjiang County]. Zhu Shengyuan, ed. 1765. Airusheng *Fangzhiku* database.

Longxi xianzhi [Gazetteer of Longxi County]. Huang Hui, ed. 1762. Reprint *Zhongguo difangzhi jicheng*. Shanghai: Shanghai shudian, 2000.

Minshu [Book of Min [Fujian]]. He Qiaoyuan, ed. 1631. Reprint Fuzhou: Fujian renmin, 1994.

Nanshu zhi [Gazetteer of the Southern Metropolitan Region]. Fan Jingwen. 1638. Reprint *Zhongguo fangzhi congshu*. Taibei: Chengwen, 1983.

Putian xianzhi [Gazetteer of Putian County]. Song Ruolin, ed. 1758. Airusheng *Fangzhiku* database.

Quanzhou fuzhi [Gazetteer of Quanzhou Prefecture]. Yang Siqian, ed. 1612. Reprint *Zhongguo shixue congshu*. Taibei: Taiwan xuesheng, 1987.

Shaowu xianzhi [Gazetteer of Shaowu County]. Zhu Shutian, ed. 1937.

Tongshan zhi [Gazetteer of Tongshan]. Chen Zhenzao, ed. Preface 1751. Reprint *Zhongguo difangzhi jicheng*. Shanghai: Shanghai shudian, 2000.

Xinghua fuzhi [Gazetteer of Xinghua Prefecture]. Zhou Ying, ed. 1503. Reprint Fuzhou: Fujian remin, 2007. [*Chongkan Xinghua fuzhi*].

Yongchun xianzhi [Gazetteer of Yongchun County]. Lin Xiyuan, ed. 1526. Reprint Taibei: Yongchun wenxianshe, 1973.

Zhangpu xianzhi [Gazetteer of Zhangpu County]. Chen Ruxian, ed. 1700. Reprint: *Zhongguo fangzhi jicheng*. Shanghai: Shanghai shudian, 2000.

Zhangpu xianzhi [Gazetteer of Zhangpu County]. Shi Xiwei, ed. 1885. Reprint Zhangpu: Zhangpu zhengxie wenshi ziliao zhengji yanjiu weiyuanhui, 2004.

Zhangzhou fuzhi [Gazetteer of Zhangzhou Prefecture]. Xie Bin, ed. 1572. Reprint *Zhongguo shixue congshu*. Taibei: Taiwan xuesheng, 1965.

Zhangzhou fuzhi [Gazetteer of Zhangzhou Prefecture]. Wu Lianxun, ed. 1877.

Zhenhai weizhi [Gazetteer of Zhenhai Guard]. Preface 1752. Dongshan museum.

Zhenhai weizhi jiaozhu [Annotated Gazetteer of Zhenhai Guard]. Preface 1752. Reprint Huang Jianlan, ed. Zhengzhou: Zhongzhou guji, 1993.

B. Genealogies

Anxi Hutou Hongshi shizu [Founding Ancestors of the Hong of Hutou, Anxi]. 1994. Photographed in Hutou.

Anxi Hushi zupu [Genealogy of the Hu of Anxi]. 1989. Photographed in Hutou.

Cangnan Wangshi zupu [Genealogy of the Wang of Cangnan]. 2006. Photocopied in Cangnan.

Changle Zhuti Linshi zupu [Genealogy of the Lin of Zhuti, Changle]. Preface 1535. Photocopy in Fujian provincial library.

Chanxian Dongshi zupu [Genealogy of the Dong of Chanxian]. 2000. Photographed in Hutou.

Fuquan Jiangshi jiamiao [Ancestral Temple of the Jiang of Fuquan]. No date. Photocopy in Shishi municipal library.

Fuquan Jiangshi Sifang Beisha Xupu [Genealogy, Recompiled, of the Northern Mansion [Subbranch] of the Fourth Branch of the Jiang of Fuquan]. Preface 1631. Photocopy in Shishi municipal library.

Fuquan Quan zongpu [General Genealogy of the Quan of Fuquan]. Preface 1877. Photocopy in Shishi municipal library.

Fuzhou Guoshi zupu [Genealogy of the Guo of Fuzhou]. 1892. Fujian provincial library.

Hengchan Sushi zupu [Genealogy of the Su of Hengchan]. 2005. Photographed in Hutou.

Huangshi zupu [Genealogy of the Huang]. Taizhong: Xin yuandong, 1962.

Jin'an Dushi zupu [Genealogy of the Du of Jin'an]. 1997. Fujian provincial library.

Jinghai Rongshi zupu [Genealogy of the Rong of Jinghai]. No date. Photographed in Jinghai.

Jinmencheng Nishi zupu [Genealogy of the Ni of Jinmencheng]. No date; preface to previous edition 1641. Photographed in Jinmencheng.

Kuishan Wang zupu [Genealogy of the Wang of Kuishan]. 1997. Photographed in Jingli, Putian.

Linyang Yanshi jiapu [Genealogy of the Yan of Linyang]. 1878. Nankai University library.

Longtancun Chenshi zupu [Genealogy of the Chen of Longtan Village]. No date. Photographed in Longtan, Pingnan, by Li Renyuan.

Meijiang Linshi zupu [Genealogy of the Lin of Meijiang]. 2002. Photographed in Meihua, Changle.

Nanyu Chenshi zupu [Genealogy of the Chen of Nanyu]. 1903. Reprinted 1985. Photographed in Dongshan.

Puqi Heshi zupu [Genealogy of the He of Puqi]. 2003. Photographed in Puqi.

Qingxi Houshan Zhengshi zupu [Genealogy of the Zheng of Houshan, Qingxi]. 1941. Photographed in Hutou.

Qingxi Lishi jiapu [Genealogy of the Li of Qingxi]. 1774. Photographed in Hutou.

Qingxi Rulin Linshi jiapu [Genealogy of the Lin of Rulin, Qingxi]. No date; preface to previous edition 1772. Photographed in Hutou.

Qingxi Zhushan Linshi zupu [Genealogy of the Lin of Zhushan, Qingxi]. 1989. Photographed in Hutou.

Ruiyun Yaoshi zupu [Genealogy of the Yao of Ruiyun]. Ca. 1628. Photographed in Ruiyun, Pingnan, by Li Renyuan.

Shejiang yanpai Fuquan Chenshi zupu [Genealogy of the Shejiang Branch of the Chen of Fuquan]. No date. Photographed in Fuquan.

Shiyou Dalun Caishi zupu [Genealogy of the Cai of Dalun, Shiyou]. Preface 1598. Reprint 1997. Photocopy in Quanzhou municipal library.

Taoyuan Hankou Linshi sixiu zupu [Fourth Edition of the Genealogy of the Lin of Hankou, Taoyuan]. 2009. Photographed in Dapu, Yongchun.

Taoyuan Hongbu Linshi baxiu zupu [Eighth Edition of the Genealogy of the Lin of Hongbu, Taoyuan]. 2009. Photographed in Dapu, Yongchun.

Taoyuan Hongbu sifang Linshi sanxiu zupu [Third Edition of the Genealogy of the Fourth Branch of the Lin of Hongbu, Taoyuan].1930. Photographed in Dapu, Yongchun.

Wugongtang Boyuancun Sushi jiapu [Wugong Hall: Genealogy of the Su of Boyuan Village]. 1986. Fujian provincial library.

Wujiang Zhengshi zupu [Genealogy of the Zheng of Wujiang]. 1973. Photographed in Xinzhu, Taiwan, by Lu Cheng-heng.

Xiaoshan Daoyuan Tianshi zupu [Genealogy of the Tian of Daoyuan, Xiaoshan]. 1837. Genealogical Society of Utah.

Yangtou Yanshi zupu [Genealogy of the Yan of Yangtou]. 2008. Photographed in Hutou.

Yanshi zupu [Genealogy of the Yan]. No date; preface to previous edition 1579. Reprint *Beijing tushuguan cang jiapu congkan, Minyue qiaoxiang juan*. Vol. 17. Beijing: Beijing tushuguan, 2000.

Yingqiao Wangshi zupu [Genealogy of the Wang of Yingqiao]. 1577. Photocopy in Wenzhou library.

Yingyang Panshi zupu [Genealogy of the Pan of Yingyang]. 1942. Photographed in Jinshan.

Yongchun Tangshi zupu [Genealogy of the Tang of Yongchun]. Preface 1917. Photographed in Dapu, Yongchun.

Yongning Nanmenjing Lishi zupu [Genealogy of the Li of Nanmenjing, Yongning]. 1907. Photographed in Yongning, by Jiang Nan.

Zhangpu Liu'ao Yingli Rongyang Zhengshi zupu [Genealogy of the Zheng of Rongyang, Yingli, Liu'ao, Zhangpu]. Preface 1829. Photocopy in Shishi municipal museum.

Zhengxing zupu kai Tai zu Zheng Yuangong yixi [Genealogy of the Zheng, with the Descendants of Zheng Yuangong the Founding Ancestor on Taiwan]. 1993. Photographed in Xinzhu, Taiwan, by Lu Cheng-heng.

C. Inscriptions

"Chongxiu Aocheng qianjian Shishi chenghuang miaoji." [Record of the Reconstruction of the Temple to the God of the Wall of Aocheng [Yongning], Relocated to Shishi] 1778. Inscription in Shishi; also in Dean and Zheng, *Fujian zongjiao beiming huibian Quanzhou fu fence*, 300.

"Chongxiu Pinghai weixue shengmiao beiji." [Record of the Reconstruction of the Pinghai Guard School and Temple to the Sage] 1519. Inscription outside Chenghuang temple, Pinghai; also in Dean and Zheng, *Fujian zongjiao beiming huibian Quanzhou fu fence*, 148.

"Chongxiu Wumiao ji." [Record of the Reconstruction of the Martial Temple] 1908. Inscription in Guandi temple, Dongshan.

"Dadudu Huang gong xingmiao huimin gongde beiji." [Stone Record of the Merit and Virtue of Commander Huang Who Erected a Temple to Benefit the People] 1681. Inscription in Guandi temple, Dongshan.

"Dingjian Tongcheng Guanwangmiao ji." [Record of the Construction of the Temple to King Guan in Tongcheng] 1516. Inscription in Guandi temple, Dongshan.

"Fengling dingjian Lijiang chenghuang miao beiji." [Stone Record of the Construction of the Temple of the God of the Wall of Lijiang in Fengling] 1680. Inscription in Chenghuang temple, Puxi.

"Gongde bei." [Inscription of Merit and Virtue] 1731. Inscription in Chenghuang temple, Dachengsuo.

"Gongli Guan Yongmao beiji." [Stone Record of the Collective Establishment of Guan Yongmao] 1713. Inscription in Guandi temple, Dongshan.

"Houshan miao bei." [Inscription of Houshan Temple] 1748. Inscription at Houshan temple, Hutou.

"Pinghai wei chenghuang miao shijin bei." [Inscription of the Prohibitions of the Temple of the God of Wall of Pinghai Guard] 1908. Inscription outside Chenghuang temple, Pinghai; also in Dean and Zheng, *Fujian zongjiao beiming huibian Quanzhou fu fence*, 357.

"Qingxi Laisuli Houshan Zhenwu miao ji." [Record of the Temple of True Martiality at Houshan in Laisuli along the Qingxi] 1621. Inscription at Houshan temple, Hutou.

"Raoping xian Zhengtang Zhou wei chengju limian liyi." [Zhou, Magistrate of Raoping, in the Matter of the [Entitlement] by Regulation for Exemption from Corvée Labor for Residents of the Town] 1730. Inscription in Chenghuang temple, Dachengsuo.

"Tong'an Dushi fuyeji." [Record of the Recovery of Property by the Du Family of Tong'an] 1546. Inscription in the Overseas Chinese University museum at Jimei.

"Xinjian Xia Chen xiaozongci xu." [Preface to the Construction of the Lesser Descent-Line Shrine of the Chen of Xia] 1806. Inscription in Yongning.

"Yixue beiji." [Stone Inscription on the Charitable School] 1725. Inscription in Zhenhai.

D. Other Premodern Chinese Sources

Cai Jiude. *Wobian shilue* [Selective Account of the Japanese Piracy]. Ming. In *Congshu jicheng chubian*, vol. 3975. Beijing: Shangwu, 1937.

Chen Shengshao. *Wensulu* [Record of Inquiry into Customs]. Ca. 1826. In *Lice huichao, Wensulu*. Beijing: Shumu wenxian, 1983.

Chen Zilong, ed. *HuangMing jingshi wenbian* [Collected Essays on Statecraft of the August Ming]. Seventeenth century. Beijing: Zhonghua, 1997.

Dai Jin. *HuangMing tiaofa shilei zhuan* [Categorized Substatutes of the August Ming]. Sixteenth century. In *Zhongguo zhenxi falü dianji jicheng*, edited by Liu Hainian and Yang Yifan. Beijing: Kexue, 1994.

DaMing Huidian [Statutes of the Great Ming]. 1587. Academia Sinica, *Hanji quanwen ziliaoku (Scripta Sinica)* database.

Fan Jingwen. [*Fan*] *Wenzhong ji* [Collected Writings of Fan Jingwen]. In *Wenyuange Siku quanshu*. Taibei: Taiwan Shangwu, 1986.

Gu Yanwu. *Tianxia junguo libing shu* [Strengths and Weaknesses of the Regions of the Realm]. Qing. In *Siku quanshu cunmu*. Jinan: Qilu, 1997.

——. *Tianxia junguo libing shu* [Strengths and Weaknesses of the Regions of the Realm]. Qing. Reprint Shanghai: Shanghai kexue jishu, 2002.

Hong Shou. *Canghai jiyi* [Surviving Records of the Vast Sea]. Preface 1568. Taibei: Taiwan guji, 2002.

Huang Yu. *Shuanghuai suichao* [Notes Made over the Years at Doubletree Pavilion]. In *Congshu jicheng chubian*. Changsha: Shangwu, 1939.

Huo Yi. *Junzheng tiaoli leikao* [Itemized Substatutes of Military Governance, Categorized]. 1552. In *Xuxiu siku quanshu*. Shanghai: Shanghai guji, 2002.

Ming shilu [Veritable Records of the Ming]. 1418–mid-seventeenth century. Academia Sinica, *Hanji quanwen ziliaoku (Scripta Sinica)* database.

Mingshi [History of the Ming]. 1736. Academia Sinica, *Hanji quanwen ziliaoku (Scripta Sinica)* database.

Pu Songling. *Liaozhai zhiyi* [Strange Stories from the Liao Studio]. Qing. Reprint Tianjin: Tianjin guji, 2004.

Qi Biaojia. *Puyang yandu* [Judgements from Puyang]. In *Lidai panli pandu*, edited by Yang Yifan and Xu Lizhi. Beijing: Zhongguo shehui kexue, 2005.

Qian Gu. *Wudu wencui xu ji* [Supplementary Collection of Literary Materials from Suzhou]. Sixteenth century. In *Wenyuange Siku quanshu*. Taibei: Taiwan Shangwu, 1986.

Shen Jing. *Shuangzhu ji* [The Double Pearl]. Late sixteenth or early seventeenth century. In *Shuangzhu ji pingzhu; Sixian ji pingzhu*. In *Liushizhong qu pingzhu*, Changchun: Jilin renmin, 2001

"Shenshi zou dengdeng potai shouyun ke" [Various Talismans for the Rituals of Eliminating the Fetus and Gathering Clouds]. Manuscript. No date. Collected in Hutou, Anxi.

Tan Lun. *Junzheng tiaoli* [Itemized Substatutes of Military Governance]. 1574. Copy in Naikaku Bunko.

Tang Shuyi, et al. *Qian shi jilue* [Brief Record of Poetry of Guizhou]. 1873. Reprint Chengdu: Sichuan minzu, 2002.

Wan Biao. *Haikou yi* [Comments on Piracy]. Sixteenth century. In *Siku quanshu cunmu*. Jinan: Qilu, 1997.

Wang Zaijin. *Haifang zuanyao* [Essential Writings on Coastal Defense]. Ming. In *Xuxiu Siku quanshu*. Shanghai: Shanghai guji, 2002.

Yan Junyan. *Mengshui zhai cundu* [Court Opinions Drafted at Mengshui Pavilion]. Seventeenth century. Beijing: Zhongguo zhengfa daxue, 2002.

Ye Xianggao. *Cangxia cao* [Drafts from Cangxia]. Ming Tiangqi period. Reprint Yangzhou: Jiangsu Guangling guji, 1994.

Yuxuan Mingchen zouyi [Imperially Ordered Collection of Memorials by Ming Officials]. 1781. In *Wenyuange Siku quanshu*. Taibei: Taiwan Shangwu, 1986.

Zhang Gang. *Zhang Gang riji* [Diary of Zhang Gang]. Shanghai: Shanghai shehui kexue, 2003.

Zheng Lichun. *Zheng Duanjian gong nianpu* [Chronological Biography of Zheng Duanjian]. In *Siku quanshu cunmu*. Jinan: Qilu, 1997.

Zheng Ruozeng. *Chouhai tubian* [Illustrated Compendium on Maritime Security]. Preface 1562. In *Zhongguo bingcheng jicheng*. Beijing: Jiefang, 1990.

Zhongguo Mingchao dang'an zonghui [General Collection of Ming Dynasty Archives]. Nanning: Guangxi shifan daxue, 2004.

Zhu Wan. *Piyu zaji* [Miscellaneous Writings to Show My Zeal]. Sixteenth century. In *Siku quanshu cunmu*. Jinan: Qilu, 1997.

E. Other References

Acharya, Viral and Matthew Richardson. "Causes of the Financial Crisis." *Critical Review* 21, nos. 2–3 (2009): 195–210.

Agnew, Christopher. "Migrants and Mutineers: The Rebellion of Kong Youde and 17th Century Northeast Asia." *Journal of the Economic and Social History of the Orient* 52, no. 3 (2009): 505–41.

Allio, Fiorella. "Spatial Organization in a Ritual Context: A Preliminary Analysis of the *Koah-Hiu* Processional System of the Tainan Region and Its Social Significance." In *Xinyang, yishi yu shehui: Disanjie guoji Hanxue huiyi lunwenji (renleixue zu)*, edited by Lin Meirong, 131–78. Taipei: Zhongyang yanjiuyuan minzuxue yanjiusuo, 2003.

Andrade, Tonio. *The Gunpowder Age: China, Military Innovation and the Rise of the West in World History*. Princeton: Princeton University Press, 2016.

Antony, Robert. *Like Froth Floating on the Sea: The World of Pirates and Seafarers in Late Imperial South China*. Berkeley: Institute of East Asian Studies, 2003.

Bai Gang, ed. *Zhongguo zhengzhi zhidu tongshi* [General History of the Political System of China]. Beijing: Renmin, 1996.

Barkey, Karen. *Empire of Difference: The Ottomans in Comparative Perspective*. Cambridge: Cambridge University Press, 2008.

Bayly, Christopher. *Imperial Meridien: The British Empire and the World, 1780–1830*. London and New York: Longman, 1989.

Beattie, Hillary. *Land and Lineage in China: A Study of T'ung-Ch'eng County, Anhwei, in the Ming and Ch'ing Dynasties*. Cambridge: Cambridge University Press, 1979.

Borges, Jorge Luis. "On Exactitude in Science" (1946). In *Collected Fictions*, translated by Andrew Hurley, 325. New York: Viking, 1998.

Bourgon, Jerome. "Uncivil Dialogue: Law and Custom Did Not Merge into Civil Law under the Qing." *Late Imperial China* 23, no. 1 (2002): 50–90.

Brandt, Loren, Debin Ma, and Thomas Rawski. "From Divergence to Convergence: Reevaluating the History behind China's Economic Boom." *Journal of Economic Literature* 52, no. 1 (2014): 45–123.

Brook, Timothy. *The Chinese State in Ming Society*. London and New York: RoutledgeCurzon, 2005.

———. "Communications and Commerce." In *The Cambridge History of China*, vol. 8, *The Ming Dynasty*, pt. 2, edited by Denis Twitchett and Frederick Mote, 579–707. Princeton: Princeton University Press, 1998.

———. *The Confusions of Pleasure: Commerce and Culture in Ming China*. Berkeley: University of California Press, 1998.

———. *Praying for Power: Buddhism and the Formation of Gentry Society in Late-Ming China*. Cambridge, MA: Council on East Asian Studies, Harvard University, 1993.

———. "The Spatial Structure of Ming Local Administration." *Late Imperial China* 6, no. 1 (1985): 1–55.

Buoye, Thomas. *Manslaughter, Markets and Moral Economy: Violent Disputes over Property Rights in Eighteenth Century China*. Cambridge: Cambridge University Press, 2000.

Cai Jialin. *Mingdai de weixue jiaoyu* [Guard School Education in Ming]. Yilan: Mingshi yanjiu xiaozu, 2002.

Calanca, Paola. *Piraterie et contrabande au Fujian: l'administration chinoise face aux problemes d'illégalité maritime*. Paris: Les Indes savantes, 2011.

Cao Shuji. *Zhongguo yimin shi* [History of Migration in China]. Vol. 5. *Ming shiqi*. Fuzhou: Fujian renmin, 1997.

Chang, Pin-Tsun [Zhang Bincun]. "Chinese Maritime Trade: The Case of Sixteenth-Century Fu-Chien (Fukien)." PhD diss., Princeton University, 1983.

Chao, Shin-yi. *Daoist Ritual, State Religion and Popular Practices: Zhenwu Worship from Song to Ming (960 to 1644)*. Abingdon and New York: Routledge, 2011.

Chen Baoliang. "Mingdai weixue fazhan shulun" [The Development of Guard Schools in Ming]. *Shehui kexue jikan*, no. 6 (2004):93–96.

Chen Chunsheng. "Cong woluan dao qianhai: Mingmo Qingchu Chaozhou difang dongluan yu xiangcun shehui bianqian" [From the Piracy Scourge to the Coastal Evacuation: Local Turmoil and Rural Social Change in Chaozhou in Late Ming and Early Qing]. *Ming-Qing luncong*, no. 2 (2001): 73–106.

———. "Mingdai qianqi Chaozhou haifang ji qi yingxiang" [Coastal Defense of Chaozhou in the Early Ming and Its Impact]. *Zhongshan daxue xuebao (Shehui kexue ban)* 47, no. 2 (2007): 24–32; no. 3, 46–52.

Chen Chunsheng and Xiao Wenping. "Juluo xingtai yu shehui zhuanxing: Ming-Qing zhiji Hanjiang liuyu difang dongluan zhi lishi yingxiang" [Village Structure and Social Transformation: The Historical Impact of Local Turmoil in the Hanjiang Basin in Ming-Qing]. *Shixue yuekan*, no. 2 (2011): 55–68.

Chen Gexin and Luo Weike, eds. *Kang wo mingcheng- Jinxiang, Pucheng* [Famous Anti-Pirate Towns: Jinxiang and Pucheng]. Special issue, *Cangnan wenshi ziliao*, no. 20 (2005).

Chen Guoqiang and Shi Yilong eds. *Chongwu renleixue diaocha* [Anthropological Investigation of Chongwu]. Fuzhou: Fujian jiaoyu, 1990.

Chen Limin. *Xunyou Pinghai* [A Tour of Pinghai]. Beijing: Zhongguo wenshi, 2006.

Chen Wenshi. "Mingdai weisuo de jun" [Soldiers in the Ming Guards]. *Zhongyang yanjiuyuan lishi yuyan yanjiusuo jikan* 48, no. 2 (1977): 177–203.

Chin, James. "Merchants, Smugglers, and Pirates." In *Elusive Pirates, Pervasive Smugglers: Violence and Clandestine Trade in the Greater China Seas*, edited by Robert Antony, 43–58. Hong Kong: Hong Kong University Press, 2010.

Clark, Hugh. *Community, Trade and Networks: Southern Fujian from the Third to the Thirteenth Century*. Cambridge: Cambridge University Press, 1991.

Cohen, Myron. *Kinship, Community, Contract and State: Anthropological Perspectives on China*. Stanford: Stanford University Press, 2005.

———. "Commodity Creation in Late Imperial China." In *Locating Capitalism in Time and Space: Global Restructurings, Polities and Identity*, edited by David Nugent. Stanford: Stanford University Press, 2002. Reprinted in *Kinship, Community, Contract and State: Anthropological Perspectives on China*, 223–51. Stanford, Stanford University Press, 2005.

Collins, James. *The State in Early Modern France*. 2nd edition. Cambridge: Cambridge University Press, 2009.

Dardess, John. *A Political Life in Ming China: A Grand Secretary and His Times*. Lanham, MD: Rowman and Littlefield, 2013.

de Certeau, Michel. *The Practice of Everyday Life*. Translated by Steven Rendall. Berkeley: University of California Press, 1984.

Dean, Kenneth. *Taoist Ritual and Popular Cults in Southeast China*. Princeton: Princeton University Press, 1993.

Dean, Kenneth and Thomas Lamarre. "Ritual Matters." In *Impacts of Modernities*, edited by Thomas Lamarre and Kang Nae-hui, 257–84. Hong Kong: Hong Kong University Press, 2004.

Dean, Kenneth (Ding Hesheng) and Zheng Zhenman. *Fujian zongjiao beiming huibian Quanzhou fu fence* [Collected Religious Inscriptions from Fujian: Quanzhou Volume]. Fuzhou: Fujian renmin, 1995.

———. *Fujian zongjiao beiming huibian Xinghua fu fence* [Collected Religious Inscriptions from Fujian: Xinghua Volume]. Fuzhou: Fujian renmin, 2003.

———. *Ritual Alliances of the Putian Plains*. Leiden: Brill, 2010.

Deleuze, Gilles and Felix Guattari. *Anti-Oedipus*. Translated by Robert Hurley, Mark Seem, and Helen Lane. Minneapolis: University of Minnesota Press, 1983.

———. *Nomadology: The War Machine*. Translated by Brian Massumi. New York: Semiotext(e), 1986.

Deng Qingping. "Zhouxian yu weisuo: Zhengqu yanbian yu Huabei biandi de shehui bianqian—yi Ming-Qing Yuzhou weili" [Subprefectures, Counties and Guards: Administrative Geography Evolution and Social Change in North China Borderlands—the Case of Yuzhou in the Ming-Qing]. PhD diss., Beijing University, 2006.

Deng Xiaonan. *Zuzong zhi fa: bei Song qianqi zhengzhi shilue* [The Law of the Ancestors: A Political History of Early Northern Song]. Beijing: Sanlian, 2006.

Dennerline, Jerry. *The Chia-Ting Loyalists: Confucian Leadership and Social Change in Seventeenth-Century China*. New Haven: Yale University Press, 1981.

Dennis, Joseph. *Writing, Publishing and Reading Local Gazetteers in Imperial China, 1100–1700*. Cambridge, MA: Asia Center, Harvard University, 2015.

Dreyer, Edward. "Military Origins of Ming China." In *The Cambridge History of China*, vol. 7, *The Ming Dynasty*, pt. 1, edited by Denis Twitchett and Frederick Mote, 58–106. Princeton: Princeton University Press, 1988.

Duara, Prasenjit. *The Crisis of Global Modernity: Asian Traditions and a Sustainable Future*. Cambridge: Cambridge University Press, 2015.

———. *Culture, Power and the State: Rural North China, 1900–1942*. Stanford: Stanford University Press, 1988.

———. "Superscribing Symbols: The Myth of Guandi, Chinese God of War." *Journal of Asian Studies* 47, no. 4 (1988): 778–95.

Dykstra, Maura. "Complicated Matters: Commercial Dispute Resolution in Chongqing, 1750–1911." PhD diss., UCLA, 2015.

Ebrey, Patricia. "China as a Contrasting Case: Bureaucracy and Empire in Song China." In *Empires and Bureaucracy in World History: From Late Antiquity to the Twentieth Century*, edited by Peter Crooks and Timothy Parsons, 31–53. Cambridge: Cambridge University Press, 2016.

Elman, Benjamin. *A Cultural History of Civil Examinations in Late Imperial China.* Berkeley: University of California Press, 2000.

Fan Wenlan and Cai Meibiao. *Zhongguo tongshi* [Survey History of China]. Beijing: Remin, 2008.

Farmer, Edward. *Zhu Yuanzhang and Early Ming Legislation: The Reordering of Chinese Society Following the Era of Mongol Rule.* Leiden: Brill, 1995.

Faure, David. *Emperor and Ancestor: State and Lineage in South China.* Stanford: Stanford University Press, 2007.

———. "The Emperor in the Village: Representing the State in South China." *Journal of the Hong Kong Branch of the Royal Asiatic Society* 35 (1995): 75–112.

Feng Menglong. *Stories to Awaken the World: A Ming Dynasty Collection*, translated by Shuhui Yang and Yunqin Yang. Seattle: University of Washington Press, 2009.

Feng Yanqun. "Cong Zhu Youdun zaju kan Mingdai weisuo junhu shengcun zhuangkuang" [The Livelihood Situation for Ming Guard Military Households as Seen from the Plays of Zhu Youdun]. *Shijiao ziliao*, no. 10 (2015): 71–74.

Foucault, Michel. "Governmentality." In *The Foucault Effect: Studies in Governmentality, with Two Lectures by and an Interview with Michel Foucault*, edited by Graham Burchell, Colin Gordon, and Peter Miller, 87–104. London: Harvester Wheatsheaf, 1991.

———. *Security, Territory, Population: Lectures at the Collège de France, 1977–78*, edited by Michel Senellart; translated by Graham Burchell. Basingstoke: Palgrave Macmillan, 2007.

———. "What Is Critique?" In *What Is Enlightenment? Eighteenth-Century Answers and Twentieth-Century Questions*, edited by James Schmidt, 382–98. Berkeley: University of California Press, 1997.

Freedman, Maurice. *Chinese Lineage Society: Fukien and Kwangtung.* London: Athlone, 1966.

Fukuyama, Francis. *The Origins of Political Order: From Prehuman Times to the French Revolution.* New York: Farrar, Straus, and Giroux, 2011.

Gao Bingzhong. "Yizuo bowuguan/miaoyu jianzhu de minzu zhi—lun chengwei zhengzhi yishu de shuangming zhi" [Ethnography of a Structure [That Is Both] Museum and Temple: Double-Naming as a Political Art]. In *Xiangcun wenhua yu xin nongcun jianshe*, edited by Li Xiaoyun, Zhao Xudong, and Ye Jingzhong, 182–98. Beijing: Shehui kexue, 2008.

Gates, Hill. *China's Motor: A Thousand Years of Petty Capitalism.* Ithaca: Cornell University Press, 1996.

Geertz, Clifford. *The Interpretation of Cultures: Selected Essays.* New York: Basic Books, 1973.

Geiss, James. "The Chia-Ching Reign. 1522–1566." In *The Cambridge History of China*, vol. 7, *The Ming Dynasty*, pt. 1, edited by Denis Twitchett and Frederick Mote, 440–510. Princeton: Princeton University Press, 1988.

Girard, Pascale, trans. and ed. *Le Voyage en Chine d'Adriano de las Cortes (1625)*. Paris: Chandeigne, 2001.

Glahn, Richard von. "Household Registration, Property Rights, and Social Obligations in Imperial China: Principles and Practices." In *Registration and Recognition: Documenting the Person in World History*, edited by Keith Breckenridge and Simon Szreter, 39–66. *Proceedings of the British Academy* 182 (2012).

———. "Imagining Pre-Modern China." In *The Song-Yuan-Ming Transition in Chinese History*, edited by Paul Jakov Smith and Richard von Glahn, 35–70. Cambridge, MA: Harvard University Asia Center, 2003.

Goldstone, Jack. "The Problem of the 'Early Modern' World." *Journal of the Economic and Social History of the Orient* 41, no. 3 (1998): 249–84.

Goodman, David. "Corruption in the PLA." In *Chinese Economic Reform: The Impact on Security*, edited by Gerald Segal and Richard Yang, 35–52. London and New York: Routledge, 1996.

Goodrich, L. Carrington and Chaoying Fang, eds. *Dictionary of Ming Biography, 1368–1644*. New York: Columbia University Press, 1976.

Goossaert, Vincent. "A Question of Control: Licensing Local Ritual Specialists in Jiangnan, 1850–1950." In *Xinyang, shijian yu wenhua tiaoshi*, edited by Kang Bao (Paul Katz) and Liu Shufen, 569–604. Taibei: Zhongyang yanjiuyuan, 2013.

Greif, Avner. *Institutions and the Path to the Modern Economy: Lessons from Medieval Trade*. Cambridge: Cambridge University Press, 2006.

Gu Cheng. "Tan Mingdai de weiji" [On Guard Registration in the Ming]. *Beijing shifan daxue xuebao*, no. 5 (1989): 56–65.

———. "Weisuo zhidu zai Qingdai de biange" [The Transformation of the Guard System in the Qing]. *Beijing shifan daxue xuebao*, no. 2 (1989): 15–22.

Guo Hong. "Mingdai de qidao zhi ji: Zhongguo gudai junshixing jisi de gaofeng" [Banner Worship in Ming: The Height of an Ancient Military Sacrifice]. *Minsu yanjiu* 111 (2013): 90–96.

Hamashima Atsutoshi. "Communal Religion in Jiangnan Delta Rural Villages in Late Imperial China." *International Journal of Asian Studies* 8, no. 2 (2011): 127–62.

———. "Dong Ya zhuguo de chenghuangshen xinyang" [Belief in the God of the Wall in the Countries of East Asia]. In *Chenghuang xinyang*, edited by Lin Weiyi, 13–48. Singapore: Feilaiba chenghuang miao, 2008.

Hansen, Valerie. *Negotiating Daily Life in Traditional China: How Ordinary People Used Contracts, 600–1400*. New Haven: Yale University Press, 1995.

Hasan, Farat. *State and Locality in Mughal India: Power Relations in Western India, c. 1572–1730*. Cambridge: Cambridge University Press, 2004.

He Mengxing.*Wuyu shuizhai: yige Mingdai Minhai shuishi zhongzhen de guancha* [Wuyu Fort: A Ming Naval Post in the Seas of Fujian]. Taibei: Lantai, 2005.

Heijdra, Martin. "The Socioeconomic Development of Rural China during the Ming." In *The Cambridge History of China*, vol. 8, *The Ming Dynasty*, pt. 2, edited by Denis Twitchett and Frederick Mote, 417–578. Princeton: Princeton University Press, 1998.

Hershatter, Gayle. "The Subaltern Talks Back: Reflections on Subaltern Theory and Chinese History." *Positions: East Asia Cultural Critique* 1, no. 1 (1993): 103–30.

Hexie chengxiang you [Tour of a Harmonious Community]. Anxi: 2007.

Higgins, Roland. "Piracy and Coastal Defense in the Ming Period, Government Response to Coastal Disturbances, 1523–1549." PhD diss., University of Minnesota, 1981.

——. "Pirates in Gowns and Caps: Gentry Law-Breaking in the Mid-Ming." *Ming Studies* 10 (1980): 30–37.

Ho, Dahpon. "Sea Lords Live in Vain: Fujian and the Making of a Maritime Frontier in Seventeenth-Century China." PhD diss., University of California, San Diego, 2011.

Hobsbawm, Eric. "Peasants and Politics." *Journal of Peasant Studies* 1, no. 1 (1973): 3–22.

Hsiao, Ch'i-ch'ing. *The Military Establishment of the Yuan Dynasty*. Cambridge, MA: Council on East Asian Studies, Harvard University, 1978.

Huang, Philip. "Between Informal Mediation and Formal Adjudication: The Third Realm of Qing Justice." *Modern China* 19, no. 3 (1993): 251–98.

——. "Centralized Minimalism: Semiformal Governance by Quasi Officials and Dispute Resolution in China." *Modern China* 34, no. 1 (2008): 9 –35.

——. *Civil Justice in China: Representation and Practice in the Qing*. Stanford: Stanford University Press, 1996.

Huang, Raymond. *Broadening the Horizons of Chinese History: Discourses, Syntheses, and Comparisons*. Armonk, NY: M.E. Sharpe, 1999.

——. *Taxation and Governmental Finance in Sixteenth-Century Ming China*. Cambridge: Cambridge University Press, 1974.

Huang Xiaodong. "Hanyu junhua gaishu" [Military Dialects of Chinese]. *Yuyan jiaoxue yu yanjiu*, no. 3: (2007) 21–27.

Huang Zhongqing. *Mingdai haifang de shuizhai yu youbing: Zhe Min Yue yanhai daoyu fangwei de jianzhi yu jieti* [Naval Forts and Soldiers in Ming Coastal Defense: The Establishment and Disintegration of Island Defense on the Zhejiang, Fujian, and Guangdong Coast]. Yilan: Xueshu jiangzhu jijin, 2001.

Hucker, Charles. *The Censorial System of Ming China*. Stanford: Stanford University Press, 1996.

Hymes, Robert. *Way and Byway: Taoism, Local Religion and Models of Divinity in Sung and Modern China*. Berkeley: University of California Press, 2002.

Jiang Bowei. "Cong junshi chengbao dao zongzu juluo: Fujian Jinmencheng zhi yanjiu" [From Military Fort to Lineage Village: The Walled Town of Jinmen, Fujian]. *Chengshi yu sheji xuebao* 13, nos. 7–8 (1999): 133–77.

Johnson, David. "The City God Cults of T'ang and Sung China." *Harvard Journal of Asiatic Studies* 45, no. 2 (1985): 363–457.

Johnston, Alastair I. *Cultural Realism: Strategic Culture and Grand Strategy in Chinese History*. Princeton: Princeton University Press, 1995.

Jones, William, trans. *The Great Qing Code*. Oxford: Clarendon Press, 1994.

Joyner, Charles. *Shared Traditions: Southern History and Folk Culture*. Urbana: University of Illinois Press, 1999.

Julien, François. *Detour and Access: Strategies of Meaning in China and Greece*. Translated by Sophie Hawkes. New York: Zone Books, 2000.

Katayama Tsuyoshi. "Shindai Kantonshō Shukō deruta no zukōsei ni tsuite: zeiryō, koseki, dōzoku" [The *Tujia* System in the Pearl River Delta in

Guangdong in Qing: Taxes, Households, Lineage]. *Tōyō Gakuhō* 63, nos. 3–4 (1982): 1–34.

Katz, Paul. *Divine Justice: Religion and the Development of Chinese Legal Culture.* London: Routledge, 2009.

Kawagoe Yasuhiro. "Mingdai junshishi de yanjiu zhuangkuang" [The Current Situation of Research on Ming Military History]. In *Ming-Qing shidaishi de jiben wenti*, edited by Mori Masao et al. Translated by Zhou Shaoquan et al., 241–259. Beijing: Shangwu, 2013.

———. "Wokou beiluren yu Mingdai de haifangjun" [Kidnap Victims of Japanese Piracy and Naval Defense Soldiers in Ming]. Translated by Li Sanmou. *Zhongguo bianjiangshi de yanjiu*, no. 3 (1998): 107–15.

Kerkvliet, Ben. "Everyday Politics in Peasant Societies (and Ours). " *Journal of Peasant Studies* 36, no. 1 (2009): 227–43.

Kishimoto Mio, *Shindai Chūgoku no bukka to keizai hendō* [Prices and Economic Change in Qing China]. Tokyo: Kenbun Shuppan, 1997.

Kuhn, Philip. *Chinese among Others: Emigration in Modern Times.* Lanham, MD: Rowman and Littlefield, 2008.

Langlois, John. "The Code and *Ad Hoc* Legislation in Ming Law," *Asia Major.* 3rd series, 6, no. 2 (1993): 85–112.

Lee, Sukhee. *Negotiated Power: The State, Elites and Local Governance in Twelfth- to Fourteenth-Century China.* Cambridge, MA: Harvard University Asia Center, 2014.

Levi, Margaret. "Conscription: The Price of Citizenship." In *Analytic Narratives*, edited by Robert Bates et al., 109–47. Princeton: Princeton University Press, 1998.

Li, Bozhong. *Agricultural Development in Jiangnan, 1620–1850.* New York: St. Martin's Press, 1998.

Li Huayan. "Jin sanshinian lai Ming-Qing ding'ge zhe ji junshishi yanjiu huigu" [A Look Back on the Last Thirty Years of Research into the Military History of the Ming-Qing Transition]. *Mingdai yanjiu* 23 (2014): 127–54.

Li Jinming. *Mingdai haiwai maoyishi* [History of Maritime Trade in Ming]. Beijing: Zhongguo shehui kexueyuan, 1990.

Li, Kangying. *The Ming Maritime Trade Policy in Transition, 1368–1567.* Wiesbaden: Harrassowitz Verlag, 2010.

Li Pengfei. "'Sanyan erpai' zhong Mingdai junshi jishu zhi yanjiu" [Military Technology in Ming as Seen in "Three Words Two Slaps" Stories]. *Heilongjiang shizhi*, no. 23 (2012): 11–13.

Li, Renyuan. "Making Texts in Villages: Textual Production in Rural China during the Ming-Qing Period." PhD diss., Harvard University, 2014.

Li, Tana. "An Alternative Vietnam? The Nguyen Kingdom in the Seventeenth and Eighteenth Centuries," *Journal of Southeast Asian Studies* 29, no. 1 (1998): 111–21.

Liang Zhisheng. *Mingdai weisuo wuguan shixi zhidu yanjiu* [The System of Inheritance of Oficer Positions in Ming Guards]. Beijing: Zhongguo shehui kexue chubanshe, 2012.

———. "Shixi Mingdai weisuo wuguan de leixing" [The Categories of Officers in Ming Guards]. *Xibei daxue xuebao (Shehui kexue ban)*, no. 5 (2001): 83–88.

Liew Foon Ming. *The Treatises on Military Affairs of the Ming Dynastic History (1368–1644).* Hamburg: Gesellschaft für Natur- und Vülkerkunde Ostasiens, 1998.

———. *Tuntian Farming of the Ming Dynasty (1368–1644)*. Hamburg: Gesellschaft für Natur- und Vülkerkunde Ostasiens, 1984.

Lim, Ivy Maria. *Lineage Society on the Southeastern Coast of China: The Impact of Japanese Piracy in the 16th Century*. Amherst, NY: Cambria, 2010.

Lin Changzhang. "Ming-Qing dongnan yanhai weisuo de difanghua - yi Wenzhou Jinxiang wei wei zhongxin" [Localization in the Guards of the Southeast Coast in Ming-Qing: The Case of Jinxiang Guard, Wenzhou]. *Zhongguo lishi dili luncong* 24, no. 4 (2009): 115–25.

Lin Renchuan. *Mingmo Qingchu de siren haishang maoyi* [Private Sea Trade in Late Ming and Early Qing]. Shanghai: Huadong shifan daxue, 1987.

Link, Perry. *An Anatomy of Chinese: Rhythm, Metaphor, Politics*. Cambridge, MA: Harvard University Press, 2013.

Liu Daosheng. *Ming-Qing Huizhou zongzu wenshu yanjiu* [Lineage Documents of Huizhou from Ming-Qing]. Hefei: Anhui renmin, 2008.

Liu, William Guanglin. *The Chinese Market Economy, 1000–1500*. Albany: State University of New York Press, 2015.

Liu Xiangru and Zhang Tianhao. *Meijiang fengqing* [The Scenery of Meijiang]. Hong Kong: Huaxing, 2003.

Liu Yonghua and Zheng Rong. "Qingchu Zhongguo dongnan diqu de lianghu guizong gaige: laizi Minnan de lizheng" [The Policy of Allocating Tax-Paying Responsibilities to the Patriline in the Early Qing in China's Southeast Region: An Example from Southern Fujian]. *Zhongguo jingjishi yanjiu*, no. 4 (2008): 81–87.

Liu Zhiwei. "Beyond the Imperial Metaphor: A Local History of the Beidi (Northern Emperor) Cult in the Pearl River Delta," translated by Maybo Ching. *Chinese Studies in History* 35, no. 1 (2001): 12–30.

———. *Zai guojia yu shehui zhijian: Ming Qing Guangdong diqu lijia fuyi zhidu yu xiangcun shehui* [Between State and Society: The *Lijia* Tax System and Rural Society in Guangdong in Ming-Qing]. Guangzhou: Zhongshan daxue, 1997.

Lu Jianyi. "Mingdai haijin zhengce yu Fujian haifang" [The Ming Coastal Prohibition and Coastal Defense in Fujian]. *Fujian shifan daxue xuebao (Zhexue shehui kexue ban)*, no. 2 (1992): 118–21.

Lu Zhengheng [Lu Cheng-heng]. "Guan yu zei zhijian: Zheng Zhilong baquan ji Zheng bu" [Between Official and Bandit: The Authority of Zheng Zhilong and the Zheng Administration]. Master's thesis, Qinghua University, 2012.

Luan Chengxian. *Mingdai huangce yanjiu* [The Yellow Registers of the Ming]. Beijing: Zhongguo shehui kexue, 1998.

Luo Xiaoxiang. "Soldiers and the City: Urban Experience of Guard Households in Late Ming Nanjing." *Frontiers of History in China* 5, no. 1 (2010): 30–51.

Makino Tatsumi. *Kinsei Chūgoku sōzoku kenkyū* [Lineages in Early Modern China]. Tokyo: Nikko Shoin, 1949.

Mann, Michael. "The Autonomous Power of the State: Its Origins, Mechanisms and Results." *Archives européennes de sociologie* 25, no. 2 (1984): 185–213.

Mann, Susan. *Local Merchants and the Chinese Bureaucracy, 1750–1950*. Stanford: Stanford University Press, 1987.

McKay, Joseph. "Maritime Pirates as Escape Societies in Late Imperial China." *Social Science History* 37, no. 4 (2013): 551–73.

McKay, Ruth. *The Limits of Royal Authority: Resistance and Obedience in Seventeenth-Century Castile*. Cambridge: Cambridge University Press, 1999.

McKnight, Brian. *Village and Bureaucracy in Southern Sung China*. Chicago: University of Chicago Press, 1971.

Menzies, Gavin. *1421: The Year China Discovered the World*. New York: Bantam, 2002.

Mitchell, Timothy. "The Limits of the State: Beyond Statist Approaches and Their Critics." *American Political Science Review* 85, no. 1 (1991): 77–96.

Muscolino, Micah. "Underground at Sea: Fishing and Smuggling across the Taiwan Strait, 1970s–1990s." In *Mobile Horizons: Dynamics across the Taiwan Strait*, edited by Wen-hsin Yeh, 99–123. Berkeley: Institute of East Asian Studies, University of California, 2013.

Needham, Joseph, ed. *Science and Civilization in China*. Cambridge: Cambridge University Press, 1954.

Nimick, Thomas. *Local Administration in Ming China: The Changing Roles of Magistrates, Prefects, and Provincial Officials*. Minneapolis: Center for Early Modern History, University of Minnesota, 2008.

Oakes, Tim. "The Alchemy of the Ancestors: Rituals of Genealogy in the Service of the Nation in Rural China." In *Faiths on Display: Religion, Tourism, and the Chinese State*, edited by Tim Oakes and Donald Sutton, 51–78. Lanham, MD: Rowman and Littlefield, 2010.

Ocko, Jonathan. "The *Missing Metaphor*: Applying Western Legal Scholarship to the Study of Contract and Property in Early Modern China." In *Contract and Property in Early Modern China*, edited by Madeleine Zelin, Jonathan Ocko, and Robert Gardella, 178–205. Stanford: Stanford University Press, 2004.

Oi, Jean and Andrew Walder. "Property Rights in the Chinese Economy: Contours of the Process of Change." In *Property Rights and Economic Reform in China*, edited by Jean Oi and Andrew Walder, 1–26. Stanford: Stanford University Press, 1999.

Oxfeld, Ellen. *Blood, Sweat and Mahjong: Family and Enterprise in an Overseas Chinese Community*. Ithaca: Cornell University Press, 1993.

Parsons, James Bunyan. *The Peasant Rebellions of the Late Ming Dynasty*. Tucson: University of Arizona Press, 1970.

Peng Yong. "Mingdai qijun jingji shenghuo tanyan—yi banjun wei xiansuo" [The Economic Life of Ming Troops: The Case of the Rotating Capital Troops]. In *Dishiyi jie Mingshi guoji xueshu taolunhui lunwenji*, edited by Tian Tao et al., 163–74. Tianjin: Tianjin guji, 2007.

Perdue, Peter. *China Marches West: The Qing Conquest of Central Eurasia*. Cambridge, MA: Harvard University Press, 2005.

———. *Exhausting the Earth: State and Peasant in Hunan, 1500–1850*. Cambridge, MA: Council on East Asian Studies, Harvard University, 1987.

Perry, Elizabeth. "Popular Protest: Playing by the Rules." In *China Today, China Tomorrow: Domestic Politics, Economy and Society*, edited by Joseph Fewsmith, 11–28. Lanham, MD: Rowman and Littlefield, 2010.

Pieke, Frank. "The Genealogical Mentality in Modern China." *Journal of Asian Studies* 62, no. 1 (2003): 101–28.

Pomeranz, Kenneth. *The Great Divergence: China, Europe, and the Making of the Modern World Economy*. Princeton: Princeton University Press, 2000.

——. "Land Markets in Late Imperial and Republican China." *Continuity and Change* 23, no. 1 (2008): 101–50.

Puk Wing-kin. *The Rise and Fall of a Public Debt Market in 16th-Century China: The Story of the Ming Salt Certificate*. Leiden: Brill, 2016.

Putian xian difangzhi biancuan weiyuan hui and Putian xian minsu xuehui, *Puxi suocheng zaji* [Miscellaneous Notes from Puxi Battalion]. Putian, 1997.

Qi Wenying. "Beiming suojian Mingdai daguan hunyin guanxi" [Marriage Relations of Ming High Officials as Seen from Stone Inscriptions]. *Zhongguoshi yanjiu*, no. 3 (2011): 167–81.

Rao Weixin. "Daoyan: zupu yu shehui wenhuashi yanjiu" [Introduction: Genealogies and Research in Social and Cultural History]. In *Zupu yanjiu* [Research on Genealogies], edited by Rao Weixin, 1-24. Beijing: Shehui kexue, 2013.

——. "Mingdai junzaoji kaolun" [The Military-Saltern Registration in Ming]. *Zhongyang yanjiuyuan lishi yuyan yanjiusuo jikan* 85, no. 2 (2014): 427–75.

——. ed. *Zupu yanjiu* [Research on Genealogies]. Beijing: Shehui kexue, 2013.

Reed, Bradly. *Talons and Teeth: County Clerks and Runners in the Qing Dynasty*. Stanford: Stanford University Press, 2000.

Reid, Anthony. "Violence at Sea: Unpacking "Piracy" in the Claims of States over Asian Seas." In *Elusive Pirates, Pervasive Smugglers: Violence and Clandestine Trade in the Greater China Seas*, edited by Robert Antony, 15–26. Hong Kong: Hong Kong University Press, 2010.

Roberts, Michael. *The Military Revolution 1560–1660*. Belfast: Marjory Boyd, 1956.

Robinson, David. *Bandits, Eunuchs, and the Son of Heaven: Rebellion and the Economy of Violence in Mid-Ming China*. Honolulu: University of Hawai'i Press, 2001.

——. "Military Labor in China, circa 1500." In *Fighting for a Living: A Comparative History of Military Labour 1500-2000*, edited by Erik Jan Zürcher, 43–55. Amsterdam: Amsterdam University Press, 2014.

Robson, James. "Hidden in Plain View: Concealed Contents, Secluded Statues, and Revealed Religion." In *The Rhetoric of Hiddenness in Traditional Chinese Culture*, edited by Paula Varsano, 117–205. Albany: State University of New York Press, 2016.

Rosenthal, Jean-Laurent and R. Bin Wong. *Before and Beyond Divergence: The Politics of Economic Change in China and Europe*. Cambridge, MA: Harvard University Press, 2011.

Rowe, William. *Hankow: Conflict and Community in a Chinese City, 1796–1895*. Stanford: Stanford University Press, 1989.

Ruskola, Teema. "Conceptualizing Corporations and Kinship: Comparative Law and Development Theory in a Chinese Perspective." *Stanford Law Review* 52, no. 6 (2000): 1599–729.

Sangren, Paul Steven. *History and Magical Power in a Chinese Community*. Stanford: Stanford University Press, 1987.

——. "Traditional Chinese Corporations: Beyond Kinship." *Journal of Asian Studies* 43, no. 3 (1984): 391–415.

Schneewind, Sarah. *Community Schools and the State in Ming China*. Stanford: Stanford University Press, 2006.

Scholte, Jan. *Globalization: A Critical Introduction*. 2nd edition. New York: Palgrave Macmillan, 2005.

Scott, James. *The Art of Not Being Governed: An Anarchist History of Upland Southeast Asia*. New Haven: Yale University Press, 2009.

———. *Seeing like a State: How Certain Schemes to Improve the Human Condition Have Failed*. New Haven: Yale University Press, 1998.

———. *Weapons of the Weak: Everyday Forms of Peasant Resistance*. New Haven: Yale University Press, 1985.

Shen Bin and Hong Zhongxin. "Mingmo de lijia yi yu bianhu duice lue" [The *Lijia* Tax System in Late Ming and the Counter-Strategy of Reorganizing the Household]. *Zhongguo shehui jingjishi yanjiu*, no. 3 (2015): 41–51.

Shishi shizhi Beijing: Fangzhi, 1998.

Sivaramakrishnan, Kalyanakrishnan. "Some Intellectual Genealogies for the Concept of Everyday Resistance." *American Anthropologist* 107, no. 3 (2005): 346–55.

So, Billy Kee-Long. *Prosperity, Region and Institutions in Maritime China: The South Fukien Pattern, 946–1368*. Cambridge, MA: Asia Center, Harvard University, 2000.

So, Kwan-wai. *Japanese Piracy in Ming China during the Sixteenth Century*. East Lansing: Michigan State University Press, 1975.

Sommer, Matthew. *Polyandry and Wife Selling in Qing Dynasty China: Survival Strategies and Judicial Interventions*. Berkeley: University of California Press, 2015.

Spivak, Gayatri Chakravorty. "Can the Subaltern Speak?" In *Marxism and the Interpretation of Cultures*, edited by Cary Nelson and Lawrence Grossberg, 271–313. Urbana: University of Illinois Press, 1988.

Stoler, Ann Laura. *Along the Archival Grain: Epistemic Anxieties and Colonial Common Sense*. Princeton: Princeton University Press, 2009.

Struve, Lynn. "Modern China's Liberal Muse: The Late Ming." *Ming Studies* 63 (2011): 38–68.

Sun Wenlong, ed. *Dongshan wenwu mingsheng zhi* [Gazetteer of the Artifacts and Famous Sites of Dongshan]. Dongshan: Fujiansheng Dongshan bowuguan, 1990.

Swope, Kenneth. *A Dragon's Head and a Serpent's Tail: Ming China and the First Great East Asian War (1592–1598)*. Norman: University of Oklahoma Press, 2009.

Szonyi, Michael. "Lineages and the Making of Modern China." In *Modern Chinese Religion II: 1850–2015*, vol. 1, edited by Vincent Goossaert, Jan Kiely, and John Lagerwey, 433–90. Leiden: Brill, 2016.

———. *Practicing Kinship: Lineage and Descent in Late Imperial China*. Stanford: Stanford University Press, 2002.

Tackett, Nicolas. "A Tang-Song Turning Point." In *A Companion to Chinese History*, edited by Michael Szonyi, 118–28. Chichester, UK: Wiley Blackwell, 2017.

Tagliacozzo, Eric. *Secret Trades, Porous Borders: Smuggling and States along a Southeast Asian Frontier, 1865–1915*. New Haven: Yale University Press, 2005.

Tam, Yik Fan. "Xianghua Foshi (Incense and Flower Buddhist Rites): A Local Buddhist Funeral Ritual Tradition in Southeastern China." In *Buddhist Funeral Cultures of Southeast Asia and China*, edited by Paul Williams and Patrice Ladwig, 238–260. Cambridge: Cambridge University Press, 2012.

Tang Wenji. *Yongningwei zashi* [Miscellaneous Historical Notes from Yongning Guard]. Fuzhou: Fujian shizhi, 2001.

Taylor, Romeyn. "Official Altars, Temples and Shrines Mandated for All Counties in Ming and Qing." *T'oung Pao* 83 (1997): 93–125.

———. "Yüan Origins of the Wei-So System." In *Chinese Government in Ming Times: Seven Studies*, edited by Charles Hucker. New York: Columbia University Press, 1969.

ter Haar, Barend. *Guan Yu: The Religious Afterlife of a Failed Hero*. Forthcoming.

———. "The Religious Core of Local Social Organization." In *A Companion to Chinese History*, edited by Michael Szonyi, 304–14. Chichester, UK: Wiley Blackwell, 2017.

Tilly, Charles. "Entanglements of European Cities and States." In *Cities and the Rise of States in Europe, A.D. 1000 to 1800*, edited by Charles Tilly and Wim Blockmans, 1–27. Boulder, CO: Westview Press, 1994.

———. "Reflections on the History of European State-Making." In *The Formation of National States in Western Europe*, edited by Charles Tilly, 3–81. Princeton: Princeton University Press, 1975.

Tong, James. *Disorder under Heaven: Collective Violence in the Ming Dynasty*. Stanford: Stanford University Press, 1991.

Wakefield, David. *Fenjia: Household Division and Inheritance in Qing and Republican China*. Honolulu: University of Hawai'i Press, 1998.

Waldron, Arthur. *The Great Wall of China: From History to Myth*. Cambridge: Cambridge University Press, 1990.

Wang Fansen. *Quanli de maoxiguan zuoyong: Qingdai de sixiang, xueshu yu xintai* [The Capillary Uses of Power: Thought, Scholarship and Ideology in Qing]. Taibei: Lianjing, 2013.

Wang Heming, ed. *Zhongguo jiapu zongmu* [General Catalogue of Chinese Genealogies]. Shanghai: Shanghai guji, 2008.

Wang Lianmao and Ye Endian, eds. *Quanzhou, Taiwan Zhang Shixiang jiazu wenjian huibian* [Collected Documents of Zhang Shixiang and his Lineage from Quanzhou and Taiwan]. Fuzhou: Fujian renmin, 1999.

Wang Mingming. "Place, Administration and Territorial Cults in Late Imperial China: A Case Study from South Fujian." *Late Imperial China* 16, no. 1 (1995): 33–78.

———. *Xicun jiazu: shequshi, yishi yu difang zhengzhi* [Lineages of Xicun: Community History, Ritual and Local Politics]. Guiyang: Guizhou renmin, 2004.

Wang Weichu. "Families and Regions of Ming *Jin-Shi* Degree Holders: A Study of the *Jin-Shi* Lists in the China Biographical Database Project." Master's thesis, Harvard University, 2016.

Wang Yuquan. *Mingdai de juntun* [The Military Colonies of the Ming]. Beijing: Zhonghua, 1965.

Watson, James. "Waking the Dragon: Visions of the Chinese Imperial State in Local Myth." In *An Old State in New Settings: Studies in the Social Anthropology of China in Memory of Maurice Freedman*, edited by Hugh Baker and Stephan Feuchtwang, 162–77. Oxford: JASO, 1991.

Weber, Max. "Politics as a Vocation" (1918). In *From Max Weber: Essays in Sociology*, translated and edited by H. H. Gerth and C. Wright Mills, 77–128. Abingdon: Routledge, 1991.

Wei Qingyuan. *Mingdai huangce zhidu* [The Yellow Register System of Ming]. Beijing: Zhonghua, 1961.

Weller, Robert. "The Politics of Ritual Disguise: Repression and Response in Taiwanese Popular Religion." *Modern China* 13, no. 1 (1987): 17–39.

———. "Responsive Authoritarianism and Blind-Eyed Governance in China." In *Socialism Vanquished, Socialism Challenged: Eastern Europe and China, 1989-2009*, edited by Dorothy J. Solinger and Nina Bandelj, 83-98. Oxford: Oxford University Press, 2012.

Wen Duanzheng. *Cangnan fangyanzhi* [Gazetteer of Cangnan Dialect]. Beijing: Yuwen, 1991.

Wilkison, Wade. "Newly Discovered Ming Dynasty Guard Registers." *Ming Studies* 3 (1976): 36-45.

Will, Pierre-Etienne and R. Bin Wong. *Nourish the People: The State Civilian Granary System in China, 1650-1850*. Ann Arbor: Center for Chinese Studies, University of Michigan, 1991.

Wills, John. *Embassies and Illusions: Dutch and Portugese Envoys to K'ang-hsi, 1666-1687*. Cambridge, MA: Council on East Asian Studies, Harvard University, 1984.

Wong, R. Bin. *China Transformed: Historical Change and the Limits of European Experience*. Ithaca: Cornell University Press, 1997.

———. "Taxation and Good Governance in China, 1500-1914." In *The Rise of Fiscal States: A Global History, 1500-1914*, edited by Bartolomé Yun-Casalilla and Patrick K. O'Brien, 353-77. Cambridge: Cambridge University Press, 2012.

Wu Daxin. "Haishang, haidao, wo—Mingdai Jiajing da wokou de xinxiang" [Merchants, Pirates, Dwarf [Bandits]: New Perspectives on the Wokou of the Jiajing Period of Ming]. Master's thesis, Ji'nan International University, 2002.

Wu Han. "Mingdai de junbing" [Soldiers of the Ming]. *Zhongguo shehui jingjishi jikan* 5, no. 2 (1937): 147-200.

Wu Yanhong. *Mingdai chongjun yanjiu* [Conscription in Ming]. Beijing: Shehui kexue wenxian, 2003.

Wu Zaoting. *Quanzhou minjian chuanshuo ji* [Popular Legends of Quanzhou]. Quanzhou: Quanshan shushe, 1933-34.

Xie Shi. "Mingdai Taicangzhou de shezhi" [The Establishment of Taicang Subprefecture in Ming]. *Lishi yanjiu*, no. 3 (2012): 29-43.

———. "Yi tun yi min: Ming Qing Nanling weisuo juntun de yanbian yu shehui jiangou" [Both Colonist and Civilian: Transformations and Social Structure of the Military Colonists of Nanling Guards in Ming-Qing]. *Wenshi*, no. 4 (2014): 75-110.

Xu Bin. *Ming Qing E-dong zongzu yu difang shehui* [Lineages and Local Society in Eastern Hubei in Ming Qing]. Wuhan: Wuhan daxue, 2010.

Xu Hong. "Mingdai Fujian de zhucheng yundong" [The Wall Construction Movement in Ming Fujian]. *Jinan xuebao* 3, no. 1 (1999): 25-76.

Xu Shuang. "Fujian chenghuang xinyang yanjiu" [The Cult of the God of the Wall in Fujian]. Master's thesis, Fujian shifan daxue, 2007.

Xu Xianyao. "Mingdai de goujun" [Recovery of Deserters in Ming]. *Mingshi yanjiu zhuankan* 6 (1983): 133-92.

Yamazaki Takeshi. "Junbu Shu Gan no mita umi—Mindai Kasei nenkan no enkai eijo to 'Daiwakō' zenya no hitobito" [The Coast from the Viewpoint of Commissioner Zhu Wan: On the Coastal Guards and the Japanese Pirates in the Jiajing Period of the Ming]. *Tōyōshi kenkyū* 62, no. 1 (2003): 1-38.

Yang Guozhen. *Ming Qing tudi qiyue wenshu yanjiu* [Research into Land Deeds in Ming-Qing]. Beijing: Renmin, 1988.

Yang Peina. "Binhai shengji yu wangchao zhixu: Ming-Qing Min-Ao yanhai diqu shehui bianqian yanjiu" [Coastal Livelihood and Imperial System: Research into Social Change in Coastal Regions of Fujian and Guangdong in Ming-Qing]. PhD diss., Zhongshan University, 2009.

Ye Jinhua. "Ming-Qing zaohu zhidu de yunzuo jiqi tiaoshi" [Operation and Adjustment of the Saltern Household System in Ming-Qing]. PhD diss., Zhongshan University, 2012.

Ye Mingsheng, ed. *Min-Tai Zhang shengjun xinyang wenhua* [Belief in Zhang Shengjun in Fujian and Taiwan]. Fuzhou: Haichao sheying meishu, 2008.

Yi Zeyang. *Mingchao zhongqi de haifang sixiang yanjiu* [Coastal Defense Thought in Mid-Ming]. Beijing: Jiefangjun, 2008.

Yin Changyi. *Zhang Shixiang jiazu yimin fazhanshi: Qingchu Minnan shizu yimin Taiwan zhiyi ge'an yanjiu* [History of Migration and Development of Zhang Shixiang and His Lineage: A Case Study of a Prominent Lineage from Southern Fujian Migrating to Taiwan in Early Qing]. Taibei, 1983.

Yu Dazhu, ed. *Yurong guqu* [Old Flavors of Yurong [Fuqing]]. Fuzhou: Haixia wenyi, 1991.

Yu Zhijia. "Bangding tingji: Mingdai junhu zhong yuding jiaose de fenhua" [Associated Males Fulfilling Service Duties: On the Diversification of Roles of the Supernumeraries in Ming Military Households]. *Zhongyang yanjiuyuan lishi yuyan yanjiusuo jikan* 84, no. 3 (2013): 455–525.

———. "Lun Mingdai de fuji junhu yu junhu fenhu" [Military Households with Attached Registration and Division of Military Households in Ming]. In *Gu Cheng xiansheng jinian ji Ming-Qing shi yanjiu wenji*, 80–104. Zhengzhou: Zhongzhou guji, 2005.

———. "Mindai gunko no shakaiteki chii ni tsuite: gunko no kon'in o megutte" [The Social Status of Ming Military Households: Marriage Relations of Military Households]. *Mindaishi kenkyū* 18 (1990): 7–31.

———. "Mindai gunko no shakaiteki chii ni tsuite: kakyo to ninkan ni oite" [The Social Status of Ming Military Households: Examination Participation and Official Service]. *Tōyō gakuhō* 71, nos. 3–4 (1990): 311–51.

———. *Mingdai junhu shixi zhidu* [The Inheritance System of Military Households in Ming]. Taibei: Taiwan xuesheng, 1987.

———. "Mingdai junhu zhong de jiaren, yi'nan" [Retainers and Adopted Sons in Ming Dynasty Military Households]. *Zhongyang yanjiuyuan lishi yuyan yanjiusuo jikan* 83, no. 3 (2011): 507–69.

———. "Ming-Qing shidai junhu de jiazu guanxi – weisuo junhu yu yuanji junhu zhijian" [Lineage Relations of Military Households in Ming-Qing: Between Guard Military Households and Those in the Native Place]. *Zhongyang yanjiuyuan lishi yuyan yanjiusuo jikan* 74, no. 1 (2003): 97–140.

———. "Shilun Mingdai weijun yuanji yu weisuo fenpei de guanxi" [On the Relationship between Native Place and Guard Assignment of Guard Soldiers in Ming]. *Zhongyang yanjiu yuan lishi yuyan yanjiusuo jikan* 60, no. 2 (1989): 367–50.

———. "Shilun zupu zhong suojian de Mingdai junhu" [Ming Dynasty Military Households as Seen from Genealogies]. *Zhongyang yanjiu yuan lishi yuyan yanjiusuo jikan* 57, no. 4 (1986): 635–67.

——. *Weisuo, junhu yu junyi: yi Ming-Qing Jiangxi diqu wei zhongxin de yanjiu* [Guards, Military Households and Military Service: Research on the Jiangxi Region in Ming-Qing]. Beijing: Beijing daxue, 2010.

——. "Zailun duoji yu chouji" [More on Conscription and Drafts]. In *Zheng Qinren jiaoshou qizhi shouqing lunwenji*, 197–237. Taibei: Daoxiang, 2006.

Zelin, Madeline. "A Critique of Rights of Property in Prewar China." In *Contract and Property in Early Modern China*, edited by Madeleine Zelin, Jonathan Ocko, and Robert Gardella, 17–36. Stanford: Stanford University Press, 2004.

——. *The Magistrate's Tael: Rationalizing Fiscal Reform in Eighteenth-Century Ch'ing China*. Berkeley: University of California Press, 1984.

Zemon Davis, Natalie. *Fiction in the Archives: Pardon Tales and Their Tellers in Sixteenth-Century France*. Stanford: Stanford University Press, 1987.

Zhang Bincun. "Shiliu shiji Zhoushan qundao de zousi maoyi" [Smuggling in the Zhoushan Archipelago in the Sixteenth Century]. *Zhongguo haiyang fazhanshi lunwenji* 1 (1984): 71–96.

Zhang Jinhong and Xu Bin. "Wang Jinghong jiqi houyi xintan" [New Perspective on Wang Jinghong and His Descendants]. *Haijiaoshi yanjiu*, no. 2 (2005): 44–54.

Zhang Jinkui. "Ershi nian lai Mingdai junzhi yanjiu huigu" [A Look Back on Twenty Years of Ming Military System Research]. *Zhongguoshi yanjiu dongtai*, (October 2002): 7–15.

——. "Junhu yu shehui biandong" [Military Households and Social Change]. In *Wan Ming shehui bianqian: wenti yu yanjiu*, edited by Wan Ming, 403–61. Beijing: Shangwu, 2005.

——. *Mingdai weisuo junhu yanjiu* [Guards and Military Households of the Ming]. Beijing: Xianzhuang, 2007.

Zhang, Lawrence. "'Power for a Price': Office Purchase, Elite Families and Status Maintenance in Qing China." PhD diss., Harvard University, 2010.

Zhang Sheng. "Weisuozhi chutan" [Preliminary Discussion of Guard Gazetteers]. *Shixueshi yanjiu*, no. 1 (2001): 50–58.

Zhang Songmei. "Mingchu jun'e kao" [On the Number of Soldiers in Ming]. *Qilu xuekan* 191 (2006): 47–52.

Zhang, Wenxian. "The Yellow Register Archives of Imperial Ming China." *Libraries and the Cultural Record* 43, no. 2 (2008): 148–75.

Zhao Shiyu. "'Bu Qing bu Ming' yu 'Wu Ming bu Qing': Ming Qing yidai de quyu shehuishi jieshi" ["Neither Ming nor Qing" and "If No Ming Then No Qing": On the Ming-Qing Dynastic Transition and Regional Social History]. *Xueshu yuekan* 42, no. 7 (2010): 130–40.

Zheng Rong. "Ming-Qing yixiang Tongshan maoyi fazhan yu wumiao jisi" [Commercial Development and Worship at the Martial Temple in Tongshan since Ming-Qing]. *Zhangzhou shifan xueyuan xuebao (Zhexue shehui kexue ban)* 72, no. 2 (2009): 65–59.

——. "Tongshan: yige junhu shehui de bianqian, 1368–1949" [Tongshan: The Social Transformation of a Society of Military Households, 1368–1949]. Master's thesis, Xiamen University, 2006.

Zheng Zhenman. *Family Lineage Organization and Social Change in Ming and Qing Fujian*, translated by Michael Szonyi. Honolulu: University of Hawai'i Press, 2001.

——. *Ming-Qing Fujian jiazu zuzhi yu shehui bianqian* [Family Lineage Organization and Social Change in Ming and Qing Fujian]. Changsha: Hunan Jiaoyu, 1992.

Zhuang Chusheng. "Shilun Hanyu fangyan dao" [On Chinese Dialect Islands]. *Xueshu yanjiu,* no. 3, (1996): 6–9.

Zurndorfer, Harriet. "Oceans of History, Seas of Change: Recent Revisionist Writing in Western Languages about China and East Asian Maritime History during the Period 1500–1630." *International Journal of Asian Studies* 13, no. 1 (2016): 61–94.

ILLUSTRATION SOURCES

Figure 1.2 (Pu Manu's archival record) is reproduced with the permission of the First Historical Archives, Beijing, People's Republic of China.

Figure 3.3 (Jinmen battalion map) was created by Jiang Bowei

All other maps were created by Jeff Blossom. Provincial borders are taken from CHGIS Version 5 © Fairbank Center for Chinese Studies and the Institute for Chinese Historical Geography at Fudan University, December 2010. The coastline, globe inset map, and Yangtze River are taken from Natural Earth (naturalearthdata.com).

All family tree figures were created by Jeff Blossom.

All photographs by the author.

A NOTE ON THE TYPE

THIS BOOK has been composed in Miller, a Scotch Roman typeface designed by Matthew Carter and first released by Font Bureau in 1997. It resembles Monticello, the typeface developed for The Papers of Thomas Jefferson in the 1940s by C. H. Griffith and P. J. Conkwright and reinterpreted in digital form by Carter in 2003.

Pleasant Jefferson ("P. J.") Conkwright (1905–1986) was Typographer at Princeton University Press from 1939 to 1970. He was an acclaimed book designer and AIGA Medalist.

The ornament used throughout this book was designed by Pierre Simon Fournier (1712–1768) and was a favorite of Conkwright's, used in his design of the *Princeton University Library Chronicle.*